ALEXANDER
THE GREAT

ALEXANDER THE GREAT

Selections from Arrian,
Diodorus, Plutarch, and Quintus Curtius

Edited, with Introduction, by
James Romm

Translated by Pamela Mensch and James Romm

Hackett Publishing Company, Inc.
Indianapolis/Cambridge

Copyright © 2005 by Hackett Publishing Company, Inc.

15 14 13 12 11   2 3 4 5 6 7

For further information, please address:
Hackett Publishing Company, Inc.
P.O. Box 44937
Indianapolis, IN 46244-0937
www.hackettpublishing.com

Cover design by Abigail Coyle, Deborah Wilkes, and Lance Brisbois
Text design by Meera Dash
Composition by Agnew's, Inc.
Printed at Versa Press, Inc.

Library of Congress Cataloging-in-Publication Data

Alexander the Great : selections from Arrian, Diodorus, Plutarch, and
Quintus Curtius / edited, with introduction, by James Romm ; translated
by Pamela Mensch and James Romm.
       p. cm.
Includes bibliographical references and index.
ISBN 0-87220-728-5 (cloth) — ISBN 0-87220-727-7 (pbk.)
    1. Alexander, the Great, 356–323 B.C. 2. Greece—History—
Macedonian Expansion, 359–323 B.C. 3. Generals—Greece—
Biography. 4. Greece—Kings and rulers—Biography. 5. Greece—
History—Macedonian Expansion, 359–323 B.C. I. Arrian. II. Romm,
James S. III. Mensch, Pamela, 1956–
    DF234.A4895 2005
    938'.07'092—dc22   2004019818

ISBN-13: 978-0-87220-728-8 (cloth)
ISBN-13: 978-0-87220-727-1 (pbk.)

Contents

Introduction

Few historical figures have been the subject of as much disagreement and dispute as Alexander the Great. Within the past sixty years alone, he has been portrayed as an enlightened humanitarian promoting universal brotherhood and as a bloodthirsty tyrant of Hitlerian proportions, and many things in between the two extremes. His phenomenal military talents and physical fortitude are beyond dispute, as is the immensity of the changes he wrought over large stretches of the inhabited world. But questions of what kind of person he was, what motivated him to undertake his campaign of conquest, and what plans he had for the lands he had mastered are still open, even after centuries of inquiry, and probably always will remain so.

Because Alexander became the founder and leader of a vast empire, these questions are of great importance to today's readers, especially those concerned with issues of leadership and empire in the modern world. We would make very different assessments of the Macedonian conquest of Asia depending on whether we regard Alexander, on the one hand, as a self-aggrandizing, obsessed, or deluded individual or, on the other, as an intelligent, well-intentioned man who believed himself capable of improving the world. There is evidence to support both points of view, and our decision as to where the weight of evidence falls is of necessity a subjective one. Readers of the Alexander story must therefore become not only historians but psychologists as well, since the story revolves, more than most accounts of the past, around the enigmas of the human character.

This edition of excerpts from the ancient Alexander sources, principally from Arrian, has been designed to help readers in both these tasks: it assembles passages illustrating not only the major actions undertaken by Alexander in the course of his reign but also those in which questions of Alexander's character are most at issue and in which Arrian tries to make judgments about that character. Indeed, Arrian's confused and conflicted attempts to arrive at an understanding of Alexander can be a useful guide to modern readers as they navigate their own confusions and conflicts. Though in the end Arrian decides that he is "not ashamed to admire Alexander," and though he has been accused by his detractors of taking an unreservedly positive view, I believe that his portrait of Alexander, if examined critically and compared at key points with other versions, reveals a balanced enough mixture of dark and light tones as to allow modern readers to frame their own moral judgments.

The goal of this edition, therefore, is to introduce readers to a complex individual, as well as to allow them to follow a series of compelling and consequential historical events. However, to properly understand those events, readers will first need to be familiar with the historical landscape as it looked when Alexander came to power, and this requires turning back the clock somewhat to the time of his father, Philip, and before. For Alexander's unique role in history derived only in part from his own innate talents, formidable though these were. He also inherited an army that was the strongest in the world and a nation that had already become the superpower and *hegemon* (leader) of a large portion of Europe, thanks to the revolution wrought by Philip over the preceding twenty-two years. Indeed, were it not for Alexander's even larger achievements, Philip instead might well have become known as "the Great," the ruler who united all Greece under a single political structure for the first time in its fifteen-hundred-year history.

Greeks and Macedonians

Macedonia, sometimes also called Macedon, was an ethnically mixed region in antiquity bounded by Greek states to the south and by a series of tribal kingdoms in other directions. It comprised the rugged terrain of the lower Balkans in its northern and western reaches as well as a fertile alluvial plain in the south, and these two very differently settled areas were often in conflict with each other before Philip firmly united them into a nation. Today the territory once known as Macedonia overlaps the borders of two modern nations that both claim its name: Greece, which calls its northernmost province Macedonia, and the country that, following a bitter dispute with Greece over nomenclature, is officially known as the Former Yugoslav Republic of Macedonia.

This dispute between modern Greece and its northeastern neighbor over the legacy of ancient Macedonia reflects a very old confusion over whether or not the Macedonians were Greek, and it is important that we clarify this issue from the start, especially since the terms "Greek" and "Macedonian" are often blurred by popular usage. In the fourth century B.C.E., however, there was no doubt as to who was who. In Philip's and Alexander's army, Greeks and Macedonians fought with different weapons, spoke the Greek language differently (or perhaps spoke a different language entirely; the linguistic evidence is slight enough to allow for either interpretation), and regarded one another as sufficiently alien as to engage in what Arrian (II.10; see page 53) describes as "ethnic rivalry." Alexander himself had been educated by a Greek intellectual, Aristotle, and cultivated Hellenic tastes in art, literature, and religion, but when he addressed his countrymen he could speak openly about the dangers they faced from a Greek rebellion or about the unreliability of the Greeks serving in their navy. The two peoples were separate and distinct, despite the fact that, for a time anyway, they fought under the same banner.

Whether the Macedonians were themselves "Greek" in some anthropological sense is debated by experts today; the evidence, in particular that pertaining to the native tongue of the region, is slight but inclines toward an affirmative answer. But Greeks or not, they had developed along very different social and political lines than their neighbors to the south. For most of their history they lacked the defining unit of Hellenic civilization, the city-state, living instead in scattered villages and rural settlements across a vast (by Greek standards) territory. Also, they retained a political institution that the Greeks had almost entirely discarded long before: hereditary monarchy. The Macedonian kingship perhaps looked familiar to the Greeks by comparison with Homer's *Iliad*, in which great rulers like Agamemnon wielded power over coalitions of lesser barons, making war only by their consent and with their participation. But they themselves had long ago rejected this system in favor of less centralized oligarchies and democracies, and by Philip's time they had come to regard one-man rule as a barbarian institution. Finally, cultural heritage and sophistication helped delineate the two peoples. Most Macedonians, beyond an aristocratic elite, knew little of the refinements of Greek philosophy, art, and literature. The Macedonian rulership had tried to import these as part of a Hellenization program in the fifth and fourth centuries, but the process was still inchoate at the time Philip came to power, as famously described in a speech Arrian imagines Alexander giving to his men:

> Philip, my father . . . took you up when you were helpless wanderers, most of you dressed in hides, pasturing a few flocks in the mountains and in their defense fighting ineptly with your neighbors, the Illyrians, Triballians, and Thracians. He gave you cloaks to wear instead of skins, led

you down from the mountains to the plains. . . . He made you city-dwellers, and by means of laws and good customs gave you an orderly way of life. (Arrian VII.9)

Because they had adopted certain Hellenic ways by the time they invaded Asia, and because the language and structure of their new imperial administration was borrowed from their southerly neighbors, Alexander and his Macedonian army are sometimes referred to, informally, as Greeks. But this mischaracterization is avoided in this volume. We may sometimes speak of a "Greco-Macedonian army" when it is important to emphasize that both peoples went into Asia together, supposedly in pursuit of common goals. But the Greeks played a relatively small role in Alexander's campaign and indeed in some battles were barely used at all, perhaps because Alexander was not sure how well they would fight in an army not truly their own.

In terms of its ability to project power, Macedonia, up until Philip's time, had always been much weaker than the leading Greek states and seems at one point to have paid tribute to Athens. Its internal disunity and frequent dynastic struggles made it seem easy prey to its aggressive Balkan neighbors, the tribes mentioned by Alexander in the passage quoted above, and it was frequently invaded by them or defeated in battle. Its one important military asset, a large population of horses and men who were expert at riding them, led to a reliance on cavalry as its primary offensive weapon, but cavalry attacks were useless against tightly closed ranks of Greek armored infantry. A further resource, great stands of wood for shipbuilding, went unused due to the Macedonians' lack of access to, or interest in, the sea; in fact, their best timber was often sold to wood-poor Athens, where it helped furnish the great trireme fleets of the imperial Athenian navy.

The Age of Philip

In 359 B.C.E. when Philip II came to the Macedonian throne, the Greeks could never have imagined that he would one day threaten and finally end their political freedom. The Macedonians had suffered a humiliating defeat at the hands of the Illyrians the previous year, and their strategic position looked shakier than ever. It was the Greek city of Thebes, using new tactics combining cavalry maneuvers with a more flexible infantry phalanx, that then dominated affairs in the region. After Thebes lost its brilliant general, Epaminondas, in battle in 362, most observers would have bet that Athens, which had partly rebuilt its old naval alliance, would emerge as the ultimate *hegemon* of the Aegean world.

But naval power had revealed its limitations in the Peloponnesian War of the previous century; supremacy was henceforth to be vied for on the land. Thebes had defeated the traditional infantry superpower, Sparta, through its innovative use of land forces, and Philip had spent several of his teenage years at Thebes observing these innovations. When he came to power in Macedonia he quickly demonstrated how much he had learned in the school of Epaminondas. He drafted ten thousand infantrymen and began drilling them to fight as a Greek-style phalanx but with newly designed equipment: a small, shoulder-slung shield and a long, heavy wooden lance called a *sarissa*. These lances, cut from hard native wood and weighted at the butt end so as to balance at a point three-quarters down the shaft, instantly changed the dynamics of land warfare, rendering the traditional Greek phalanx obsolete. An infantry soldier wielding it with both hands could jab his opponent from a distance of twelve feet; the Greek hoplite ("armed foot soldier"), whose left hand was employed in holding a heavy shield, could manage a weapon of only half that length. Thus, whereas the Greek phalanx maintained a balance between offensive and defensive weaponry, the Macedonians concentrated their offensive power so as to make defense (or so they hoped) unnecessary.

Philip's new infantry phalanx proved its effectiveness in his very first battle, and he went on to employ it, in many kinds of terrain and against many opponents, for the next twenty years. Constant drill and frequent battlefield experience brought the core of his new force to a state of seasoned, toughened professionalism. In most engagements Philip deployed this massive phalanx, bristling with its enormous spikes, at the center of his line, with cavalry contingents at either wing; while the phalanx pinned down and immobilized the opponent's center, the cavalry waited and watched for weak points at which to launch its devastating strikes. Meanwhile, contingents of lighter, more mobile infantry, dubbed the shield-bearers, helped fill in the spaces between phalanx and cavalry. In time, as Philip's land empire expanded, new contingents were added to the army from the subject peoples or hired from abroad: additional cavalry from the Thessalians and Paeonians, javelin-throwers and archers from Balkan neighbors, slingers from Crete, and a crack infantry force from the Agrianians. At the time of Philip's death the Macedonian army had swelled to thirty thousand men and had attained a degree of complexity and flexibility never before seen on European battlefields.

As Philip's dominance of the northern Aegean grew, so did his wealth. Gold mines captured in Thrace subsidized his substantial levies and also enabled him to buy political support in the Greek cities to his south. Ever the cunning diplomat, he preferred to pay for his victories with cash rather than blood and is said to have remarked that the greatest weapon in his arsenal was a donkey laden with gold. The mounting surpluses also helped attract the most talented engineers of the Greek world into Philip's service, and a new generation of weapons began to take shape: catapults that could hurl a bolt or stone with terrifying force and siege machines that threatened even the strongest of city walls. The technologized warfare that would flourish in the Hellenistic age began its evolution here, in Macedonia, in the age of Philip.

The army inherited by Alexander was thus the creation of Philip, developed, trained, and kept in almost continuous use over two decades of Macedonian expansion. All that Alexander required in order to become the most powerful man in Europe was the skill to command this army—a skill that, as it would turn out, he possessed in phenomenal measure.

The New Order in Europe

The Greek city-states watched the growth of Philip's power with some alarm but took no concerted action to stop it until too late. They were too accustomed to fighting one another to drop their differences and make common cause in the face of the new threat. At Athens, Demosthenes began a series of public speeches in the late 350s to alert his fellow citizens to the growing danger. Often he persuaded them to take some partway measure, but there were many in the city who would have been happy to reach an accommodation with Philip, just as Philip hoped not to have to fight Athens. Serious confrontations were avoided by both sides for a long time. Finally, in 339 the pressure on Athens reached a breaking point when Philip, while campaigning in northern Greece, made a sudden and belligerent swerve in the direction of Attica. Athens hastily forged an alliance with Thebes, and the two cities stood shoulder to shoulder on the battlefield of Chaeronea—where Philip's army soundly thrashed them. The man whom many Athenians considered a drunken, loutish barbarian was now fully in control of the city's destiny.

But Philip did not intend to terrorize or crush the Greeks, least of all Athens, whose navy he would need in order to carry through the project he was then planning—an invasion of the western portions of the Persian empire. He ceded full political autonomy to most of the Greek states (while taking steps to make sure they did not use it against him) and summoned their representatives to a council at Corinth, where he established a new collective body, the Greek League, under his leadership. For the first time ever, the Greeks— with the important exception of the Spartans, who had refused to join anything convened by Philip—were required by treaty to deal with frictions between cities by means of a legal process rather than by warfare, and they voted on enterprises to be undertaken in common. Philip, as the elected *hegemon* or leader of the League, quickly got them to endorse his planned invasion of Asia and to grant him full decision-making powers as its commander in chief. Macedonia thus set itself up not as the conqueror but as the unifier of Greece and the champion of a panhellenic—or so Philip hoped—crusade.

The idea of a Hellenic union that could direct its collective energies against the Persians had been discussed by Greek intellectuals for decades. Isocrates, an Athenian rhetorician and political essayist, had agitated for it in his speeches since 380 B.C.E., and in the 340s he had begun to address his editorials to Philip, urging him to lead both the union and the invasion. Only by a panhellenic attack on Persia, Isocrates wrote, could the Greeks overcome the entrenched rivalries and divisions that set them at each other's throats year after year, war after war. Greece was destroying itself from within, he wrote, and spawning a new generation of violent, vagrant mercenary soldiers with no goals or ideals other than the promotion of eternal strife. These ills, moreover, were proving a boon to the Persians, who eagerly attached to their own forces the soldiers made stateless in Greek wars. Without such hired Greek soldiery, Isocrates argued, the Persians would be easy prey, as demonstrated in the invasion led by King Agesilaus of Sparta (396–395 B.C.E.), who had made steady progress into western Asia before events back in Greece forced him to return home. And, Isocrates wrote, the moral legitimacy of such an invasion would be beyond question, since it could be considered payback for the massive and highly destructive invasions of Greece mounted by the Persians in the preceding century.

Philip hardly needed the treatises of Isocrates to guide his foreign policy, but the fact that such a respected Greek intellectual had promulgated these ideas was immensely valuable to him. It enabled him to cast both his political control of the Greeks and his planned invasion of Asia as a crusade to save Hellenism from itself and restore the fortunes of Europe, now fallen so far since the glorious victories of 480 and 479. The Persians could again become, as they were then, the common enemy against which the fractious states of Greece could at last unite.

The Persian "Enemy"

The Persians, imperial masters of Asia from the Aegean to the Indus River and of Egypt as well, the ravagers of Greece in 480 and the sackers of Athens, were easily vilified in the rhetoric of politicians such as Isocrates, but the reality was more complex. Since the late years of the fifth century and all through the fourth, the Persians had in fact been sought as allies by one side or another in Greece's internecine struggles. Persian financial support of Sparta had in large part decided the outcome of the Peloponnesian War, and, in exchange, Sparta had ceded back to Persia control over the Greek cities of Asia, the same cities liberated from Persia at such great cost by earlier generations. In 387 B.C.E. the Spartans had negotiated an even more conciliatory treaty with Persia, known as the King's Peace, which set up the Persian monarch as the arbiter of disputes in the Greek world. The Greeks, in other words, had willingly given up some of their freedom and autonomy to the Persians in exchange for the stability that, as they had come to suspect, only a strong, centralized regime could provide.

Over decades of close interaction in Asia, the Greeks and Persians became increasingly interdependent and intertwined. As discussed above, Greek mercenary soldiers came to form the core units of the Persian armed forces, and some rose to high positions of command. Coastal cities such as Miletus and Ephesus thrived as junctures of East–West trade, and in their busy marketplaces native Hellenes mingled freely with Persian garrison troops and administrators. Life under Persian rule was comfortable and prosperous for these Asian Greeks, though they may have resented the powers of the puppet rulers installed by their masters and chafed at the need to pay tribute to a distant Great King. But in their eyes, Persia could hardly be defined as an enemy, as Alexander was to find when he often had to use force to secure their cooperation.

On the Greek mainland, neighboring Macedonia struck many Greek observers as a greater threat than distant Persia, and several cities sought alliances with the Persian empire in their efforts to stop Philip's expansion. In Athens, Demosthenes conspired with Persia's western satraps to stir up resistance to Philip's regime (Alexander later captured a batch of letters that had passed between these parties). Later, Thebes also received Persian money to help support the rebellion of 335, and the rebels shouted from the city walls a proclamation of their solidarity with Persia in opposition to Macedonia. Eventually Sparta, too, tried to ally with Persia in order to overthrow Macedonian rule (as related below, page 56). Though all three cities had been threatened by the forces Xerxes led into Greece in 480, and Athens had actually been sacked and Thebes occupied, subsequent Great Kings had made clear that they had no interest in attacking the mainland Greeks; hence, many in the Greek world were inclined to side with the Persians if doing so would help them resist the Macedonians. All these circumstances reveal the ways in which Philip's definition of the Asian campaign as a war of liberation was an oversimplification at best, a cynical propaganda campaign at worst.

Whatever the political motives for Philip's planned invasion, the economic motives were clear enough to all concerned. Persian tax collectors had soaked up the wealth of Asia over the course of two centuries, and great heaps of gold now sat idle in the treasuries of the imperial capitals. Even if these cities seemed too far away to be sacked, Philip might well reckon that, once his armies had made inroads into Persian territory, the Great King would pay him handsomely to fold up his tents and go home. And he could be confident that such inroads would be made. Wealth had made the Persians soft, or at least so the Greeks thought. Like the Egyptians before them, they had taken to hiring foreigners to fight their battles for them, preferring not to stray far from their banquet tables and harems. Even in their glory days, the Persians had not been able to defeat the Greeks in a set battle; now their glory days were past, and they would be facing an army more powerful than those of the Greeks, as the battle of Chaeronea had proven.

What was more, the Persians found themselves plunged into a leadership crisis at precisely the moment that Philip was preparing to invade. In 338, right after the battle of Chaeronea, Philip learned that the Persian king, Artaxerxes III, also known as Ochus, had been poisoned by a palace eunuch named Bagoas. His successor, who also took the name Artaxerxes, was as yet an unknown quantity, and within two years he, too, would fall victim to Bagoas' poisoned chalice. Ochus had been a strong monarch during his twenty-year reign and had largely restored Persia's fortunes—for example, by recovering rule over the rebellious province of Egypt. His sudden disappearance left a great power vacuum, which in an empire as vast and diverse as Persia posed great dangers—or, from Philip's perspective, offered great opportunities.

Alexander: The Man and the Myth

Such was the geopolitical landscape at the time Philip's reign ended and Alexander's began, the year 336 B.C.E. The circumstances by which Philip was suddenly removed from the scene and replaced by his twenty-year-old son form the first part of the story contained in this volume, followed by Alexander's twelve-year reign, in which the Macedonian army carried out Philip's planned attack on Persia with a degree of success no one, not even Alexander, could have dreamed possible. Rather than anticipate these events, however, let us consider briefly the dimensions of the legend that has sprung up around Alexander's reign and the problems this legend poses for modern-day interpreters.

The Alexander legend was already taking shape during the king's life, but his sudden death at the age of thirty-two, still full of youthful vigor and as yet undefeated on the field of battle, swelled it to gigantic proportions. There is nothing quite so compelling as a heroic life cut off in its prime, the principal theme of tragic literature since the *Epic of Gilgamesh* and the *Iliad*. Alexander indeed became a tragic hero, almost inevitably, by dying "at the height of his fame and most longed for by humankind," as Arrian puts it (VII.16). He had fulfilled the destiny defined by Solon, in Herodotus' *Histories*, as the best that mortals can hope for: to die at a peak moment, when a glorious deed has been achieved and has won the acclaim of all observers, before one's luster can dim or be eclipsed by the banalities of a long, slow decline into old age.

Moreover, Alexander's premature departure from the world's stage, when his plans for the empire he had conquered were still incomplete and unclear, made him a kind of blank canvas, onto which the classical world could project its deepest hopes, fears, and fantasies.

Some immediately elevated him to divine stature, assimilating him to the handsome, beardless youths of mythology: Adonis, Perseus, and above all Dionysus. Others enshrined him as the virtuous philosopher-king longed for by Plato and like-minded thinkers who had grown weary of democracy's blunders and squabbles. To those who still stood by the old democratic ideology, however, he represented the barbarian at the gates, the bloodthirsty tyrant, the enemy of all the values the Greek world held dear. And to the growing ranks of Stoics who sought to strengthen the rational mind and control the passions, he embodied the utter loss of that control, the descent into madness and chaotic emotion, the final, irreversible abandonment of divine Reason. All these views colored the various accounts of Alexander's life published just after his demise and led their authors (as discussed in more detail below) to magnify either his faults or his virtues as far as credibility would permit.

Not only the Greco-Roman world indulged in these collective fantasies of Alexander. As the ages passed, his ghost reappeared in the folk tales and legends of the Persians, Armenians, and Egyptians he had conquered. He took on new, more exotic forms: a clever thief, an amorous lover, a superhero with magic powers, a slayer of monsters. In pursuit of knowledge he voyaged down into the depths of the sea and up into the sky. In Arabic literature he sprouted horns and became Dhul-Quarnain, The Two-horned One; in Hebrew lore he turned into a humble penitent who learned the secret of happiness from a Jewish priest. Persia, the land he had once ravaged, came to regard him as one of its own wise and virtuous kings, celebrated in the national epic *Shah Nemah*. And though the Indians preserved no trace of his invasion in their own literature, many cultures, especially that of the early Christians in the Near East, built up elaborate dialogues and exchanges of letters out of Alexander's brief encounter with the "Naked Sages," the religious devotees he had met in Taxila (Arrian VII.1–3 is a precursor of such texts).

Each nation, and each age, has made of Alexander what it most wanted, or dreaded, to see in him; and today we continue to reshape him according to our own historical perspective. For many of today's scholars, who dwell, like all of us, in the shadow of the Second World War, that has meant a tendency to see Alexander's regime in light of the Fascist dictatorships of Europe in the 1930s and 1940s; one often senses the specter of Nazi Germany looming behind their accounts of the Macedonian empire, whether or not this parallel is openly acknowledged. The advent of Hitler has, perhaps inevitably, colored our attempts to understand and to morally assess an ancient leader who also undertook a program of world conquest. That is not to say that there are no valid comparisons between the two figures, only that we must tread cautiously, with an awareness of the biases the last century has instilled in us, before making them.

Other comparisons, too, will no doubt be drawn by modern readers of the Alexander story, particularly when they see how much of the world conquered by Alexander is once again the theater of Western military operations. At the time of this writing, U.S. troops are engaged in action in places Alexander knew as Babylonia, Susiana, Areia, and Bactria; enemies of America are being sought in the same mountain fastnesses where Bessus and Spitamenes once hid. Thus the study of Alexander, in whatever light he is regarded, can usefully illuminate the present historical moment and, it is to be hoped, inform the difficult choices that lie ahead as America shapes its role in the world.

About This Edition

I have striven in this volume to achieve two somewhat contradictory goals: first, to present a consecutive and reasonably complete narrative of Alexander's life, and second, to acquaint readers with an important ancient text. In pursuit of the latter I have declined to use the synoptic approach of some other Alexander guidebooks, which assemble parallel episodes from multiple sources and allow the reader to compare different accounts. Such an approach has great value to the historical scholar but disappoints the *reader* of history who wants to follow a coherent narrative line. The life of Alexander is, above all else, a great story, one of the greatest found anywhere in fact or fiction. So I have tried to preserve the integrity of that story by basing the edition on a single ancient source, supplementing it with other material only where needed for the sake of completeness.

The decision to draw, insofar as possible, from a single ancient source is, however, a problematic one, since historians can rely on no one text as the basis of a history of the Alexander period (as they rely on Herodotus for the Persian Wars or Thucydides for the Peloponnesian War). All the surviving ancient accounts date from three centuries or more after Alexander's death, and all make use of now-lost primary sources that were in varied measures biased, incomplete, or romanticized to please a wide reading public. The differences between the extant versions are thus fairly wide, though one group of three texts—by Diodorus Siculus (a Greek), Quintus Curtius (a Roman), and Pompeius Trogus (a Roman whose work survives only in the form of a summary by a later writer)—clearly derive from a common source and thus are collectively known as the "vulgate" tradition. Two very different sources stand behind Arrian's account, usually titled *Anabasis* (or "March into the Interior") *of Alexander*, and a welter of various materials, overlapping with both the "vulgate" texts and with Arrian, gave rise to the biography of Alexander composed by Plutarch for his *Parallel Lives*. None of these works carries overriding authority with scholars; a thorough investigation of the Alexander period requires reading all of them critically, with a sharp eye for the bias of their sources. Nonetheless, most modern historians give priority to Arrian in their attempts to reconstruct the events of 334 to 323 B.C.E., and so Arrian, despite all his inadequacies, has been adopted as the basis of this edition.

Arrian lived at the end of the first century C.E. and the beginning of the second—that is, more than four centuries after Alexander's death. For much of his adult life he was a general and a provincial governor, serving the Roman empire as commander of a large army in the region today comprising eastern Turkey and Armenia. But he also made time for literary pursuits and authored works on hunting, cavalry tactics, and his own campaign to repel an invasion by the Alan tribes beyond Rome's borders, in addition to the biography of Alexander and a variety of other works. As a young man he studied under the great Stoic sage Epictetus, and the *Discourses of Epictetus* and *Encheiridion* ("Handbook"), still read for inspiration today, are actually records Arrian made of his master's teachings. He was thus a complex man, a seeker of spiritual truths at one point in life, at another a man of action devoted to protecting the frontiers of a great land empire. One can see why he was attracted to Alexander as a subject, a man who had studied under Aristotle as a youth and went on to found a great land empire.

Arrian tells his readers at the outset of his narrative that he had read widely the primary sources on Alexander's life and found two of them, those of Ptolemy and Aristobulus—two members of Alexander's staff on the campaign through Asia—by far the most reliable. So he based his own account on those two while also including the occasional choice anecdote drawn from other authors. Since the original texts of these two works have perished, we cannot fully judge whether Arrian was right to trust them. In certain places both Ptolemy and

Aristobulus undoubtedly indulged in the exaggerations to which all Alexander historians were prone, and Ptolemy at least seems to have prettied up his account, knowing that his own position in later life, king of Egypt, relied in part on the strength of Alexander's reputation. Incidents in which some believe Alexander committed war crimes or ordered wanton executions were apparently given only summary treatment by these two men or else were "spun" in such a way as to exonerate their commander. However, Ptolemy and Aristobulus were at least eyewitnesses of the events they described, which the author of the work from which the three "vulgate" texts derived, a man most scholars identify as a Greek named Cleitarchus, most likely was not.

Arrian's text, then, has been adopted as the basis for this volume, but an attempt has been made to present this text in a critical light. Important points on which the other sources contradict it have been indicated in the footnotes, and in one case—the murder of Parmenio, which Arrian barely mentions—a selection from one of these sources has been provided as a corrective. The speeches put in the mouths of Alexander and other characters by Arrian are characterized in the notes as largely fictitious, and the inconsistencies and/or inadequacies of Arrian's moral judgments are also highlighted. Arrian, it must be admitted, was not a terribly deep thinker, and his insights into both Alexander's personality and his historical significance are not profound. Indeed, at times he can seem almost comically naïve, as for example when he asserts in his preface that Ptolemy's memoir deserves to be trusted because Ptolemy ruled Egypt at the time he wrote, and kings are deterred by fear of dishonor from telling lies. And despite the fact that his narrative concerns the collision of two great empires spanning much of the civilized world, Arrian gives maddeningly little attention to the great geopolitical implications of Alexander's conquests, preferring instead a narrow, almost microscopic focus on the actions of his main character.

Yet the very ordinariness of Arrian's dimensions are in another sense part of what makes his text so appealing. Though writing in an age known for its rhetorical excesses, Arrian avoided (as Quintus Curtius did not) the impulse to load down his story with elaborate speeches. His style is pleasingly sober, straightforward, and direct, and his descriptions of military maneuvers are often remarkably clear and captivating. Even the inconsistency of his judgments about Alexander can be seen as one of his strengths, for it prefigures, as discussed above, the ambivalence many modern readers feel in the face of such a titanic and inscrutable personality. Given that most ancient writers gravitated toward extremes, surrounding Alexander with either radiant glow or pitch-black shadow, Arrian at least achieved a certain degree of balance. He presents a figure who is, in the end, fully human, despite having achieved things that seemed possible only for a god.

* * * * * * * *

The translation of all selections—with the sole exception of the Quintus Curtius passages, which I translated—was prepared by Pamela Mensch, with my occasional suggestions and revisions. As editor I take responsibility for any inaccuracies or omissions. We have tried to retain some of the flavor of Arrian's style, which is elevated, sober, and somewhat archaic, without losing the liveliness and intensity that arise from the events described. In battle scenes, we have elected to preserve the great detail and precision of Arrian's descriptions, even at risk of alienating any modern reader who finds such detail superfluous or confusing. Those who wish to understand a great battle as it unfolds, step by step and blow by blow, can do no better than to follow these magnificent descriptions, written by a man who had himself commanded troops in combat on many occasions.

Selections from all texts are preceded by the chapter number, or book and chapter number, which will allow interested readers to locate them in a full version of that text. Omissions within a chapter are marked by an ellipsis, but between chapters such elisions are not marked. Italicized summaries connecting the selections are my own compositions. The chapters into which the volume has been divided do not correlate with the book divisions of Arrian's text but rather, after the first chapter, follow a geographic and political breakdown of the phases of Alexander's campaigns.

The Latin and Greek texts that served as the basis of the translations are in three cases those published in the Loeb Classical Library series: the edition of Arrian done by P. A. Brunt, of Diodorus by C. B. Welles, and of Quintus Curtius by John C. Rolfe. For Plutarch the Teubner text of Konrat Ziegler was used.

I wish to thank Leslie Clockel for her typing assistance, Deborah Wilkes and Meera Dash for their help in the preparation of the manuscript, the anonymous reader for suggestions on the Introduction, and, as always, my loving wife, Tanya, with whom I have found a happiness that Alexander never knew.

James Romm

Chronology

(All dates are B.C.E.)

Events Referred to in the Text

GREECE	MACEDONIA/BALKANS	ASIA/EGYPT
600–400		
490 Persians invade Greece by sea; defeated at Marathon		c. 550 Persian empire founded by Cyrus
480 Persians under Xerxes invade Greece by land and sea; Athens sacked		521–486 Reign of Darius I
479 Final defeat of Persians at Plataea		486–465 Reign of Xerxes
431–404 Peloponnesian War between Athens and Sparta		401 Xenophon and the Ten Thousand Greek mercenaries win battle of Cunaxa
400–360		
396–395 Invasion of western Asia led by Agesilaus	382 Birth of Philip	396–395 Invasion of western Asia led by Agesilaus
387 King's Peace, treaty giving Persia the right to arbitrate Greek disputes	367–365 Philip resident at Thebes	387 King's Peace, treaty giving Persia the right to arbitrate Greek disputes
380 Isocrates delivers *Panegyricus* urging panhellenic war on Persia		
371 Theban victory over Sparta at Leuctra		
362 Battle of Mantinea; death of Epaminondas		

GREECE	MACEDONIA/BALKANS	ASIA/EGYPT
360–350		
351 Demosthenes begins his *Philippic* speeches at Athens	359 Philip succeeds to throne	
	358 Reform of Macedonian army	358 Accession of Artaxerxes III (Ochus) to Persian throne
	357 Philip marries Olympias	
	356 Birth of Alexander	
350–340		
Demosthenes continues to deliver *Philippics*	Continued expansion of Macedonian hegemony	345 Persian troops recapture Egypt
346 Isocrates publishes *Philippus* urging Philip to lead Greece against Persia	343–341 Alexander educated by Aristotle	
340–335		
339 Philip seizes Elataea and gains easy entry into northern Greece	337 Philip weds Cleopatra; rift between Alexander/ Olympias and Philip; Alexander goes briefly into exile in Illyria	338 Assassination of Artaxerxes by Bagoas; Arses takes throne
338 Theban–Athenian coalition defeated at battle of Chaeronea	336 Reconciliation of Philip and Alexander	336 Arses assassinated, Darius III takes throne
337 Greek League convened at Corinth, elects Philip as head; at second meeting, Greek League votes to authorize Asian campaign	Parmenio and Attalus sent to liberate Greek cities in Asia	Parmenio and Attalus arrive to liberate Greek cities in Asia; Memnon sent to counter them
	Betrothal of Cleopatra to Alexander of Epirus	
335 Revolt of Thebes	Assassination of Philip Accession of Alexander	
	335 Alexander's campaigns in Thrace and Illyria; crossing of Danube	

The Asian Campaign

334 Crossing of Hellespont by Macedonian army
Battle of the Granicus (April)
Alexander dismisses Greek navy
Siege of Halicarnassus
Arrest of Alexander of Lyncestis

333 Alexander undoes the Gordian knot
Persian naval war in Aegean ends with death of Memnon
Battle of Issus (October)

332 Sieges of Tyre and Gaza
Alexander enters Egypt

331 Founding of Alexandria
Alexander visits Siwah oasis and shrine of Ammon
Macedonians return to Asia
Battle of Gaugamela (October 1)
Alexander enters Babylon, Susa, Persepolis
(in Greece) Revolt led by Agis of Sparta put down by Antipater

330 Burning of palace at Persepolis
Pursuit of Darius into Bactria
Assassination of Darius by Bessus and others
Alexander begins dressing in Persian royal garments
Trial of Philotas/execution of Parmenio

329 First crossing of Hindu Kush by Alexander; pursuit of regicides
Capture and punishment of Bessus
Destruction of Maracanda garrison by Spitamenes

328 Killing of Cleitus (autumn)
Spitamenes murdered by Scythian allies

327 Conspiracy of the pages; arrest of Callisthenes
Capture of Sogdian Rock; wedding of Alexander and Roxane
Second crossing of Hindu Kush; invasion of India
Capture of Aornos Rock

326 Alexander enters Taxila
Battle of the Hydaspes (April or May)
Siege of Sangala

Hyphasis mutiny
Launching of Indus River fleet

---

325 Campaign against the Malli; Alexander seriously wounded
Descent of Indus
Gedrosia march/voyage of Nearchus' fleet

---

324 Alexander's return to Persian capitals; purge of satraps
Flight of Harpalus
Susa weddings
Opis mutiny; banquet of reunification
Death of Hephaestion
(in Greece) Exiles' Decree announced at Olympic Games

---

323 Death of Harpalus
Alexander dies in Babylon (June)
Philip III and Alexander IV succeed to throne with Perdiccas
    as regent
(in Greece) Athens revolts, begins Lamian War (defeated 322)

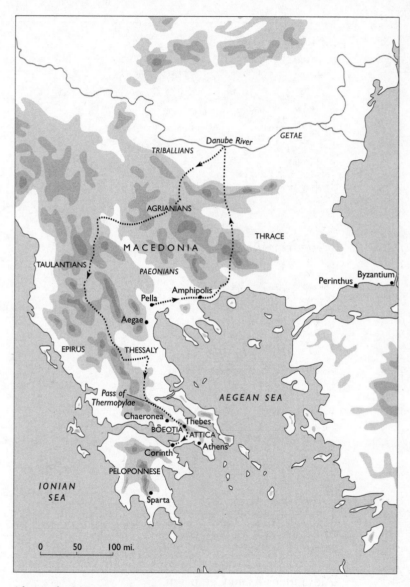

Alexander's European Campaign

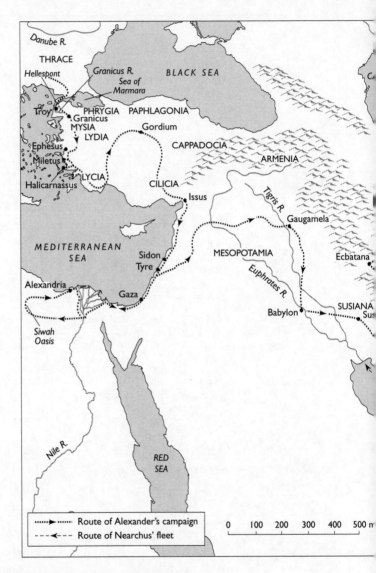

Alexander's Asian Campaign

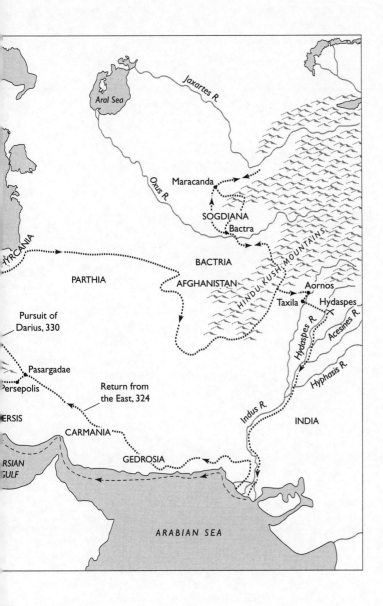

Aral Sea

Jaxartes R.

Oxus R.

Maracanda

SOGDIANA

Bactra

HYRCANIA

BACTRIA

PARTHIA

AFGHANISTAN

HINDU KUSH MOUNTAINS

Aornos

Taxila

Hydaspes

Pursuit of
Darius, 330

Hydaspes R.

Acesines R.

Pasargadae

Persepolis

Return from
the East, 324

Hyphasis R.

PERSIS

CARMANIA

Indus R.

INDIA

PERSIAN
GULF

GEDROSIA

ARABIAN SEA

I

Alexander, Prince of Macedonia

(356–336 B.C.E.)

a. The youth and upbringing of Alexander

For the first chapter of the Alexander story, the birth and childhood of the Macedonian prince, we have only one sound authority on which to rely, the Life of Alexander by Plutarch; and even this famous biography is rooted less in fact and more in romantic legend than historians would like. Plutarch lived about four centuries after Alexander, and from his readings of the primary historians he composed a literary pastiche designed to capture the personality of his subject rather than to present a complete record of events. So his patchwork of materials is only as reliable as the sources from which it was drawn, and some of these, in particular Cleitarchus and Callisthenes, seem to have cherished luridness and sensation far more than factual accuracy. Nonetheless, the early chapters of Plutarch's work paint a fairly plausible portrait of the future world conqueror as a youth, astounding all observers with his enormous talent and poise and, eventually, stirring up a tense rivalry with his father, the reigning king.

[Plutarch 2] That Alexander, on his father's side, was a descendant of Heracles by Caranus, and on his mother's a descendant of Aeacus by Neoptolemus,[1] has never been called into question. It is said that Philip was initiated into the mysteries[2] in Samothrace at the same time as Olympias. Though he was still a boy and she an orphan child,

1. Heracles and Aeacus were both sons of Zeus. Heracles was thought to have fathered the line that included Philip, Alexander's father, while Aeacus had been grandfather to Achilles, who in turn sired Neoptolemus, claimed as a distant ancestor by Olympias, Alexander's mother.
2. "The mysteries" here refers to a secret religious cult, into which newcomers were admitted by way of elaborate rituals. As a setting for Philip's first

he is said to have fallen in love with her and betrothed himself to her at once, on persuading her brother Arymbas. The night before they confined her in the bridal chamber, thunder was heard. The bride dreamed that a thunderbolt fell on her belly and kindled a great fire, which burst into flames that darted everywhere and finally died away. Some time later, Philip dreamed he was affixing a seal-ring to his wife's belly and imagined that the device carved on the ring was the image of a lion. All the other seers viewed the dream with suspicion and urged Philip to keep more careful watch over his marriage; but Aristander of Telmissus declared that Olympias was pregnant (since empty things are not sealed) and that she had conceived a son naturally courageous and lionlike.

At one point a serpent was seen stretched out beside Olympias when she had retired to bed, and this was said to have seriously impaired Philip's passion and affection, with the result that he paid fewer visits to the marriage bed, abstaining either because he feared his wife's magic spells and potions, or in the belief that she was consorting with a higher being.[3]

[3] Alexander was born early in the month of Hecatombaeon (Lous is its Macedonian name), on the sixth—the very day the temple of Ephesian Artemis was burned down.[4] In referring to that event, Hegesias the Magnesian made a witty remark, the coolness of which might have extinguished that blaze. For he said that the temple was

encounter with his future wife, Olympias, the mysteries create an aura of high emotion and a sense of the presence of divinity.

3. The story of Olympias' serpentine bedmate has a number of layers of historical significance. First, it evokes the well-attested fact that Olympias indulged heavily in ecstatic religious rites, some of which involved the handling of live snakes. Second, the story, at least as Plutarch presents it, helps explain the disaffection and even antagonism that arose in later years between Philip and Olympias. Finally, it is not clear at what point, or even whether, Alexander came to think of himself as the son of a god, but there is some suggestion in the historical sources that Olympias encouraged him in this belief. She (or others with a similar goal) may even have promulgated a rumor about a god coming to her bed in the form of a serpent on the night that Alexander was conceived.

4. The temple of Artemis at Ephesus was a huge structure, one of the largest ever built in the ancient world. A madman apparently burned it down as a way to gain notoriety. Alexander later made provisions for its restoration (see page 43 below).

probably burned down because Artemis was occupied with Alexander's delivery. All the Magi who were currently residing in Ephesus believed that the destruction of the temple foreshadowed another disaster, and ran through the town striking their faces and shouting that that day had given birth to ruin and dire misery for Asia.

On the same day, three pieces of news reached Philip, who had just captured Potidaea: Parmenio's defeat of the Illyrians in a great battle; the victory of Philip's racehorse at the Olympic Games; and the birth of Alexander. Pleased as he surely was with these tidings, Philip was even more elated by the prophets, who declared that his son, as he had been born on the day of a triple victory, would be unconquerable.

[4] Alexander's physical appearance was best represented in the statues of Lysippus, the only artist Alexander thought worthy to sculpt his likeness. And in fact the traits which many of his successors and friends tried to imitate later on[5]—the tilt of his neck, which inclined slightly to the left, and the moistness of his eyes—have been accurately observed by the artist. Apelles, who painted Alexander wielding the thunderbolt, did not capture his complexion, but made it too dark and swarthy. For they say he was fair and that his fairness took on a rosy tinge particularly around his chest and in his face. Moreover, we have read in the *Memoirs* of Aristoxenus that a delightful fragrance breathed from his skin and that a sweet smell, wafting from his mouth and all his flesh, permeated his garments.

When he was still a boy, his self-control manifested itself in the fact that, though violent and impetuous in other respects, he was unmoved by the pleasures of the body and partook of such things very sparingly.[6] His ambition kept his spirit grave and magnanimous beyond his years. For he was not eager for fame of every kind or from every quarter, unlike Philip, who, like a sophist, prided himself on his eloquence and had his Olympic victories in chariot-racing engraved on his coins. Instead, when the men who attended Alexander asked if he wanted to compete in the footrace at the Olympic Games (for he was swift-footed), he replied, "Only if I can compete with kings."

5. The portrait bust done by Lysippus did indeed spawn many imitations.
6. This self-restraint, especially in sexual matters, is the chief virtue flaunted by the ancient sources who most admire Alexander, just as the opposite quality, inability to govern the passions, is pointed out by his detractors. Indeed, the complexity of Alexander's character is revealed by the fact that he came to exemplify perfectly opposed features in different portrayals.

[5] In Philip's absence, Alexander entertained and became acquainted with envoys from the Persian king, who were won over by his affectionate nature and impressed that he asked no childish or trivial question, but inquired about the lengths of the roads and the manner of their journey, and about the King himself, his manner of dealing with enemies, and the Persians' power and prowess.[7] The envoys were so dazzled that they thought nothing of Philip's famed severity as compared with the drive and high ambition of his son.

Whenever Philip was reported either to have captured a notable city or to have won a famous battle, Alexander appeared by no means elated, but would say to his comrades, "Boys, my father will get everything first and will leave no great or glorious deed for *me* to perform with your help." As it was neither pleasure nor wealth, but excellence and reputation that attracted him, he supposed that the more he received from his father, the less he would accomplish in his own right. Accordingly, as he felt that his father's growing prosperity meant that the latter was using up opportunities, he desired to inherit an empire that afforded not riches, luxuries, and amusements, but struggles, wars, and ambitions.

[6] When Philonicus of Thessaly had brought Bucephalas to Philip and offered to sell him for thirteen talents,[8] they went down to the plain to make trial of the horse. Bucephalas seemed savage and altogether intractable: he let no rider approach him, and submitted to the voice of no man in Philip's suite, but reared up against everyone. In his annoyance, Philip ordered the animal to be led away, thinking him utterly wild and undisciplined, whereupon Alexander, who was present, said, "What a horse they are losing because in their inexperience and softness they cannot manage him!" At first Philip kept silent, but when Alexander continued to interrupt and to murmur indignantly, he said, "Do you criticize your elders in the belief that you are more knowledgeable and better able to manage a horse?" "I would manage this one, at any rate, better than anyone else,"

7. These questions all have ironic significance in view of the fact that Alexander would one day march down these roads and fight the Persian king hand to hand.
8. A fantastically large sum for a horse. Thessaly, the Greek province nearest to Macedonia toward the south, was famous for its horses, and a particularly fine breed was branded with the sign of an ox's head, from which came the name "Bucephalas" (or "Ox-head").

replied Alexander. "And if you fail, what penalty will you pay for your indiscretion?" "By Zeus," said he, "I'll pay the price of the horse." This raised a laugh, and they then came to an agreement as to the amount. Thereupon, running right up to the horse and taking hold of the rein, Alexander turned him toward the sun, having apparently guessed that Bucephalas was confused by his own shadow as it fell in front of him and darted about. Alexander ran alongside him for a little way as he trotted, and stroked him with his hand. When he saw that Bucephalas was full of courage and spirit, he quietly flung off his cloak, leaped up, and bestrode him securely. Pulling gently on the reins, he held Bucephalas back without striking him or tearing his mouth. And when he saw that the horse had dropped his threatening demeanor and was eager for a run, Alexander gave him free rein, urging him on with a bolder voice and a touch of his foot. At first there was silence and anguish among the men of Philip's suite. But when Alexander had rounded the turning post and turned back properly, elated and swaggering, they all cheered, and his father is said to have wept for joy and to have kissed his son when he dismounted. "Son," said he, "seek a kingdom equal to yourself; for Macedonia cannot contain you."

[7] Observing that his son's nature was uncompromising and that he resisted the use of force, but was easily led by reasoned argument to do what was proper, Philip tried to persuade rather than command him; and since he was by no means willing to entrust Alexander's training and discipline to the masters who were instructing him in the arts and general studies, as he considered it a matter of greater importance . . . Philip sent for Aristotle, the most celebrated and reputable of the philosophers,[9] and paid him a handsome and suitable fee: though he had destroyed Stagira (Aristotle's native place), Philip resettled it and restored those of its citizens who had fled or been enslaved.

9. This statement distorts the actual circumstances for sensational effect. Though Aristotle later became a great name in philosophy, he was still relatively unknown at the time Philip hired him; he was known to Philip through his father, Nicomachus, who had been court physician to the Macedonian royal family. Plutarch is certainly not alone, however, in his desire to romanticize the relationship between Aristotle and Alexander; legends about their friendship sprang up everywhere in late antiquity and the Middle Ages, including a spurious set of letters said to have passed between them.

[8] Alexander was literary by nature and fond of reading. As he regarded and spoke of the *Iliad* as a manual of warfare, he traveled with Aristotle's edition[10]—the so-called *Iliad* "of the casket"[11]—and kept it, with his dagger, under his pillow, as Onesicritus has recorded. And when other books were not easy to come by in upper Asia, Alexander ordered Harpalus to send him some. Harpalus sent him the books of Philistus, many works by the tragedians Euripides, Sophocles, and Aeschylus, and the dithyrambs of Telestes and Philoxenus.[12] Admiring Aristotle at first, and loving him no less than his own father, since (as he said) on his father's account he lived, but on account of Aristotle he lived nobly, Alexander viewed the philosopher with suspicion later on. Not that Alexander did Aristotle any harm, but his earlier deep affection for him, which did not last, became proof of an estrangement.[13] Yet the bent for philosophy, which had been implanted in Alexander and had developed in him from an early age, did not fade from his soul, as the honor he accorded Anaxarchus, the fifty talents he sent Xenocrates, and his courting of Dandamis and Calanus sufficiently demonstrate.[14]

10. It is doubtful that Aristotle did indeed edit the text of the *Iliad*.

11. So called because it was stored in some sort of small box.

12. Philistus wrote a historical narrative centered on the tyranny of Dionysius I and his son, men whom Alexander might easily have considered political role models. The tragedies of Aeschylus, Sophocles, and Euripides are well-known. The dithyrambic poetry of Telestes and Philoxenus have survived only in fragments.

13. In 327 Aristotle's nephew Callisthenes was arrested and, quite probably, executed by Alexander on a charge of treasonous conspiracy (see pages 109–10 below); this undoubtedly led to a breakdown in the king's relationship with Aristotle, whatever that consisted of at the time.

14. Dandamis and Calanus were Indian holy men supposedly offered inducements to join Alexander's retinue (see pages 152–3 below); Calanus in fact agreed to do so. Anaxarchus was a court philosopher who traveled with the expedition into Asia, like Callisthenes (whom Plutarch here leaves discreetly unmentioned). Xenocrates was head of the Platonic Academy in Athens; Alexander sent bequests to him and various other Athenian citizens after capturing the treasuries of the Persian capitals. Whether Alexander maintained a substantial interest in philosophy or merely appeared to do so for public-relations purposes is hard to determine; Plutarch, though, was deeply attached to the former view, as can be seen from his two youthful essays extolling Alexander as a "philosopher in arms" (*On the Fortune or the Virtue of Alexander*, parts 1 and 2, found in vol. 4 of the Loeb edition of Plutarch's *Moralia*).

[9] While Philip was making war on Byzantium,[15] Alexander, who was sixteen years old and had been left behind in Macedonia as regent and master of the seal-ring, subdued the rebelling Maedians and, after seizing their city, expelled the barbarians, settled a mixed population there, and named the city Alexandropolis. Present at Chaeronea, Alexander took part in the battle against the Greeks and is said to have been the first to assault the Theban Sacred Band. . . .[16] These exploits naturally endeared Alexander to Philip, who rejoiced to hear the Macedonians calling Alexander their king, but Philip their general.

b. The battle of Chaeronea

The story of Alexander's military career begins at Chaeronea, the first battle in which he played a leadership role. Though only eighteen years old at the time, he had so completely earned the confidence of his father, King Philip, as to be appointed to command one of the two wings of the Macedonian line, in effect the second most crucial position after that of the king himself. The only description we have of the battle is the frustratingly vague account of Diodorus Siculus, given below.

In the two years preceding the battle, the uneasy truce between Macedonia and the city of Athens had finally broken down, principally because Philip's moves in the Hellespont region threatened a trade route by which Athens got its food supplies. Philip finally precipitated a crisis by suddenly and without provocation seizing the Greek city of Elatea, a place he had no business occupying unless he had designs on Boeotia and Attica to the east. On learning of his advances there, Athenians were so terror-struck that, in a hastily convened assembly, no one spoke for a long time. Finally it was Demosthenes, the leader of the anti-Macedonian party and the most trusted statesman of the time, who put forward a proposal: to seek an alliance with Thebes, the other major power in the region, and to meet Philip head-on with all the force that could be mustered.

Demosthenes himself spoke to the Thebans in assembly and succeeded in winning the vote for an alliance, out-arguing the Macedonian speaker who had been sent by Philip to prevent this outcome. But the rhetorical brilliance Athenians such as himself had honed over the decades was not matched by the military talent of the city's leadership. Land warfare had been a rare event for Athens in recent years and was often conducted on its

15. In 340 B.C.E.
16. See the episode from Diodorus that follows for a fuller description of the battle and background on the Sacred Band.

*behalf by hired mercenaries. So when its army took the field in 338, many
citizens, including Demosthenes himself, found themselves in combat for
the first time ever. Philip's troops, by contrast, had seen almost constant action, many of them over the course of ten or twenty years.*

*The best hope of the Greeks rested on the Theban infantry, and in partic-
ular on the Sacred Band, a corps of three hundred shock troops who had
been drilled and trained at state expense (unlike most warriors who fought
as private citizens, paid but not trained by their cities). It is noteworthy, therefore, that Philip, in arranging his own forces for the battle, stationed Alexander opposite the Theban position, while he himself faced the Athenians. His
strategy is hard to discern from the blurry account given by Diodorus below,
but it seems likely that he intended Alexander to deliver the decisive blow
that would break the Greek line—which is indeed exactly what transpired.*

[Diodorus Siculus 16.85] By means of the Theban alliance, the Athenians had doubled their existing fighting force and regained confidence in their prospects. They immediately appointed Chares and
Lysicles as generals and sent all their forces under arms to Boeotia. As
all their young men were eager for the struggle, they marched in haste
and reached Chaeronea in Boeotia. Amazed at how quickly the Athenians had reached their country, the Thebans showed themselves just
as eager and went out with their weapons to meet them. Encamping
together, the allies awaited the enemy's approach.

Though Philip had lost the support of the Boeotians, he was
nonetheless determined to take on both allies together. He waited for
his own late-arriving allies and reached Boeotia with more than thirty
thousand foot soldiers and no fewer than two thousand horsemen.
Both sides, in their resolution and zeal, were ready for the battle, and
in valor they were well matched; but in numbers and in generalship
the king had the advantage. For as Philip had contended in a great variety of pitched battles, most of which he had won, he had gained a
wide experience in military actions. On the Athenian side, their best
generals had died—Iphicrates, Chabrias, and even Timotheus—and
of those who remained, though Chares held first place, he did not sur-
pass the average private soldier in martial energy and determination.

[16.86] At daybreak, when the forces were drawn up in battle array, the king posted his son Alexander—a mere boy, but notable for
courage and quickness of action—at one of the wings, placing his
most distinguished generals beside him, while he himself, keeping the
picked troops with him, led the other division and deployed the other

battalions as the occasion demanded. The Athenians, on the other side, had arrayed their forces tribe by tribe. Giving one division to the Boeotians, they themselves retained command of the other. The battle was strongly contested for a considerable time, and many fell on both sides, the struggle affording hopes of victory now to one side, now to the other.

Then Alexander, anxious to show his father his valor, and harboring a boundless ambition, was the first to break through the enemy line, though his many comrades-in-arms were equally brave. Striking down many, he subdued the troops arrayed opposite him. As the men stationed beside him did the same, gaps in the enemy's line were constantly opened. While many corpses were piling up, the foremost men around Alexander pressed hard and routed the enemy divisions ranged against them. Thereupon the king himself, bearing the brunt of the battle and not yielding the credit of the victory even to Alexander,[17] began by forcing back the troops stationed opposite him, and in helping put them to flight became responsible for the victory. More than a thousand Athenians fell in the battle, and no fewer than two thousand were captured. Likewise, many of the Thebans were killed, and no small number were taken prisoner. After the battle Philip set up a trophy, gathered the corpses for burial, offered sacrifices to the gods for the victory, and honored according to their deserts those who had fought bravely.

Though he could have now gone on to sack and destroy Athens, Philip chose instead to be magnanimous in victory. He sent Alexander as envoy to Athens at the head of an honorary procession bearing the ashes of the Athenian dead. The first, and only, visit of Alexander to the city that had become the "school of Hellas" has unfortunately not been recorded by any of our extant sources. We can only surmise what he thought of the Athenians; they, however, were quite eager to fawn on him and eagerly erected statues of the

17. Diodorus probably anticipates somewhat by implying that Philip was jealously seeking to outshine his son on the field of Chaeronea. The roles each man had played at the battle did indeed become a source of rivalry later on, but it seems clear that Philip and Alexander were operating in tandem according to a well-orchestrated plan. One theory of the battle holds that Philip feigned a retreat on the right wing in order to draw the Athenians out of position, creating a wide gap in the Greek line into which Alexander's cavalry could charge.

*young prince and his father in the market square. The fate of the Athenians,
as they knew, was now dependent on the good favor of the Macedonians,
and they made great show of courting that favor, while still keeping their
eyes open for the opportunity to revolt.*

*Philip now solidified his Greek power base by inaugurating the Greek
League at Corinth, as described in the Introduction (page xiii). His plans for
an invasion of Asia were already in motion; an advance force under Parmenio was making ready to cross the Hellespont and secure a bridgehead into
Persian territory. He needed to have some of the Greeks on his side, and the
rest at least too complacent or too intimidated to act against him, before he
could make the crossing himself with the bulk of his army. The League gave
him a position of legitimate authority and forced a stable status quo on the
Greek world under pro-Macedonian leadership.*

c. The rift between Philip and Alexander

*Though Philip had always given Alexander all the honors due to an heir ap-
parent, including the leadership of his left wing at Chaeronea, the relationship between father and son mysteriously broke down in the months
following the battle. An important cause, or perhaps a result, of the rift was
Philip's decision to take yet another wife, Cleopatra, a member of a high-
ranking Macedonian family. He had married several other women since
Olympias but had as yet sired no other children who might rival Alexander
as his successor. But his marriage to the young, highborn Cleopatra made
this prospect more real and created new tensions at court, as seen in the following episodes from Plutarch's Life of Alexander.*

[Plutarch 9] Philip's domestic troubles—his marriages and love affairs somehow infected the kingdom with the concerns of the
women's quarters—occasioned many accusations and serious quar-
rels. These were aggravated by the harshness of Olympias, a jealous
and sullen woman, who egged Alexander on. Attalus precipitated a
notorious clash at the wedding of Cleopatra, a young girl Philip was
taking to wife[18] (he had fallen in love with her when well past his

---

18. The Macedonian kings of this era practiced polygamy, largely because
there were so many foreign powers with whom marriage could be used to
forge useful alliances. In this case, however, Philip was marrying a member
of the Macedonian aristocracy, and the presumption might easily have arisen
that any children begotten from that union, being full-blooded Macedonian nobility, would rank first in the line of succession. Hence the tensions

prime). Attalus was the bride's uncle.[19] Having drunk deep at the carousal, he called on the Macedonians to ask the gods for a legitimate son to be born of Philip and Cleopatra, to be a successor to the throne. Provoked, Alexander cried, "Villain, do you consider *me* to be a bastard?" and threw a cup at Attalus. Philip then rose up, his sword drawn, to confront Alexander. But luckily for both, owing to his anger and the wine, Philip slipped and fell. Alexander now insulted him, saying, "This man, gentlemen, was preparing to cross from Europe to Asia, yet he is overturned merely crossing from couch to couch." After this drunken episode, Alexander took Olympias away and established her in Epirus. He himself took up temporary residence in Illyria.[20]

Meanwhile, Demaratus the Corinthian, a plainspoken friend of the family, paid Philip a visit. After their first affectionate greetings, Philip asked Demaratus how the Greeks were getting along with one another. Demaratus replied, "How appropriate, Philip, for you to concern yourself about Greece, now that you have filled your own house with such strife and misery." Pulling himself together, Philip sent for Alexander and brought him home, having persuaded him through Demaratus to return.

[10] When Pixodarus, the Carian satrap, sought to insinuate himself through kinship into Philip's military alliance,[21] he planned to offer his eldest daughter in marriage to Philip's son Arrhidaeus,[22]

---

between Alexander and the bride's family, as illustrated in the episode that follows.

19. Her father seems to have died, leaving Attalus, her uncle, as her guardian. Attalus was son-in-law to Parmenio, Philip's most senior general, and went on to serve as co-commander with him in the advance expedition into Asia (see page 15).

20. This breach between father and son, just before the end of Philip's life, was evidently quite a serious matter. It is not clear why, or even whether, Philip sought to remove Alexander from his long-held position as presumptive heir to the throne, though his increasing estrangement from Olympias must have played a role.

21. As satrap of Caria (in western Turkey), Pixodarus was a high official of the Persian empire, but he evidently surmised that Philip's planned invasion of Asia would be successful and tried to switch sides before the war had truly begun.

22. Arrhidaeus was Philip's illegitimate son and Alexander's half-brother. He was a mental defective who, against all odds, eventually came to be proclaimed king of the vast Macedonian empire as Philip III (see page 170).

and to that end dispatched Aristocritus to Macedonia. Rumors and slanders again reached Alexander from his friends and his mother to the effect that Philip, by means of an illustrious marriage and important state affairs, was grooming Arrhidaeus for the throne. Perturbed by these hints, Alexander sent Thessalus, the tragic actor, to Caria to converse with Pixodarus and advise him to reject the bastard, who was not even sound of mind, and choose Alexander instead to be his connection by marriage (a prospect far more gratifying to Pixodarus than the other).[23] When Philip learned of this, he visited Alexander's bedchamber. Taking along one of his son's closest friends, Philotas, son of Parmenio,[24] he admonished Alexander severely and accused him of being ignoble and unworthy of his privileges if he was content to become the son-in-law of a Carian fellow, the slave of a barbarian king. Philip then wrote to the Corinthians, ordering them to send Thessalus back, bound in shackles. As for Alexander's other companions—Harpalus, Nearchus, Erigyius, and Ptolemy, whom at a later time Alexander brought back and held in the highest esteem—Philip banished them from Macedonia.[25]

The relationship between Philip and Alexander, though damaged in the two episodes above, was at least superficially restored by the beginning of 336, though Alexander's mother, Olympias, remained in exile in her native Epirus, where she was reportedly agitating for war. As a diplomatic gesture

23. Alexander's behavior in this peculiar episode is interesting and somewhat obscure. By trying to supplant his half-brother as the bridegroom of Pixodarus' daughter, he was openly subverting his father's express wishes and risking another break with Philip, just after the first had been patched up. Perhaps he felt that his position as heir really was in jeopardy—Cleopatra, Philip's new wife, had already borne a daughter and may have been pregnant again by this time—and that he had better start building his own power base to prepare for a succession struggle.
24. It is curious to hear Philotas here described as a close friend of Alexander. Nowhere else do we see evidence of such a friendship. Eight years later Philotas would become the principal victim of one of Alexander's most notorious purges (see below, pages 94–6).
25. Philip seems to have suspected that Alexander's friends had conspired with him in the illicit communications with Pixodarus. Three of the four friends mentioned here would go on to play major roles in Alexander's Asian campaign, and Ptolemy went on after Alexander's death to found a dynasty in Egypt that endured for three centuries (see Glossary).

*Philip offered the hand of his daughter by Olympias, Alexander's sister, to
the king of Epirus, and this offer was accepted. Philip prepared a wedding
celebration in his capital of Aegae that would demonstrate his power and
greatness before the assembled notables of the Greek world. At the same
time he wished to rally support among these wedding guests for his grand
scheme, the invasion of Asia, which he had already begun by sending an
advance force under Parmenio and Attalus across the Hellespont. But things
were about to take an unexpected turn.*

d. The assassination of Philip

*The events surrounding Philip's assassination remain obscure today, and con-
spiracy theories continue to be debated among modern historians. Some of
these theories regard Alexander, his mother Olympias, or both together as
the originators of the plot that led to Philip's death, on the grounds that they
had the most to gain from it now that Alexander's succession was in doubt.
Such theories can be neither proven nor refuted given the available evidence,
which, once again, comes largely from the account of Diodorus Siculus.*

[Diodorus Siculus 16.91] Philip arranged the wedding of Cleopatra,
his daughter by Olympias, having betrothed her to Olympias' legitimate brother Alexander, the king of Epirus.[26] As he wanted as many
Greeks as possible to take part in the festival, he organized magnificent
contests in the arts and ordered the preparation of a lavish banquet for
his friends and guests. He invited friends from all corners of Greece
and urged them to extend his invitation to as many distinguished foreigners as possible. For he was exceedingly anxious to treat the Greeks
affectionately and to express, by means of a proper entertainment, his
appreciation for their having honored him with the supreme command.

[16.92] At last, throngs of celebrants streamed together from all
directions to the festival, and the games and wedding were celebrated
at Aegae in Macedonia. Not only did illustrious individuals, one after
another, present Philip with golden crowns, but most of the noteworthy cities, including Athens, did so as well. And when the Athenians'
crown was being announced, the herald ended by saying that anyone
who plotted against King Philip and fled to Athens would be handed
over to the authorities. By means of this offhand remark, the gods, with
their divine foresight, were revealing the coming plot to Philip. . . .

26. The bride was thus also the niece of her future husband. Note that this
Cleopatra is a different person than the woman Philip had recently wed.

The procession formed at daybreak. Paraded among the other magnificent displays were statues of the twelve gods, wrought with outstanding artistry and adorned with all the brilliant and impressive trappings of wealth. Accompanying these was a thirteenth statue, suitable for a god—a likeness of Philip himself, the king having represented himself enthroned among the twelve gods.[27]

[16.93] The theater was filled when Philip himself appeared in a white cloak, having ordered his bodyguards to follow at a distance. For he was showing everyone that as he was protected by the goodwill of the Greeks, he had no need of his bodyguards. Then, though such an air of authority surrounded him, and everyone was praising and thinking him blessed, a deadly plot against the king, unexpected and utterly unforeseen, came to light. In order to present a clear account of these events, we will begin by mentioning the causes of the plot.

One of the king's bodyguards, a Macedonian named Pausanias, from the district known as Orestis, had become a favorite of Philip's on account of his beauty.[28] When Pausanias saw that another man, also named Pausanias, was endearing himself to the king, he railed at the man, saying he was a hermaphrodite and would readily welcome the erotic overtures of any interested party. The other man, unable to bear such insolence, kept silent for the moment; but after consulting with Attalus, one of his friends, about what he intended to do, he ended his life willingly and unexpectedly: a few days later, when fighting alongside Philip against Pleurias, the king of the Illyrians, this Pausanias, standing in front of Philip, received all the blows aimed at his sovereign and died.

The incident was much talked of, whereupon Attalus, who belonged to the court and was influential with the king, invited Pausanias[29] to dinner. Filling him with unmixed wine,[30] Attalus gave his

27. Scholars are not sure what Philip intended by this unusually arrogant gesture, and some have doubted the credibility of the story. But others believe Philip may have been trying to institute the practice of worshiping the ruler as a god, something not previously seen in Europe, though after Alexander's time it would become commonplace.
28. A sexual relationship is implied, as subsequent events make clear.
29. The first Pausanias is meant here, i.e., the man rejected by Philip in favor of the second.
30. Wine was normally drunk mixed with water, and unmixed wine was considered a powerful intoxicant.

body to the mule drivers to abuse in their drunken revel. When Pausanias came to his senses, he was outraged at the violence he had suffered and accused Attalus in the king's presence. Philip was vexed at the recklessness of the deed, but because of his relationship with Attalus and his present need of the man, he hesitated to condemn his misbehavior. For Attalus was the nephew of Philip's new wife, Cleopatra.[31] He had also been elected as a general of the advance force being sent to Asia[32] and was a formidable warrior. Accordingly, as the king wished to soothe Pausanias' righteous anger, he gave him noteworthy gifts and promoted him to a position of honor in the bodyguard.

[16.94] Pausanias, however, nursed an inexorable anger and was eager to take vengeance not only on the man who had offended him, but also on the one who had failed to avenge him. The sophist Hermocrates played a key role in the formation of Pausanias' plan. For Pausanias attended his lectures, and when he inquired, in the course of his studies, how one might become very famous, the sophist replied, "by killing a very famous man," for the famous man's murderer would be forever associated with his memory. Connecting this saying with his own wrath, Pausanias had no intention of postponing his plan, but carried it out at the festival itself in the following manner:

Posting horses beside the gates, he approached the entrance to the theater, having concealed a Celtic dagger about his person. As Philip had ordered the friends who were accompanying him to enter the theater ahead of him, and the guards were at a distance, Pausanias noticed the king standing alone, ran up to him, delivered a home-thrust through the ribs, and laid him out a corpse, whereupon he ran toward the gates to the horses standing ready for his flight. Some of the bodyguards immediately rushed to the king's body, while the rest, including Leonnatus, Perdiccas, and Attalus,[33] poured out in pursuit of the murderer. Having got the start of his pursuers, Pausanias would have leaped onto his horse before they reached him had he not fallen, his shoe entangled in a vine. The men with Perdiccas caught up with Pausanias as he was getting to his feet and dispatched him with their daggers.[34]

---

31. Plutarch, as we have seen above (page 11), calls Attalus Cleopatra's uncle, which is more likely correct.
32. That is, as one of Parmenio's co-commanders.
33. A different Attalus than the one sent over to Asia with Parmenio.
34. Those who regard the murder of Philip as the result of a conspiracy

Such was the death of Philip, who in the course of a twenty-four–year reign became the most powerful European king of his day and by virtue of the vastness of his empire came to see himself as enthroned with the twelve gods.

---

naturally point out the convenience to the plotters of having Pausanias thus forever silenced. (A similar set of circumstances surrounding the modern-day assassination of JFK has left room for multitudes of conspiracy theories.) An undisturbed tomb that appears to be that of Philip has recently been excavated, producing the king's skeleton (though some scholars claim it belongs to Philip's illegitimate son, Arrhidaeus) and many important works of art.

II

Alexander in Europe

(Autumn 336–Winter 335 B.C.E.)

a. The northern campaigns

Philip's sudden death at the wedding festival of his daughter left Alexander the leading, but by no means the only, claimant to the Macedonian throne. The army immediately hailed him as its new monarch, but to secure his position, Alexander took the precaution of eliminating several rivals. Among others put to death during the opening months of his reign was Attalus, the uncle of Philip's new bride Cleopatra, with whom Alexander had quarreled so bitterly (see page 11 above). Cleopatra herself was reportedly dispatched along with her young daughter, and perhaps a second child as well, by Olympias, Alexander's tempestuous mother.

Meanwhile, trouble was brewing for Alexander in the Balkans and in Greece. The territories won by Philip in his long years of campaigning now saw an opportunity to reclaim their independence. The tribal kingdoms to the north of Macedonia went into revolt almost immediately. The Greeks were more cautious, but they openly celebrated the death of Philip—Demosthenes appeared in the Athenian assembly wearing a festive cloak, even though he was mourning the death of a daughter—and began plotting ways to release themselves from the League he had founded. At the same time the Persians, eager to rid themselves of the Macedonian advance force already entrenched in their western provinces, made clear they would give generous support to any Greek cities wishing to rebel. By any measure, Alexander's reign, and the Macedonian hegemony in Europe, were at a moment of extreme crisis.

At this point begins the record of Alexander's campaigns made by Arrian, the ancient source deemed by most historians to give the clearest and most reliable picture of this remarkable period. The strengths and weaknesses of Arrian's account have already been discussed in the Introduction to this volume and will be further elucidated in the footnotes that follow. It is a very flawed history by modern standards, biased at many points by its author's explicit admiration for, and even identification with, his subject; and it

17

focuses so intensely on that subject that anything not directly connected
with Alexander himself is lost sight of. Nonetheless, there is no better an-
cient account available, and so we shall follow Arrian almost exclusively,
though not uncritically, in the remainder of this volume.

Arrian begins by explaining to his readers that he has chosen to rely on
the primary accounts of Ptolemy and Aristobulus for his information, hav-
ing judged these to be the most credible and least sensationalized. But he
also gives himself leave to record certain stories and reports he finds note-
worthy even if they come from outside these two sources. Having clarified
his method, he launches into his narrative from the point at which Alexan-
der began his campaigns as leader of the Macedonian army (omitting dis-
cussion of the political murders carried out beforehand to secure
Alexander's position on the throne).

[Arrian I.1] Philip is said to have died during the archonship of Pyth-
odelus at Athens.[1] When Alexander, Philip's son, had succeeded to the
throne, he visited the Peloponnese. He was then about twenty years
old. On his arrival he assembled all the Peloponnesian Greeks and
asked them for the leadership of the Persian campaign, which they had
already given to Philip.[2] All the Greeks granted his request except the
Spartans, who replied that it had never been their custom to follow
others, but to take the lead themselves. Athens, too, showed signs of
rebelling, though at Alexander's first approach the awestruck Athenians ceded him honors even greater than those granted to Philip. Returning to Macedonia, Alexander prepared for his campaign to Asia.

In the spring he marched to Thrace against the Triballians and
Illyrians.[3] Having learned that they were meditating revolt, he

1. 336 B.C.E. Arrian, like other ancient historians, dates events by giving the
names of important officeholders elected in the same year; no system yet existed for numbering years.
2. In 337, following his victory at Chaeronea, Philip had established a league
of all the major Greek states except Sparta and convened a meeting of their
representatives at Corinth. A vote of the council members had affirmed
Philip's planned invasion of Asia and bestowed on Philip the power to act as
its commander in chief. As the heir to Philip's throne, Alexander now sought
affirmation from the Greeks that he had also inherited the leadership of the
expedition.
3. Tribal peoples dwelling along the northern and eastern borders of Macedonia proper; long a threat to Macedonian security, they had been partially
subdued by Philip's armies.

considered it unwise, when embarking on a campaign far from home, to leave neighboring tribes behind unless they had been thoroughly humbled. Setting out from Amphipolis, he invaded the region of Thrace inhabited by the so-called autonomous Thracians, keeping Philippi and Mount Orbelus on his left. Ten days after crossing the river Nestus, he is said to have reached Mount Haemus. And there, at the narrow path leading up the mountain, he was met by many armed [. . .][4] and autonomous Thracians standing ready to bar his way; they had occupied the height of Haemus at the very point where the army had to pass around the mountain. The tribesmen had brought a number of wagons together to form a barricade from which they could defend themselves if they were pressed hard. They also planned to send the wagons down against the ascending Macedonian phalanx[5] at the steepest part of the mountain, thinking that the more tightly packed the phalanx, the more forcibly the wagons, as they hurtled down, would disperse it.

Alexander gave thought to how he could safely cross the mountain. When he realized that the risk had to be run (as there was no other way around), he relayed his instructions to the hoplites: when the wagons came rolling down the slope, the men in the wide part of the path were to break ranks, move to either side, and let the wagons pass down the middle; the hoplites in the narrow part were to crouch down (some were even to fall to the ground) and lock their shields tightly together. For when the wagons hurtled down, their momentum would likely cause them to leap over the men and pass by without injuring them.[6] The outcome justified Alexander's advice and conjectures. Part of the phalanx divided, and the wagons, as they rolled over the shields, did little harm; indeed, no one was killed. As they had especially dreaded the wagons, and these had proved harmless,

---

4. A word denoting some other tribe is missing from the manuscripts here.
5. The phalanx is the infantry contingent of the army, which fought in a block formation of varying size.
6. A. B. Bosworth imagines this formation as a kind of ramp composed of "a line of men lying on the ground and a second standing over them, their shields interlocking" (*Commentary* I.56), but he does not believe it could actually have succeeded in the manner described. However we envision the stratagem, what is perhaps most remarkable is Alexander's willingness to experiment with a configuration that, if unsuccessful, would have resulted in many deaths among his troops.

the Macedonians now took courage, raised a shout, and attacked the Thracians. Alexander ordered the archers to move from the right wing to the front of the phalanx (a more convenient position for them) and to shoot at the Thracians wherever they attacked. He himself collected the *agema*, the shield-bearers, and the Agrianians[7] to form his left wing, with himself in command. The archers, shooting at the Thracians who sallied forth from the ranks, succeeded in driving them back. The phalanx now joined battle and had no difficulty thrusting back the barbarians, who were lightly or poorly armed. The latter no longer awaited Alexander, who was advancing from the left, but threw away their arms and fled as best they could down the mountain. Nearly fifteen hundred of them perished. On account of their speed and knowledge of the country, few were seized, though all the women who had been accompanying them were captured with their young children and all the property that could be carried off.

[I.2] Alexander sent the plunder back to the cities at the coast, appointing Lysanias and Philotas to take charge of it. He himself, after crossing the peak, passed over the river Haemus, continued his march against the Triballians, and reached the river Lyginus, which lies a three days' journey from the Danube in the direction of the Haemus. Syrmus, the Triballians' king, who had long since learned of Alexander's expedition, sent the Triballians' wives and children to the Danube, where they were to cross to Peuce, one of the river's islands. The Triballians' Thracian neighbors had fled to this island well in advance of Alexander's approach, and Syrmus himself now joined them with his suite. But most of his subjects fled back to the Haemus, from which Alexander had himself set out the day before.

When he learned of their move, Alexander turned back, led his men against the Triballians, and came upon them already encamped. Though caught, the Triballians drew themselves up in battle array at the glen beside the river. Alexander himself, having deepened the phalanx,[8] led his men forward and commanded the archers and slingers to run out ahead and fire their arrows and stones at the barbarians, thinking this might draw them into the open from the glen. As they

---

7. See Glossary for explanations of all names of military contingents.
8. The Macedonian phalanx could be "deepened" as needed by the shifting of its manpower to add to the rear of the formation. By this kind of shift the width of the front line could be reduced and the impetus of the whole formation increased.

came within range of these missiles, the Triballians ran out to engage the archers in hand-to-hand combat (as archers do not wear armor). When Alexander had thus drawn the barbarians out, he ordered Philotas[9] to lead the Upper Macedonian cavalry against the enemy's right wing, where they had advanced farthest after emerging from the glen, and ordered Heraclides and Sopolis to lead the cavalry from Bottiaea and Amphipolis against the left wing. Having marshaled the remaining cavalry in front of the infantry phalanx, he led both forces against the enemy's center.

While the two sides assailed one another from a distance, the Triballians were holding their own; but when the tightly arrayed phalanx attacked them with force, and Alexander's cavalry, no longer using their javelins, were thrusting the enemy this way and that with the horses themselves,[10] the Triballians were routed and fled through the glen to the river. Three thousand died in the rout, but only a few were taken alive, as the woods beside the river were dense, and the gathering darkness impaired the Macedonians' pursuit. Eleven Macedonian horsemen died, according to Ptolemy, and about forty foot soldiers.[11]

[I.3] The third day after the battle Alexander reached the Danube. Europe's largest river, the Danube traverses the most territory and bounds the most warlike races, principally the Celtic tribes (in whose territory the river's springs emerge). There Alexander found his warships, which had come from Byzantium through the Black Sea. After filling them with archers and hoplites, he sailed for the island to which the Triballians and Thracians had fled, and tried to force a landing. But the barbarians met his ships wherever they drew near shore. The warships, which were few in number, carried a modest force; the island, in most places, was steep for a landing; and the river's current, as it was confined in a narrow space, was swift and hard to deal with.

---

9. Not the Philotas who had been deputed to convey spoils in the previous chapter, but the son of Alexander's most senior general, Parmenio; he will later come to play a crucial part in the Alexander story (see pages 94–6 below).

10. The Macedonian cavalryman carried a javelin and a slashing sword into battle, but at close quarters the forward motion of his horse was often his most powerful weapon.

11. Arrian's casualty figures, here and throughout the narrative, are extremely lopsided, much more so than the figures given by other sources for the same engagements. Most likely his sources, Ptolemy and Aristobulus, minimized Macedonian losses in order to enhance Alexander's reputation.

So, after withdrawing his ships, Alexander decided to cross the Danube and march against the Getae, who dwelt on its farther side. For he had noticed many of them gathered together at the bank as though to bar his way should he try to cross—they had nearly four thousand horsemen and more than ten thousand foot soldiers—and at the same time a sudden longing seized him to pass beyond the Danube.[12] He himself went aboard the ship. Having collected the leather tents used in camp, Alexander had them filled with hay, gathered as many as possible of the local vessels made from solid trunks (there were many of these, since the neighboring tribes used them for fishing, for visiting one another up and down the river, and especially for plundering), and ferried across as much of his army as he could. Nearly fifteen hundred horsemen and four thousand foot soldiers made the crossing with Alexander.

[I.4] They crossed at night where a deep cornfield afforded them cover as they touched at the bank. Toward dawn, Alexander led the men through the field, having ordered the foot soldiers to flatten the corn, holding their pikes aslant, until they reached untilled ground. As long as the phalanx advanced through the field, the cavalry followed; but once both forces had passed it, Alexander himself led the cavalry to the right wing and ordered Nicanor to lead the phalanx in rectangular formation. The Getae did not even await the first cavalry charge. For Alexander's daring—his having so easily crossed the largest of rivers in one night without bridging it—confounded their expectations,[13] and they found the phalanx, with its locked shields,

12. This is the first occurrence in Arrian of a formula that will be repeated numerous times, on occasions when great exploits or crossings into unknown territory present themselves: "A great desire [*pothos*] seized Alexander." Some scholars have seen this recurring motif as Arrian's attempt to capture language actually used by Alexander; others consider it a gratuitous romanticization of the king's insatiable desire for conquest. In any case, the form of the expression is interesting: Arrian says "a longing seized Alexander," as if an irresistible outside force was at work, rather than that Alexander felt a desire to go farther. In this case, the crossing of the Danube, a river that Philip had always adopted as the limit of Macedonian territory, is very much a step into terra incognita.

13. A hallmark of Alexander's genius was to move his forces so quickly as to utterly demoralize his opponents before even striking a blow. Time and again his army appeared sooner than his enemies had anticipated or arrived in places it was never expected to go.

utterly daunting and the cavalry's impetus forceful. At first the Getae fled to their city, which lay a few miles from the Danube. But when they saw Alexander rapidly leading the phalanx along the river (lest his infantry be surrounded by the Getae, who were lying in ambush), with the cavalry in front, they abandoned their poorly fortified city after taking up on horseback as many of their children and women as the horses could carry. They rushed as far as they could away from the river into the wilderness.

Alexander seized their city and gave all the plunder they had left behind to Meleager and Philip[14] to convey back to camp, and he himself, after razing the town, offered sacrifices at the bank of the Danube to Zeus the preserver, to Heracles, and to the Danube itself for letting him cross, and that same day led all his men safely back to camp.

Envoys now visited Alexander from all the other autonomous tribes settled near the Danube and from Syrmus, the king of the Triballians. Envoys also arrived from the Celts, who dwelt on the Ionic Gulf. Men of enormous stature, these Celts had a high opinion of themselves. All the envoys declared they had come desiring Alexander's friendship, and he exchanged pledges with one and all. He asked the Celts what human thing they feared the most, expecting, since his great name had reached the Celts and gone even farther, that they would say they feared him beyond everything. But the Celts' reply disappointed him. For as they dwelt far from Alexander in a place hard to reach, and saw that he was drawn in other directions, they said they feared only that the sky might fall on them; and though they admired Alexander, neither fear nor any concern for their advantage had moved them to send him envoys. Having declared these men his friends and allies, Alexander sent them off, though he remarked under his breath, "Big talkers, these Celts!"

Having settled matters on Macedonia's northeastern frontier, Alexander now had to deal with problems in the northwest: a revolt led by Cleitus, the son of an ancient enemy king named Bardylis, aided by the neighboring Taulantian tribe under their king, Glaucias. Here, for the first time in his life, Alexander found himself in serious difficulties. His two enemies succeeded in trapping him in between strong positions, in a spot where they could deprive his army, and his horses, of food. Alexander used a number of crafty moves to get out of this jam, including an interesting form of what are now

14. A different Philip than Alexander's recently killed father.

called "psychological operations": knowing that the Taulantians were
watching from the ridges above, he ordered his infantry to form into a deep
phalanx and execute a series of complex drill maneuvers and then charge
the surrounding heights. The Taulantians were so astonished and intimidated
by the precision of the Macedonian drills that they abandoned their strong-
hold and fled as soon as the attack was launched. That left Alexander free to
deal with Cleitus, whom he soon overcame.

b. The Theban revolt

After the defeat of Cleitus and Glaucias, Alexander had nothing further to
fear from the tribes on his northern frontier, and indeed he had cemented
strong friendships with some of them, especially the Agrianians, who had
long been, and would long remain, his nation's most reliable foreign allies.
The entire campaign had taken about five months and was concluded just
in time for Alexander to take on his next challenge, the Theban revolt (recounted below).

While Alexander was solidifying his power base in Europe, his general
Parmenio was hard at work in Asia trying to fulfill the mission Philip had sent
him on, to seize and hold a bridgehead for the coming invasion. The newly
installed Persian king, Darius III, had sent a force of hired Greek soldiers under the command of a brilliant Greek general, Memnon, to oust this expe-
ditionary force from Asia Minor (the western coast of Turkey). Though
successful in winning back some of these "liberated" Greek cities, Memnon
was ultimately unable to bar the pathway into Asia that Parmenio and his
Macedonians had opened.

At the same time, Darius sought to employ the long-successful Persian
strategy of keeping the Europeans out of Asia by keeping them at war with
each other. His agents secretly brought money to both Thebes and Athens
to be used in inciting revolt against Macedonia. These agents, though unmentioned by Arrian, undoubtedly played some part—how large is unclear—in the disastrous events about to unfold at Thebes.

[I.7] Meanwhile, a number of Theban exiles, slipping into Thebes by
night with the help of certain persons who sought to stage a revolt,
seized and killed Amyntas and Timolaus, two members of the force
occupying the Cadmeia.[15] (As these men anticipated no hostilities,

---

15. The Cadmeia was the citadel of ancient Thebes, the highest and therefore most easily defended section of the city. A Macedonian garrison had been
established there in 338, after the battle of Chaeronea, as a way for Philip to

they were roaming outside the garrison.) Coming forward in the assembly, the exiles incited the Thebans to revolt from Alexander, invoking "freedom" and "autonomy"—noble old words—and encouraging them to rid themselves of their Macedonian oppressors. The people found the exiles persuasive, especially since they insisted that Alexander had died in the land of the Illyrians. This rumor was indeed making the rounds; it had gained currency because Alexander had been away for a considerable time and no news had come from him. The result was just what always happens under such circumstances: in the absence of accurate information, people formed conjectures in keeping with their wishes.

When Alexander learned what was afoot at Thebes, he decided that the developments there could not be neglected. For he had long been suspicious of Athens and considered that the Thebans' enterprise would be dangerous if the Spartans, who had long ago become rebels in spirit if not in fact,[16] joined other Peloponnesians (and the Aetolians, whom he did not consider reliable) in support of the revolt. Marching past Eordaea and Elimiotis and the heights of Stymphaea and Parvaea, Alexander reached Pelinna in Thessaly on the seventh day. Setting out from Pelinna, he entered Boeotia on the sixth day, so that the Thebans did not learn that he had entered the gates until he had reached Onchestus with his entire army. Then the men who had fomented the revolt declared that the army from Macedonia was Antipater's; they continued to insist that Alexander was dead. They angrily contradicted those who reported that Alexander himself was leading the army, and maintained that a different Alexander had come—namely, Alexander the son of Aeropus.

Starting from Onchestus the next day, Alexander led his army to Thebes and encamped at the grove of Iolaus, giving the Thebans time, in case they repented their bad decisions, to send him an embassy. But the Thebans were so far from conceding anything that might lead to an agreement, that their horsemen, sallying out from the city with a considerable number of light-armed troops, skirmished with his advanced guards and killed a few Macedonians. Alexander

---

keep the Thebans in line with his political agenda, and the two men mentioned here belonged to that garrison.

16. Referring to Sparta's unwillingness to join the Greek League established by Philip after the battle of Chaeronea.

sent out some light-armed troops and archers to deflect the attack, and his men easily repulsed the Thebans, who were by now approaching his camp. The next day, Alexander marched the entire army around to the gates that led to Eleutherae and Attica. Even then he did not assault the city walls but encamped not far from the Cadmeia, so that its Macedonian occupiers would have help nearby. For the Thebans had blockaded the Cadmeia with a double palisade and were keeping watch so that no outside aid could reach those who were penned in there, nor could those inside run out and injure them when they were under attack from beyond their walls. Having encamped near the Cadmeia, Alexander continued to delay, as he still wished to approach the Thebans through friendship rather than threat of harm.[17]

At that point, the Thebans who realized what was in their state's best interest were moved to come out to Alexander and to seek forgiveness for their people's revolt. But the exiles and all who had summoned them (especially those among them who were officers of the Boeotian League), supposing that they would meet with no kindness from Alexander, were doing all they could to drum up popular support for the war. But even so, Alexander did not attack the town.

[I.8] Ptolemy, however, says that Perdiccas, who had been put in charge of guarding the Macedonian camp and stood with his own battalion not far from the enemy's palisade, did not wait for Alexander's signal but assaulted the palisade, tore it down, and attacked the Thebans' forward guard. When Amyntas, son of Andromenes, saw Perdiccas advancing within the palisade, he followed him. (Amyntas had been posted with Perdiccas and commanded his own battalion.) Taking note of these developments, Alexander led up the rest of the troops, lest they be cut off and find themselves at the Thebans' mercy.[18] He signaled the archers and the Agrianians to run inside the

17. Arrian's account of Alexander's siege of Thebes differs markedly from those of Diodorus and other writers in portraying Alexander, and the Macedonians generally, as moderate and restrained in responding to Theban provocations. Diodorus, by contrast, shows Alexander becoming enraged and personally directing the worst atrocities of the siege in a spirit of vengeance.
18. Again emphasizing Alexander's restraint, Arrian depicts a sequence of events in which the general attack on Thebes commenced not on Alexander's orders, but as the result of an unauthorized sally by the subcommander, Perdiccas. Diodorus, by contrast, claims that Perdiccas acted under orders from Alexander. Such differences indicate that the destruction of Thebes was

palisade, but kept the *agema* and the shield-bearers outside. When Perdiccas had forced his way into the second palisade, he was wounded; having fallen there, he was brought back to camp in serious condition, and his life was saved only with difficulty. But the men under his command, falling on the Thebans at the hollow road that runs past the temple of Heracles, hemmed them in with the aid of Alexander's archers. They followed the retreating Thebans as far as the temple of Heracles, but at that point the Thebans wheeled around with a shout, and the Macedonians were put to flight. Eurybotas, the Cretan captain of the archers, perished with nearly seventy of his men. The remainder fled to the Macedonians' *agema* and the royal shield-bearers.

At that point Alexander, seeing his men fleeing and the Thebans, having broken ranks, in pursuit, attacked with his phalanx in formation and thrust the Thebans inside the gates. The retreat proved so terrifying to the Thebans that when they were driven into the city they did not bar the gates in time, and all the Macedonians who were following close on their heels rushed with the Thebans into the fortress. (Because the Thebans had posted so many advance guards, their walls were not manned.) Having reached the Cadmeia, some of the Macedonians proceeded on to the Ampheion;[19] joined by the troops posted in the Cadmeia,[20] they entered the adjacent sections of the city; those at the walls (held now by the troops who had rushed in with the fleeing Thebans) scaled them and rushed to the marketplace. For a short while the Thebans posted at the Ampheion held their ground, but when they were pressed hard on all sides by the Macedonians and by Alexander, who could be seen here and there, some of the Theban horsemen, escaping through the city, went out into the plain; the foot soldiers saved themselves as best they could. After that, it was not the Macedonians so much as the Phocians, the Plataeans, and the other Boeotians[21] who, in a rage,

---

widely considered a black mark on Alexander's reputation and that some writers had sought to mitigate it.

19. A hill adjoining the Cadmeia.

20. The members of the garrison, who had now been set free.

21. Another point on which the different viewpoints of the various Alexander historians can be discerned. Diodorus, while agreeing that the slaughter of the Thebans was aided by the city's Greek enemies, places primary responsibility on the heads of the Macedonians and in particular on Alexander, who,

slaughtered the Thebans helter-skelter even when the latter made no move to defend themselves, falling upon some in their houses (where some resistance was met with) and upon others who tried to approach the temples as suppliants. They spared neither women nor children.

[I.9] This tragedy, both with regard to the size of the captured city and the quickness of the action, and not least in its outcome, unexpected by both the victims and the perpetrators, astonished all the other Greeks no less than those who took part in it. For if the reverses that befell the Athenians in Sicily[22] were no less of a calamity in terms of the number of casualties, at least their army was destroyed far from home and included more allied troops than native Athenians, and their city survived and managed to hold out for a long time afterward against the Spartans, their allies, and the Great King;[23] hence it did not afford its victims the same sense of disaster, nor did it evoke the same terror in the other Greeks. Athens' subsequent defeat at Aegospotami,[24] moreover, took place at sea, and though the Athenians were humbled by the pulling down of their Long Walls, the surrender of many ships, and the loss of their empire, their city nevertheless retained its ancient form and before long regained its former power, completely fortified its Long Walls, and again prevailed at sea; it was then *their* turn to save from the direst dangers the Spartans who had once terrified them and nearly annihilated their city. The Spartan defeats at Leuctra and Mantinea[25] astonished them more

---

he says, had been driven into a murderous rage by the taunts flung at him prior to the battle's onset.

22. Arrian here refers to the destruction of the Athenian expedition to Sicily in 413 B.C.E., in which tens of thousands lost their lives.

23. "The Great King" is the standard Greek term for the ruler of the Persian empire. Persia had thrown its financial resources behind the Spartans in the final years of their twenty-seven–year war with the Athenians, the so-called Peloponnesian War.

24. The battle in 405 in which Athens lost its entire navy at one stroke and therefore had to accept defeat in its war against Sparta.

25. The Spartan infantry, though reputed to be invincible in a set land battle, was finally defeated at Leuctra (371 B.C.E.) and Mantinea (362 B.C.E.) by a Theban army led by Epaminondas. After Leuctra, Epaminondas had further humiliated the Spartans by leading his army straight into their formerly unassailable territory, an event referred to in the second part of this sentence.

by the disaster's unexpectedness than by the number of casualties, and the attack of the Boeotians and Arcadians with Epaminondas against Sparta frightened the Spartans and their allies more by the surprise of such an unusual sight than by the keenness of their danger. The conquest of the Plataeans' city²⁶ was no great tragedy, both because of the smallness of the city and [. . .]²⁷ of those confined in it, the majority having fled to Athens long before. And the capture of the island cities, Melos and Scione,²⁸ brought more disgrace to its perpetrators than any great surprise to the Greek world as a whole.

But in Thebes, the hasty and unpremeditated character of the revolt, and the suddenness of the capture, which came about with little effort on the part of the conquerors,²⁹ and the wholesale slaughter of the kind perpetrated by members of the same race taking vengeance for an ancient enmity,³⁰ and the complete enslavement of the city that was then preeminent among the Greeks for power and renown in warfare—all of these elements were attributed, not unreasonably, to the wrath of the gods. For it was said that the Thebans had paid the full penalty, long after the fact, for their betrayal of the Greeks in the Persian War, and for their occupation of the Plataeans' city during the

---

26. In the opening phase of the Peloponnesian War (427 B.C.E.), Plataea, an ally of Athens, was captured by Sparta after a long siege, and all its surviving inhabitants were executed.

27. A word or phrase has fallen out of the text here.

28. More notorious episodes from the Peloponnesian War: Athens conducted mass executions after the capture of the rebel city of Methone (not actually an island) in 412 and after the conquest of Melos in 415. It is noteworthy that, in the above catalog of annihilations, Arrian lists only those conducted by the great Greek states; he might equally well have mentioned the destruction of Olynthus by Philip in 348, but his point seems to be that Greek warfare, just as much as that conducted by the Macedonians, could at times sanction the mass killing of civilians or prisoners of war.

29. A further point on which Arrian has "spun" the siege of Thebes differently than other authors: Diodorus shows the Thebans mounting a very stern counteroffensive and inflicting heavy losses on the Macedonians.

30. "Members of the same race" implies that Greeks were butchering fellow Greeks; Arrian uses the phrase as though the Macedonians had not been involved. The "ancient enmity" mentioned sprang from the forceful and arrogant foreign policies Thebes had followed during the height of its power in the 360s.

armistice and their complete enslavement of that city, and for their butchery, uncharacteristic of Greeks, of those who had surrendered to the Spartans, and for laying waste the Plataeans' countryside, in which the Greeks, drawn up opposite the Persians, had repulsed the danger threatening Greece, and because they had voted to destroy Athens when a motion was proposed among the Spartans' allies concerning the city's enslavement.[31] Even before the disaster, many warning signs were said to have been sent by the gods; these had been ignored at the time, but afterward the memory of them led people to conclude that the event had been prefigured long before.

The allies who had taken part in the action and to whom Alexander entrusted the disposition of affairs in Thebes[32] decided to garrison the Cadmeia and to raze the city to the ground and distribute its territories (except for consecrated ground) to the allies. All the children, women, and Theban survivors (except for the priests and priestesses, all the guest-friends[33] of Philip or Alexander, and all who had served as *proxenoi*[34] of the Macedonians) were enslaved. They say that

31. Arrian here takes the opportunity to remind his readers of the wrongs committed by Thebes in the 150 years before its destruction: (1) It had sided with the Persians in 480–479 B.C.E., during Xerxes' great invasion of mainland Greece; (2) it had made an unprovoked attack on its neighbor, Plataea, in 431, at the outset of the Peloponnesian War; (3) it had collaborated with Sparta in the later annihilation of the Plataeans (see n. 28 above); (4) again in the Persian Wars, Thebes had aided the enemies of Greece just prior to the decisive battle of Plataea; (5) again in the Peloponnesian War, after Sparta had defeated the Athenians and consulted its allies about the terms of a peace settlement, Thebes had voted for the total destruction of Athens (404).
32. As a rebellious member of the Greek League established by Philip, Thebes was subject to a punishment chosen by the other members of the League, and it seems likely that Alexander did institute some sort of judiciary proceeding before acting. But it was hardly possible under the circumstances to refer the matter to the main body of the League, seated far away at Corinth. Most likely the Greek contingents of Alexander's army were summoned to form a kind of ad hoc judicial body, but among these there was a high proportion of states that had suffered in the past from Theban aggression, and so a harsh verdict was assured.
33. A "guest-friend" in this context means someone who had received Philip or Alexander into his home or had been received by them.
34. The *proxenoi* were citizens of Thebes who had undertaken to represent Macedonian interests in Thebes, hence supporters of Alexander.

Alexander saved the house of Pindar the poet and spared his descendants out of reverence for Pindar.[35] In addition to these measures, the allies decided to rebuild and fortify Orchomenus and Plataea.[36]

[I.10] When the Thebans' misfortune was reported to the other Greeks, all the Arcadians who had rushed from home to the Thebans' rescue condemned to death those who had encouraged them to do so; the Eleans received back their exiles because the latter were friendly to Alexander; and the Aetolians, having sent embassies of their own, tribe by tribe, begged Alexander's forgiveness because they, too, had revolted on learning of the Thebans' revolt. The Athenians, who were then celebrating their great mysteries, were thunderstruck when some of the Thebans arrived straight from the action itself. Abandoning the mysteries, they began transporting their goods and chattels from the fields to the city. The people assembled and on Demades' motion selected ten envoys from among all the Athenians and sent them to Alexander (having chosen men known to be especially friendly to him) to convey the delight he had afforded the people of Athens by his safe return from the Illyrians and Triballians (though they had not expressed this sentiment at the time) and by his punishment of the Thebans' revolt.[37]

Alexander responded in kindly fashion to the embassy, but wrote a letter to the Athenian people demanding the surrender of Demosthenes and Lycurgus. He also demanded Hyperides, Polyeuctus, Chares, Charidemus, Ephialtes, Diotimus, and Moerocles, as he considered these men responsible both for the city's disaster at Chaeronea and for the later offenses committed at Philip's death against himself and Philip. He also argued that these men were no less guilty of the Thebans' revolt than the Theban rebels themselves. The Athenians

---

35. If true, undoubtedly a propaganda move by Alexander, who wished to appear high-mindedly Hellenic in cultural outlook even while overseeing the destruction of a Greek city. But the legend is unknown to Diodorus and other "vulgate" sources.

36. Cities formerly destroyed by Thebes.

37. These sudden and demonstrative pro-Macedonian moves on the part of the Greek states most sympathetic to the Theban revolutionaries show that Alexander's strategy in destroying Thebes had worked. Diodorus summarizes this strategy as follows: "Alexander decided to destroy the city completely and, by means of the fear that would result, to nip in the bud any further ventures by rebels" (17.9.4).

did not give up the men, but sent a second embassy to Alexander, entreating him to relax his anger against those whose surrender he had demanded. And Alexander relented, perhaps out of reverence for the city, or because he was eager for the expedition to Asia and wanted to leave no cause for resentment behind in Greece.[38] Of those men, however, whose surrender had been demanded but not granted, Alexander ordered Charidemus alone to go into exile. Charidemus fled to Asia, to the court of King Darius.

38. Alexander's change of heart in this matter, which would have caused a grave rift with Athens had it gone forward, is interesting. It resembles another policy change in the early phases of the Asian invasion involving the treatment of Greek mercenaries who had fought on the Persian side (see page 42 with note 22 below). In his dealings with the Greeks and with Athens in particular, Alexander seems to have felt torn between his rage at those who opposed him and his respect for the pluralism and outspokenness natural to Greek political life.

III

The War with Darius— Phase I

(Spring 334–Autumn 332 B.C.E.)

a. The battle of the Granicus

[Arrian I.11] Having settled these matters, Alexander returned to Macedonia, where he performed the sacrifice to Olympian Zeus established by Archelaus and celebrated the Olympic Games at Aegae.[1] Some say that he also held a contest in honor of the Muses. Word now came that the statue in Pieria of Orpheus, son of Oeagrus the Thracian, was sweating continuously. The prophets interpreted this in a variety of ways, but Aristander, a Telmissian seer, urged Alexander to take heart, as it had been made clear that the epic and lyric poets and all who concerned themselves with song would have plenty of work composing verses celebrating Alexander and his exploits.[2]

In early spring, Alexander marched to the Hellespont,[3] having entrusted Macedonian and Greek affairs to Antipater, while he himself led the infantry, which with the light-armed troops and archers numbered not much more than thirty thousand, with more than five thousand horsemen. His route passed alongside Lake Cercinitis in the direction of Amphipolis and the outlets of the river Strymon. After crossing the Strymon, he passed Mount Pangaeum on his way to Abdera and Maroneia, Greek cities settled on the coast. From there he

---

1. The games were in fact held at Pella; Arrian's sources were in error here.
2. Orpheus was a legendary poet and musician, hence the point of Aristander's interpretation.
3. See the map on pages xxviii–xxix. The Hellespont (modern-day Dardanelles) is the strait connecting Europe and Asia, both sides of which were held at this point by the advance Macedonian force under Parmenio.

reached the Hebrus and crossed the river easily. Marching through Paetica, he headed for the Black River, crossed it, and arrived in Sestus twenty days after setting out from home. On reaching Elaeus, he sacrificed to Protesilaus at the latter's grave, as Protesilaus is thought to have been the first Greek, of those who came with Agamemnon to make war on Troy, to have crossed into Asia. The offering was made in the hope that Alexander's landing might have a more favorable outcome than that of Protesilaus.[4]

Parmenio had been assigned to transport the cavalry and most of the infantry from Sestus to Abydus. These troops crossed in 160 triremes[5] and many other merchant vessels. A popular story has it that when crossing from Elaeus to the Achaean harbor, Alexander himself took the helm of the admiral's ship, and that when he was halfway across the Hellespont he sacrificed a bull to Poseidon and the Nereids and poured a libation from a golden bowl into the sea. It is also said that he was the first to disembark with his weapons onto Asian soil and that he built two altars—one where he had set out from Europe, the other where he had landed in Asia—in honor of Zeus Protector of Landings, Athena, and Heracles. Having made his way up to Troy, he sacrificed to Trojan Athena, dedicated his armor in the temple, and took down, in exchange for it, some of the sacred weapons preserved from the Trojan War. They say that his shield-bearers used to carry these weapons before him into battle.[6] He is also said to have sacrificed to Priam at the altar of Zeus of the Courtyard, hoping to appease

4. This sacrifice is the first of many gestures performed by Alexander in an effort to highlight parallels between his own invasion of Asia and the Greek expedition against Troy some eight hundred years earlier. Just as Agamemnon and his troops had gone east to avenge a wrong—the Trojan abduction of Helen—so now Alexander sought to avenge the Persian sack of Athens and other Greek cities in 480 and 479 B.C.E. It should be remembered that Alexander considered himself a direct descendant of Achilles, the greatest of the Greeks who fought at Troy, and carried a copy of Homer's *Iliad* with him wherever he went on campaign. Protesilaus was thought to have been killed immediately upon disembarking onto Asian soil.

5. A trireme is a Greek warship powered by 150 rowers. In this case the ships were used as ferries, rather than, as in the crossing engineered by Xerxes in 480, as supports for a pontoon bridge.

6. It is hard to visualize how this would be accomplished, but Arrian depicts the arrangement still in force eight years after this (VI.9; see page 141 below).

⎡Priam's wrath against the family of Neoptolemus,[7] to which he himself belonged.⎤

[I.12] When Alexander reached Troy, Menoetius the pilot
crowned him with a golden crown, and then Chares the Athenian,
having arrived from Sigeum, and certain others, some of them
Greeks, others local residents. . . ⎡Some say that Alexander placed a
wreath on the tomb of Achilles, and Hephaestion is said to have
placed one on Patroclus' tomb.⎤Legend has it that Alexander accounted Achilles happy for having had Homer to herald his renown
to posterity. And, indeed, Alexander was right to account Achilles
happy on that score especially; for though Alexander was fortunate in
other respects, here there was a void, and his exploits were not published to humankind in a worthy manner either in prose or in verse.
Nor were his praises sung in lyric poetry as were those of Hieron,
Gelon, Theron,[8] and many others who do not bear comparison with
him. Consequently, Alexander's exploits are much less well-known
than the paltriest of ancient deeds. For the expedition of Cyrus' Ten
Thousand against King Artaxerxes, and the sufferings of Clearchus
and the men captured with him, and the march to the coast of those
same men under Xenophon's command[9] are much better known,
thanks to Xenophon, than Alexander's exploits. Yet Alexander never
campaigned in another man's service, nor did he flee the Great King
and merely defeat those who impeded his march to the coast.[10] One
can point to no other man, Greek or barbarian, who performed

---

7. Neoptolemus, according to legend, was the son of Achilles and hence
Alexander's ancestor. In the myths of the Trojan War he had cruelly slain King
Priam, the elderly ruler of Troy.
8. Famous athletes whose victories have been celebrated in the odes of Pindar and other poets.
9. Arrian here refers to the events of Xenophon's *Anabasis*, in which a band
of ten thousand Greek mercenary soldiers were conveyed into Mesopotamia
to fight on behalf of a claimant to the Persian throne and then had to make
their way home unassisted through alien and often hostile territory after the
leader who had hired them was killed in battle.
10. That is, Xenophon's band of ten thousand cannot compare in greatness
with Alexander, since (1) they fought as mercenary soldiers rather than in a national cause, (2) they withdrew from Persia without overthrowing the reigning
monarch, as they had set out to do, and (3) most of their struggles were against
disorganized tribes who happened to be blocking their route homeward.

exploits so numerous and so momentous. It was this, I affirm, that spurred me on to write this history, and I have not considered myself unworthy to make Alexander's exploits known to humankind. That much I have discerned about myself, whoever I may be. I need not set down my name, for it is not unknown to men, nor is my country nor my family nor the offices I have held in my own land. But this I do put on record: that these chronicles are my country and my family and my offices, and have been from my youth. And that is why I do not consider myself unworthy of a foremost place in Greek letters, if indeed Alexander merits a foremost place in the annals of warfare.

As Alexander begins his long trek eastward, following for now the coastline of the Sea of Marmara, Arrian gives us a rare look inside the camp of the Persians gathering to oppose him. In few places does his narrative thus "cut away" from Alexander to consider what is happening elsewhere; like a movie director working with a cinematic superstar, he prefers to keep his focus on Alexander as much as possible.

The Persian commanders were Arsames, Pheomithres, Petenes, and Niphates. With them were Spithridates, the satrap of Lydia and Ionia, and Arsites, the governor of Hellespontine Phrygia. These men had encamped near the city of Zeleia with the barbarian cavalry and the Greek mercenaries. They took counsel when Alexander's crossing had been reported, and Memnon of Rhodes[11] advised them not to take a chance against the Macedonians, whose infantry, he said, was far superior to their own; besides, the Macedonians had Alexander present, while on their side Darius[12] was absent. He advised them to march ahead, destroy the fodder by having the horses trample it, and burn the standing harvest, not even sparing the cities themselves, as Alexander would not remain in the country if provisions were scarce.[13] It is said that Arsites declared at the meeting that he would

11. A Greek strategist who, like many Greek military experts of the day, had gone into the service of the Persian king. In his youth, Memnon had apparently lived for a time at Philip's court in Macedon, and so he knew firsthand the strength of the army he was now about to face.
12. The reigning king of Persia, who had not yet seen fit to personally assume leadership of the resistance forces.
13. This "scorched-earth" strategy most likely would have worked, since

not permit one house to be burned by the men posted with him. The Persians reportedly sided with Arsites because they suspected that Memnon was intentionally delaying the war on account of the honor he held from the king.

[I.13] In the meantime, Alexander was advancing to the Granicus River, having arrayed the hoplites in two phalanxes, with the horsemen at the wings. He had given orders for the baggage train to follow behind. The reconnaissance force under Hegelochus included the horsemen armed with pikes[14] and five hundred light-armed troops. When the army neared the Granicus, the party from the lookout places galloped up to report that the Persians had taken up a position, arrayed for battle, beyond the far bank of the river. Alexander now drew up his entire army in battle order. Parmenio approached him and spoke as follows:[15]

"Under the circumstances, sire, I think it would be wise to encamp at the bank of the river as we are. For I doubt our enemies, who are far outnumbered by our infantry, would dare to bivouac near us, and at dawn we will be able to cross the stream easily and will make it across before they are in formation. It would be unsafe, I feel, for us to attempt the crossing now, since we will not be able to keep the army in line as it crosses. For one can see that the river has many deep spots, and you notice that the banks themselves are high and steep. So as we climb out in disarray and in column—the weakest possible formation—the enemy horsemen, arrayed for battle, will charge. Our

---

Alexander had very little money with him when he came over into Asia; he needed a quick engagement and victory in order to secure the sustenance of his forces.

14. Though most Macedonian cavalrymen carried shorter javelins, some, like those mentioned here, wielded the fearsome fourteen-foot *sarissas* that were standard equipment for infantry. They apparently held these weapons with both hands while gripping the horse with their legs.

15. The plan here urged by Parmenio, for an overnight rest and a dawn attack, is precisely what Alexander *did*, according to the very different account of the Granicus battle given by Diodorus. Scholars are very much in a quandary over this difference and disagree as to which version is more reliable. Arrian's version gives Alexander credit for a much bolder and riskier strategy: crossing the Granicus right in the teeth of armed Persian opposition when his men and horses were badly in need of rest. But it was not unlike Alexander to run such risks when he thought he could intimidate his enemy by lack of hesitation.

first stumble would create immediate difficulties and might even spoil the outcome of the larger war."

But Alexander replied, "I know all that, Parmenio. But I would be ashamed, after having easily crossed the Hellespont, if this piddling stream"—such was the phrase he used to disparage the Granicus—"keeps us from crossing as we are. I would consider it unworthy of the Macedonians' renown and of my quickness in the field. And I think the Persians would take courage and think themselves a match for the Macedonians in battle, having suffered nothing in the present instance to justify their fear."[16]

[I.14] So saying, he sent Parmenio to lead the left wing, while he himself led the right. Philotas, son of Parmenio, had been stationed ahead of the right wing with the Companion Cavalry, the archers, and the Agrianian javelin men. Amyntas was stationed next to him with the horsemen armed with pikes, the Paeonians, and Socrates' cavalry squadron. Next came the Companion shield-bearers under the command of Nicanor, son of Parmenio. Then came the phalanx of Perdiccas, then that of Coenus, that of Craterus, that of Amyntas, and finally that of Philip, son of Amyntas. On the left wing, the Thessalian cavalry, led by Calas, was stationed first. Then came the allied cavalry under the command of Philip, son of Menelaus, followed by the Thracians under Agathon. Next came the infantry battalions of Craterus, Meleager, and Philip, which extended to the center of the entire line.

The Persians had nearly twenty thousand horsemen and an only slightly smaller force of foreign mercenary foot soldiers.[17] The horsemen were drawn out in a long line parallel to the riverbank, and the foot soldiers were posted behind them, on the high ground overlooking the river.[18] They could see Alexander himself; the brightness of

16. Whether Alexander actually spoke these words is doubtful, but they do capture his characteristic insights into the psychological side of warfare, in particular the benefits of preventing one's opponent from gaining confidence.
17. These hired infantrymen were mostly Greek hoplites, as will become clear below. The Persians had never developed any strength of their own in infantry warfare.
18. The disposition of the Persian forces is another feature of this battle that remains obscure. In contrast to Arrian, Diodorus reports that the Persians stationed their cavalry in the foothills some distance from the river, which in some ways makes better sense, given that charging horses need open ground

his weapons and the bustle of the men who attended him were unmistakable. As he was aiming at their left, it was there that they concentrated their cavalry squadrons.

For a time both armies stood quietly at the river's edge, shrinking from what lay ahead. There was a great silence on both sides. For the Persians were waiting for the Macedonians to enter the river, as they intended to attack them when they climbed out. But Alexander, leaping onto his horse and urging his suite to follow him and show themselves brave, ordered the mounted guides and the Paeonians under Amyntas to charge into the river with one infantry battalion and follow Socrates' squadron under Ptolemy, son of Philip. (Socrates' squadron happened to hold the command of the entire cavalry on that day.) Alexander himself, leading the right wing to the sound of war trumpets and the men raising their battle cry, entered the stream and extended his line continuously at an angle opposite to that in which the current was dragging them, so that the Persians might not fall upon his men climbing out in column, while he might himself assault *them* with the phalanx formed up as tightly as possible.

[I.15] When the first troops with Amyntas and Socrates touched the bank, the Persians shot at them from above, some hurling javelins into the river from the bank, others descending to the lower ground at the water's edge. There was a close contest between the horsemen —some emerging from the river, others barring their way—and a dense shower of javelins hurled by the Persians, while the Macedonians assailed the enemy with their spears. But as they were far outnumbered they suffered in the first assault. Defending themselves from the river, they occupied an insecure and lower position, whereas the Persians were assailing them from above. In fact, the strongest contingent of the Persian cavalry had been stationed there; Memnon's sons, and with them Memnon himself, were putting their lives on the line. Accordingly, the first Macedonians who engaged the Persians, though they showed themselves brave, were cut to pieces, except for those who wheeled back toward Alexander, who was approaching. Bringing up the right wing, Alexander now drew near and himself

---

to gain speed and momentum. It is also totally unclear why the Persians would have placed their armored infantry behind the cavalry, where they could do little except watch the engagement (which is exactly what Arrian pictures them doing).

launched an attack on the Persians where the mass of their cavalry had
been posted and where the Persian commanders had been stationed.
A fierce battle was joined around Alexander, and meanwhile battalion after battalion of Macedonians succeeded in crossing the river
with no difficulty. Though the battle was fought on horseback, it
looked more like an infantry engagement. For in a confined space
horses contended with horses, men with men, the Macedonians trying to drive the Persians from the bank and force them into the plain,
the Persians trying to hem the Macedonians in and thrust them back
to the river. And in this struggle Alexander and his men gained the
upper hand not only because of their strength and experience but because they were using spears made of cornel wood, whereas the Persians fought with light javelins.[19]

At a certain point Alexander's spear was shattered. He asked
Aretis, a royal groom, for another, but as Aretis' spear had also been
shattered—he was fighting valiantly with the remaining half of his
broken spear—he showed it to Alexander and urged him to ask for another's. Demaratus the Corinthian, one of the Companions, gave
Alexander his spear. Taking it up and catching sight of Mithridates,
Darius' son-in-law, riding out in front of the other horsemen and
bringing on a wedge-shaped mass of cavalry, Alexander also rode out
ahead of his own horsemen and struck Mithridates down, hitting him
in the face with his spear. Rhoesaces now rode at Alexander and struck
his head with a scimitar; Alexander's helmet, though partially broken,
checked the blow. Alexander now slew Rhoesaces, striking with his
spear through the man's breastplate and into his chest. Spithridates
then raised his scimitar against Alexander from behind, but Cleitus,
son of Dropides, struck Spithridates' shoulder first, cutting off his
arm,[20] and in the meantime all the horsemen who had managed to
emerge from the river joined the troops with Alexander.

[I.16] And now the Persians, their faces, and those of their
horses, torn by the lances striking them from all sides, were thrust
back by the Macedonian horsemen. Injured as well by the light-armed

---

19. The point of this comparison seems to have less to do with the strength
of the Macedonian cavalry lances (though cornel is a very hard wood) than
with their length; Persian horseman carried short *palta* designed for throwing while Alexander's bore true lances.
20. This episode will later be recalled by Cleitus, to his woe (IV.8, page 101
below).

troops who were mingled with the cavalry, they gave way first where Alexander was bearing the brunt of the battle. When their center gave way, both cavalry wings were also broken and a desperate flight began. Nearly a thousand Persian horsemen died. No serious pursuit was undertaken, for Alexander had turned his attention to the foreign mercenaries who had remained in formation where they were first drawn up—not so much from any sound calculation as from terror at the unexpected turn of events.[21] Leading the phalanx against these men after commanding his horsemen to attack them from all sides, he hemmed them in and quickly cut them to pieces. No one escaped, unless someone was overlooked among the corpses. About two thousand were taken alive.

Among the Persian commanders, the fallen included Niphates and Petenes; Spithridates, the satrap of Lydia; Mithrobuzanes, the governor of Cappadocia; Mithridates, Darius' son-in-law; Arbupales, son of Darius and grandson of Artaxerxes; Pharnaces, the brother of Darius' wife; and Omares, the commander of the mercenaries. Arsites escaped from the battle to Phrygia, and there he died by his own hand, the story goes, because the Persians considered him responsible for their defeat.

On the Macedonian side, some twenty-five of the Companions died in the first attack. Bronze statues of these men stand at Dium. At Alexander's command, these statues were sculpted by Lysippus, who was also the only sculptor selected to fashion a likeness of Alexander. Among the other horsemen, more than sixty died, while the infantry lost some thirty men. Alexander buried these men the next day with their weapons and other decorations, and he granted their parents and children exemption from land taxes and all other personal duties or property taxes. He also showed great care for the wounded. He visited them, examined their wounds, inquired how each man came to be wounded, and encouraged them to recount and even embellish their exploits. He honored the Persian commanders with funeral rites

21. Yet another difficulty in Arrian's account of the Granicus battle. It is hard to imagine that battle-seasoned Greek mercenaries would be so much taken by surprise, and left so resourceless, by the defeat of the Persians. Plutarch gives a more plausible account, in which the mercenaries expected and asked for terms of surrender, as was usual when they found themselves on the losing side; but they soon learned to their horror that Alexander was not offering such terms.

and also buried the Greek mercenaries who died fighting on his enemies' behalf. As for the mercenaries he had captured, he had them
bound in shackles and sent to Macedonia to serve as laborers, because
though they were Greeks they had disregarded the common resolves
of their countrymen and fought against Greece on behalf of the
barbarians.[22] He also sent three hundred sets of Persian armor to
Athens as a dedicatory offering to Athena on the Acropolis, and even
ordered the following inscription: "Alexander, son of Philip, and the
Greeks, except for the Spartans, dedicated these spoils from the barbarians dwelling in Asia."[23]

b. The war at sea

*With all of Asia Minor now under his control, Alexander set about determin-
ing the political status of the various cities in the region, some with Greek
or mixed Greco-barbarian populations, others largely barbarian. The Greek
cities, having been "liberated" from Persian rule (even if, on some occasions,
unwillingly), now had democracies installed, not because Alexander believed in democracy, but rather because the Persians had opposed it. Of
course, Alexander took care to ensure that pro-Macedonian factions would
lead these democracies, and in many cases he left garrisons behind to bol-
ster the position of his supporters. Thus, the cities of Asia Minor gained autonomy from Persia but little true freedom, much as they had done almost
150 years earlier when an Athenian-led naval force liberated them for the
first time.*

*Nor did they gain economic freedom, for the tribute they had paid to the
Persian king was, in many cases, reimposed by Alexander—though the*

---

22. Evidently Alexander hoped to make an example of these men to all other
Greeks fighting in Persian service (as Arrian reports at I.29, not in this volume). In 331 B.C.E., while preparing for his final assault on the forces of Darius, Alexander released the Athenians, at least, from among this unfortunate
group of prisoners (III.6).
23. A public-relations ploy designed to isolate and embarrass the Spartans,
the sole holdouts from Alexander's coalition of Greek allies, as well as to reinforce the idea that the Asian expedition was a war of revenge undertaken
on behalf of the Greek states attacked by Persia in 480 B.C.E. The Athenians
had lost most in that attack—indeed, the temple of Athena, the very site
where Alexander's dedication was placed, had been sacked and burned—and
so now would regard themselves (or so Alexander hoped) as the primary ben-
eficiaries of the "counterattack."

payments were now labeled "contributions" to the Macedonian-led military campaign. Whether these "contributions" were meant to end after the war's conclusion is anyone's guess. In some cases, where Alexander wanted to win Greek hearts and minds to his cause, a genuine release from tribute was granted; at the important city of Ephesus, for example, Alexander ordered that the payments formerly sent to Persia be redirected to a building fund for the restoration of the ruined temple of Artemis. (The temple had supposedly been destroyed by fire on the very day of Alexander's birth—a portent of the upheavals that the new Macedonian prince would bring to the lands of Asia.) Not coincidentally, Ephesus had been the most eager of the major Greek cities to welcome Alexander and to throw out its Persian-supported ruling claque.

Having won sovereignty over Asia Minor at the Granicus battle, Alexander was now responsible for administration and governance of his new territory, and here, too, he adapted the Persian system that had been in place for two centuries. The Persians had divided their empire into provinces called satrapies, each overseen by a satrap who combined the duties of governor, chief tax collector, and commander of the regional armed forces. Alexander retained the basic outlines of the satrapal system but replaced existing satraps with his own Greek or Macedonian officers or, in some cases, with local leaders whose loyalty to him seemed beyond question (such as the Carian queen Ada, who received the satrapy of Caria after adopting Alexander as her own son). Often he separated the powers of the former satrap into three parts, appointing different officials to take charge of governance, taxation, and military defense. Garrisons of several thousand troops, drawn from the army Alexander had brought from Europe, were stationed in each province to protect the new political order of the region. Alexander made all these dispositions in great haste, as his war with Darius had only just begun and a new phase, in which the Persian navy would inevitably come into action, was about to begin.

The Persians at this point controlled the eastern Aegean with a fleet of several hundred ships manned by expert Phoenician and Cyprian sailors. Alexander, by contrast, had access to far fewer ships, and these were manned by Greeks whose loyalty to him was open to question. In an all-out naval battle, he might very well have been defeated, but such a battle never took place, for reasons that will emerge in what follows.

Alexander was in the midst of preparing for a siege of Miletus, a coastal Greek city that had insisted on neutrality in the Perso-Macedonian War, when the Persian navy made its appearance. By that time, however, his own ships had already occupied a strong position in the city's harbor, forcing the Persians to anchor at another spot far away from the action. At that point, according to Arrian, the following debate took place—a rare instance in which Alexander apparently showed restraint and declined a challenge from his opponent.

[I.18] The barbarians' ships numbered about 400 [compared with 160 Greek ships available to Alexander]. Nevertheless, Parmenio advised Alexander to fight at sea. Expecting that the Greeks would prevail with their fleet for a variety of reasons, he had been particularly impressed by an omen: an eagle had been seen sitting on the shore near the sterns of Alexander's ships. It was Parmenio's view that if they were victorious, it would be of great advantage to their enterprise as a whole, whereas a defeat would not much matter, since in any case the Persians held sway at sea. He asserted that he himself was ready to embark with the fleet and run the risk. But Alexander declared that Parmenio was mistaken in his judgment and that his interpretation of the omen did not accord with what was probable. For it would not make sense, with so few ships, to fight at sea against a much larger fleet and to engage the well-trained navies of the Cyprians and Phoenicians when their own was out of practice. Furthermore, he had no wish to commit the Macedonians' experience and daring to the barbarians on a footing so uncertain. A naval defeat would considerably harm their early renown in the war, particularly because the Greeks, elated by news of a naval defeat, would revolt. Taking these points into account, Alexander argued that this was not the proper time to engage the enemy at sea. Besides, he interpreted the omen differently: the eagle was presumably on his side, but because it was seen sitting on the ground, he was inclined to think that the omen meant he would prevail over the Persian fleet from the land.

Alexander succeeded in his operation against Miletus without having to risk a naval battle; his land-based troops seized the coastal supply stations the Persian ships relied on and forced them to move even farther away from the sphere of action. Alexander came to realize that in this way, by controlling the coast and depriving enemy ships of anchorage, his land army could render the Persian fleet useless—in which case he had no need of a fleet at all, as Arrian relates:

[I.20] Alexander decided to disband the fleet, as he was now short of money. Moreover, he observed that his own fleet was not fit to do battle with that of the Persians, and he was unwilling to endanger any portion of his forces. He also reflected that as he now controlled Asia with his infantry, he would have no further need of a navy. As he captured the coastal cities he would dissolve the Persian fleet, since they would find no crews to man their ships, nor would they have any place to land along the coast of Asia. Besides, he had interpreted the omen of the eagle to mean that he would overpower the ships from the land.

This strategy spared Alexander from paying his sailors and perhaps also from relying on Athenians and other Greek citizens whose support of the Macedonian cause might waver, especially in a fight to control their sister cities in Ionia. His land forces, by contrast, were absolutely reliable and had proven their tactical superiority at the battle of the Granicus. Nevertheless, the course Alexander now took was a risky one, in that it required him to control each and every port along the east shore of the Aegean; to allow the Persian navy to operate safely from even a single harbor might mean losing control of the entire region. Thus, in the autumn of 334 Alexander set out down the coast of Asia Minor, determined to capture every town along the way at whatever cost.

His first major challenge came at the port city of Halicarnassus, where the Persians had stationed a sizable contingent under the command of their chief general in the Aegean theater, Memnon of Rhodes. A determined siege operation was commenced against the walls of the city, but the defenders— a mix of Carians, Persians, and Greeks who supported the Persian cause— resisted with ingenuity and grit. On several occasions they sallied outside the walls and set fire to the siege machinery that Alexander was using to attack them; at the same time they built new walls inside the perimeter of the old, so that if Alexander's army should open a breach in the outer circuit, they would still be protected by the inner one. Finally, though, after a desperate sally had failed, the defenders of Halicarnassus realized that their city was about to fall, and Memnon fled under cover of darkness together with a few other high commanders. Alexander took possession of the town without a struggle the next morning; his goal had been won, but an important Persian asset had also slipped through his fingers.

The rest of the Asia Minor littoral went over willingly to the Macedonian side, and in late 334 Alexander moved his forces inland, in two detachments: Parmenio led a sweep through Phrygia in northern Anatolia while Alexander himself followed a more southerly route. The two armies then rendezvoused in the spring of 333 in Gordium, where they were also joined by reinforcements from Europe—the first of many cohorts who trekked across the Hellespont in order to join the victorious Macedonian army.

While in Gordium, Alexander tested himself against the challenge of the Gordian knot, as recounted by Arrian below. What is interesting about the incident is not so much Alexander's solution to the problem—indeed, Arrian is not even sure what solution was adopted—as the fact that, for public-relations purposes, Alexander felt it would be unwise to let the knot

*remain tied. After a solid year of victories in Asia he now had a reputation
to uphold and an image that needed to be protected.*

[II.3] When Alexander reached Gordium, a desire seized him to
ascend to the citadel, the site of the palace of Gordias and of his son
Midas, and to see Gordias' wagon and the knot of the wagon's yoke.
A popular local legend had sprung up about that wagon. . . . The legend included a prophecy: the man who untied the knot of the wagon's
yoke was destined to rule over Asia. The knot was made from cornel
bark, and its end and beginning were nowhere visible. At a loss to un-
tie the knot, Alexander was unwilling to let it remain intact lest this
create public unrest. Some say that on striking the knot he cut
through it and then claimed that it had been untied. Aristobulus, however, says that after removing the peg from the pole—for the peg that
held the knot together had been driven right through the pole—he
separated the yoke from the pole. How Alexander managed to undo
the knot I cannot say with certainty. But he and his suite undoubtedly
left the wagon believing that the prophecy about the untying of the
knot had been fulfilled. And this was indicated that night by thunder
and flashes of lightning. Alexander sacrificed the next day to the gods
who had revealed these signs and shown him how to undo the knot.

*The spring of 333 brought an unexpected piece of good news to Alexander:
Memnon, the very capable commander of Persian forces in western Asia,
had died of a sudden illness. Memnon was at the time in the midst of a successful naval campaign in the Aegean, which threatened to raise all of
Greece in an anti-Macedonian revolt and force Alexander to return to Europe.
(A similar strategy had worked for the Persians some sixty years earlier when
a Spartan general, Agesilaus, had begun to make inroads into their empire.)
After Memnon's death, however, the effort collapsed; King Darius, lacking
a new naval commander who could follow through on Memnon's promising beginning, abandoned the sea war in the Aegean and elected instead to
meet Alexander on land. He began assembling an enormous army in the region around Babylon, intending to fight a head-to-head battle against the
Macedonians as they progressed eastward.*

*Meanwhile, in the Macedonian camp, the first dark hints of conspiracies
against Alexander were starting to emerge. Already during the previous winter, information had come to Alexander that a Macedonian nobleman, also
named Alexander, had been paid by the Persians to assassinate him. This*

man, known to history as Alexander of Lyncestis, had been duly arrested and placed under guard, the evidence against him not being strong enough to permit a trial and Alexander not yet inclined toward summary execution of his apparent enemies. Now, in the summer of 333, new rumors reached Alexander about a plot against his life, as Arrian relates in the passage below. Whether there was any substance to the rumors and, if not, what Parmenio intended by fostering them are questions that will forever remain unanswerable.

[II.4] Alexander now fell ill from exhaustion, according to Aristobulus, though others say that, craving water, as he was sweating and overheated, Alexander flung himself into the river Cydnus for a swim. (The Cydnus flows through the center of the city, and as it has its sources in Mount Taurus and flows through open country, its water is cool and clear.) In any event, it is said that Alexander suffered from cramps, high fever, and continuous insomnia.[24] His other doctors doubted he would live, but Philip of Acarnania, a doctor who kept company with Alexander and who was especially trusted for his professional expertise and carried weight in the army for his grasp of affairs in general, wanted to treat Alexander with a purge, and Alexander urged him to do so. While Philip was preparing the cup, Alexander was given a letter in which Parmenio warned him to be on his guard against Philip, having heard that Philip had been bribed by Darius to poison Alexander. Alexander read the letter, and while still holding it, took the cup containing the drug and gave the letter to Philip to read. And while Philip was reading Parmenio's letter, Alexander swallowed the dose. Philip quickly made it clear that the drug was harmless. For he was not disconcerted by the letter, but merely encouraged Alexander and advised him to follow all his other instructions, as he would recover if he did so. The medicine took effect and Alexander's illness lifted, and he showed Philip that he was trusted as a friend, and made it clear to the others in his suite that he firmly refused to mistrust his friends and had the strength to face death.

24. Modern scholars suspect that Alexander had contracted malaria. If so, the illness would have remained with him throughout the rest of his life and very possibly would have been the primary cause of his death (see below, page 168).

c. The battle of Issus

While Alexander recovered from his illness at Tarsus, Darius' army was on the move, led this time by the Great King himself. A huge force—Arrian says more than six hundred thousand, though this is undoubtedly an exaggeration—prepared now to stop Alexander from moving through the mountain "gates" that led eastward into Syria and into the heartland of his empire. In the maneuverings that preceded the battle, Darius found himself lucky (for a change) when the two armies inadvertently passed by one another and the Persians ended up to the rear of the Macedonians, cutting off their retreat and their lines of supply; but Darius soon managed to squander this advantage by trading the broad field on which he had chosen to fight for a narrower one, in which his numerical superiority would be useless. Arrian begins his account by explaining how this switch of battlefields happened.

[II.6] When he was still at Mallus, Alexander received word that Darius had encamped at Sochi with all his forces. . . . Meanwhile, Darius was passing his time with the army, having selected a plain in Assyria that was open on all sides, spacious enough to accommodate his army's vast numbers, and suitable for cavalry maneuvers. Amyntas, son of Antiochus, who had deserted from Alexander,[25] advised Darius not to leave this site, as it furnished an open field for the Persians' numbers and equipment. Accordingly, Darius remained there. But when Alexander had lingered for a long time in Tarsus on account of his illness and had spent considerable time in Soli, where he sacrificed, held parades, and launched an attack on the mountain Cilicians, Darius' resolution faltered. He was won over, and not against his will, to a view that in fact gratified him enormously. Encouraged by those associates who sought to please him—the sort who are always consorting with kings, to their detriment[26]—he concluded that Alexander

---

25. Amyntas, a Macedonian nobleman, had fled to Darius in 336 after Alexander assumed the throne, probably because he was too closely associated with a rival claimant to feel safe under the new regime. Such Greek and Macedonian expatriates tend to pop up in the writings of the Greek historians as advisers to the Persian crown whose valuable counsel gets ignored; Demaratus, the exiled Spartan king, plays this role in Herodotus, Amyntas here, and the Athenian general Charidemus in Diodorus Siculus (17.30).

26. Arrian, who had observed the court of the Roman emperor Hadrian firsthand, comments on several occasions in the *Anabasis* on how flatterers always harm reigning monarchs (see pages 101 and 172 below).

was no longer willing to advance and that the news of Darius' approach was giving him pause. One courtier after another incited Darius, declaring that he would trample down the Macedonian army with his cavalry. Amyntas, however, assured the King that Alexander would appear, regardless of Darius' whereabouts, and he urged Darius to remain where he was. But the worse advice won out, as it gave Darius the most immediate pleasure. And perhaps, too, some deity was leading Darius to a position where his cavalry would not be of much use to him, nor his vast numbers of javelins and arrows, and where he would not be able to display the brilliance of his army, but would cede Alexander and his men an easy victory.[27] For the Persians' power over Asia had now to be wrested from them by the Macedonians, just as the Medes' power had been wrested by the Persians, and at an earlier period that of the Assyrians by the Medes.[28]

[II.7] After crossing the mountains at the so-called Amanic Gates, Darius advanced toward Issus and reached the rear of Alexander's army without being observed. Having gained possession of Issus, he captured the Macedonians who because of illness had been left behind, and had these men tortured and killed.[29] He advanced, the next day, to the river Pinarus. When Alexander heard that Darius was at his back, he did not credit the report, but embarked some of his Companions in a thirty-oared ship and sent them to Issus to find out if it was true. As the coastline there forms a bay, they learned the more easily that the Persians were encamped there, and reported to Alexander that Darius was at hand.

Calling together the generals, cavalry commanders, and his allies' officers, Alexander urged them to draw courage from their record

27. One of few instances in the *Anabasis* where Arrian openly espouses the idea, more common in the legendary accounts, that the Macedonian conquest was preordained and/or guided by divine forces.

28. The idea of *translatio imperii*, the inexorable transfer of imperial power from one race to another, is common to many of the Greek and Roman historians as well as to the authors of the Hebrew Bible. The Medes defeated the Assyrians in 612 B.C.E. and were themselves defeated by the Persians under Cyrus the Great about sixty years later.

29. Other sources tell us that Darius had the hands of these unfortunate men cut off and the stumps sealed with hot tar, thus forever disabling them from military service; they were then dispatched to Alexander to warn him of his enemy's strength.

of risks successfully run. Their struggle, he pointed out, would be between their own conquering army and men they had already once conquered, and the god was pursuing a better strategy on their behalf, having inspired Darius to move his army from an open space into a narrow one,[30] where the terrain would be just wide enough for the deployment of his phalanx, and where the Persians would derive no advantage from their superior numbers. Nor were these men to be compared with the Macedonians either in physical strength or fighting spirit. For the Macedonians would be coming to blows with the Persians and Medes, men who had long lived in luxury, while the Macedonians, accustomed to the toils of war, were well versed in its dangers. Above all, they were free men fighting against slaves. As for the Greeks who would be fighting Greeks,[31] they would not all be fighting for the same cause, since some would be taking their chances with Darius for a wage, and a meager one at that, while those siding with *them* would be fighting willingly in defense of Greece. As for their barbarian troops (the Thracians, Paeonians, Illyrians, and Agrianians), the strongest and most warlike tribes in Europe would be drawn up against the laziest and softest tribes of Asia. And Alexander, as general, would be matched against Darius.

Thus Alexander enumerated the Macedonians' advantages in the coming struggle. He then pointed out that the rewards of running the risk would be great. For it was not Darius' satraps they were now to overpower, nor the cavalry that had been marshaled at the Granicus, nor the twenty thousand foreign mercenaries, but the cream of the Persians and Medes and all the Asian tribes who were their subjects.[32] And the Great King himself would be present. Accordingly, nothing would be left for them after this struggle but to rule all of Asia and put an end to their many toils. He also reminded them of their brilliant accomplishments for the common good and mentioned any

30. The space in which the battle was fought today measures about nine miles of open ground between the mountains and the sea.
31. Meaning the Greek mercenaries who formed the core of Darius' infantry forces and who would now be fighting against the Greeks on Alexander's side.
32. This argument might seem at first glance to be the exact opposite of the one advanced in the previous paragraph. What Alexander means is that, since the very best of the Asian forces will be present at this battle, victory over them—which will be easily won—will mean the ultimate defeat of the Persian empire.

conspicuously daring and noble exploit, naming the man who had performed each deed. He then touched as lightly as possible on the danger he had himself incurred in their battles. He is said to have recalled Xenophon and the Ten Thousand,[33] a force not to be compared with their own either in numbers or any other quality, having had no cavalry, neither Thessalian, Boeotian, Peloponnesian, Macedonian, nor Thracian, nor as many cavalry from other nations as had been posted in their ranks, nor archers or slingers apart from a few Cretans and Rhodians, whom Xenophon had deployed on the spur of the moment when his situation became desperate. Yet those Ten Thousand had routed the King with all his forces at Babylon itself and had defeated all the tribes they encountered on their march to the Black Sea. He said everything a brave leader would naturally say to hearten brave men on the eve of a dangerous venture, and his troops approached him from all sides, clasped their king by the hand, and with excited words urged him to lead them out at once.

Both kings now arrayed their troops for battle. Alexander, who was moving his army forward, had greater flexibility in this than Darius in his fixed position, and he continued making changes as he drew nearer and learned more about the Persian dispositions. Some of these changes were deliberately screened from the view of the Persians, so that the position of key contingents would remain unknown to the enemy until the very moment of engagement. As in all his battles, Alexander gave close consideration to the psychological aspect of warfare, the importance of keeping his opponent off-balance and nervous while giving his own forces grounds for confidence. In the event, it was the fear he instilled in his opposite number, King Darius, that decided the battle of Issus.

[II.10] When his men had been posted in order, Alexander led them forward, though regular halts made his approach seem quite leisurely. For Darius was not yet advancing the barbarians from their original positions; instead he remained at the river's banks, which were steep in many places, and extended a palisade along the stretches that appeared more assailable. This made it clear to Alexander's men that

33. The Greek mercenary army that had fought successfully against the armies of the Great King at Cunaxa in 401 B.C.E.—the only other occasion on which a large European army had fought a pitched battle against Persian forces on their own territory.

Darius was at heart already vanquished.[34] Just before the armies met, Alexander rode all along the line, exhorting his troops to be brave and calling out the names and appropriate honors not only of the commanders, but of all the squadron leaders, company commanders, and chiefs of the foreign mercenaries who were distinguished for rank or bravery. A shout went up on all sides to delay no longer but to charge the enemy. At first, though Darius' forces were already in sight, Alexander led his men in order at a walking pace, lest the surging of the phalanx in a quicker advance throw it into disarray. But when they were within range, Alexander and his suite, who were stationed on the right, were the first to charge on the double to the river[35] in order to astonish the Persians with the speed of their approach; and by coming to blows more swiftly, they hoped to sustain fewer casualties from the Persian archers.

And it turned out as Alexander had guessed. For as soon as the battle was joined, the Persians posted at the left wing were routed; there Alexander and his men won a decisive victory. Meanwhile, the Greek mercenaries with Darius attacked the Macedonians where a gap appeared in the phalanx's right wing. While Alexander was dashing into the river, coming to blows with the Persians posted there and driving them off, the Macedonians at the center did not engage the enemy with equal force, and when they came upon the banks, which were steep at many points, they could not keep their front line in proper order. Spotting the worst breach in the Macedonian phalanx, the Greeks attacked. The action there was desperate, as the Greeks tried to drive the Macedonians back to the river and to recover the victory for their own men who were already fleeing, while the Macedonians, eager not to fall short of Alexander, whose success was already apparent, tried to preserve the good name of the phalanx, which

34. That is, Darius had erected defensive ramparts designed to protect his infantry but also to prevent them from moving to the attack. His reliance on a holding strategy in the center of his line, despite a numerical advantage, betrayed to the Macedonians his lack of confidence and fighting spirit.
35. There is some question as to whether Alexander was on foot or on horseback when he led this charge. Nigel Hammond, who has inspected the site of the battle in some detail, believes that "cavalry at the charge would have broken the horses' legs in the boulder-strewn riverbed," and that this initial rush must have been by infantry instead (*Alexander the Great: King, Commander and Statesman*, p. 104).

at the time was reputed to be invincible. And to some extent the Macedonians and Greeks were engaged in an ethnic rivalry.[36] It was there that Ptolemy, son of Seleucus, fell, having proved his bravery, along with nearly 120 other notable Macedonians.

[II.11] At that point the battalions from the right wing, seeing the Persians opposite them already routed, wheeled about toward Darius' foreign mercenaries, where the Macedonian center was in distress, and drove them back from the river. Having outflanked the breached Persian line, they attacked at an oblique angle and cut down the mercenaries. The Persian horsemen posted opposite the Thessalians did not remain on the opposite bank in the actual engagement, but after boldly fording the stream attacked the Thessalian squadrons. A desperate cavalry battle ensued, and the Persians did not give way until they noticed that Darius had fled[37] and that their mercenaries, decimated by the phalanx, were cut off. By then the flight was conspicuous and general. The Persians' horses suffered in the retreat, carrying their heavily armed horsemen. As for the horsemen themselves, their enormous numbers created panic and disorder. Retreating along narrow roads, they sustained more injuries from one another, when trampled underfoot, than from their pursuers. The Thessalians attacked them stoutly, and just as many horsemen as foot soldiers were slaughtered in the retreat.

As for Darius, the moment his left wing was thrown into a panic by Alexander and he saw it cut off from the rest of the army, he was among the first to flee, just as he was, on his chariot.[38] As long as he was fleeing on level ground, the chariot conveyed him away in safety; but when he encountered ravines and other difficult terrain, he stripped off his shield and cloak, abandoned the chariot, and left his bow behind as well. Mounting a horse, he fled. Night fell shortly thereafter, and thus he eluded capture. For Alexander pursued him with all his strength while it was still light, but he returned to camp

---

36. That is, the Greeks fighting on the Persian side were trying to demonstrate their prowess against Macedonians, a race many of them considered non-Greek and therefore less estimable as warriors, despite the evidence of the battle of Chaeronea.

37. With the words "Darius had fled" Arrian anticipates the events of the following paragraph.

38. The drama of Darius' escape from Alexander in his chariot has been superbly depicted on a famous mosaic found in the ruins of Pompeii.

when it grew too dark to see ahead. He seized Darius' chariot, however, and his shield, cloak, and bow. (Alexander's pursuit had been delayed, as he had turned back when the phalanx was breached. The pursuit began in earnest once he had seen the foreign mercenaries and the Persian cavalry thrust back from the river.)

Among the Persian dead were Arsames, Rheomithres, and Atizyes, who had served as cavalry officers at the Granicus. Two Persian nobles, Babaces and Sauaces, the satrap of Egypt, also perished. Among the rank and file, roughly a hundred thousand men were lost, including more than ten thousand horsemen.[39] Indeed, Ptolemy, son of Lagus, who was then with Alexander, reports that when the men who were pursuing Darius reached a certain ravine, they crossed it over the corpses. Darius' camp was captured on the first attempt, and Darius' mother, wife (who was also his sister), and infant son were taken prisoner. Two daughters were also captured along with a few Persian gentlewomen, as the other Persians had recently sent their women and baggage to Damascus. Since Darius had also sent off the greater part of his treasure and all the other luxurious trappings that accompany the Great King on campaign, no more than three thousand talents were confiscated. But Darius' treasure was soon seized in Damascus by Parmenio, who had been sent there for that purpose.

So ended the battle, which was fought in the month of Maemacterion, during Nicocrates' archonship at Athens.[40]

[II.12] The next day, though he had received a sword wound in the thigh,[41] Alexander visited the wounded, and when the corpses had been gathered he honored them with splendid funeral rites, the entire army drawn up in its brightest battle array. In his speech Alexander cited everyone who had performed an illustrious exploit in battle, whether he had himself seen the deed performed or had learned of it from general report. He also rewarded the men with gifts of money, honoring each man according to his deserts. He appointed one of his

---

39. Arrian's Persian casualty figures, both here and elsewhere, seem to be greatly exaggerated, though in this instance they are echoed by other sources. Arrian does not give a Macedonian body count for the battle of Issus, but other sources report figures ranging from 280 to 1,200 killed and missing.
40. Late autumn, 333 B.C.E.
41. Arrian says nothing about how Alexander received this wound, but an eyewitness to the battle, Chares of Mytilene, reports that Darius himself wounded Alexander before taking to flight.

bodyguards, Balacrus, son of Nicanor, as satrap of Cilicia, and enlisted Menes, son of Dionysius, to fill his place in the bodyguard. In place of Ptolemy, son of Seleucus, who had died in the battle, he appointed Polyperchon, son of Simmias, to head his battalion. . . .

Nor did he neglect Darius' mother, wife, and children. Some writers relate that on the night he gave up the pursuit of Darius, Alexander went to Darius' tent, as it had been reserved for him. Hearing the sound of women lamenting and a similar moaning not far from the tent, he asked who the women were and why their tent had been pitched so near. One of his men said, "Sire, since it was reported to Darius' mother, wife, and children that you have Darius' bow and his royal cloak, and that Darius' shield has been retrieved, they have been wailing for Darius in the belief that he is dead." On hearing this, Alexander sent Leonnatus, one of the Companions, to the women, having instructed him to inform them that Darius was alive, that he had left the weapons and cloak in his chariot when he fled, and that these were all Alexander had. Leonnatus visited the tent, informed the women how matters stood with respect to Darius, and reported that Alexander had given his consent that they be waited upon, honored, and addressed as royalty, since the war against Darius had not sprung from enmity but was a lawful struggle for the sovereignty of Asia.[42] So say Ptolemy and Aristobulus. But it is also reported[43] that on the next day Alexander himself entered the tent, accompanied only by Hephaestion. Darius' mother, in doubt as to which of the two was the king (for they were dressed alike), approached Hephaestion and prostrated herself before him because he appeared the taller. And when Hephaestion drew back and one of her attendants pointed to Alexander and said that *he* was Alexander, the queen, ashamed of her error, drew back. But Alexander declared that she had not erred, as Hephaestion, too, was an "Alexander."[44]

Though I have recorded these incidents, I do not claim that they are either authentic or entirely implausible. But if they did take place, I commend Alexander for the compassion he showed the women and

---

42. An interesting, but spurious, distinction on Alexander's part. Certainly Darius would dispute the notion that Alexander had attacked him "lawfully."
43. Arrian thus marks an instance where he has included "reports" or legends from outside his two main sources, the works of Aristobulus and Ptolemy.
44. This comment puns on the root meaning in Greek of the name Alexander, "protector of men."

the trust and respect he showed his companion. And if the chroniclers of his career think it credible that Alexander would have acted and spoken in this way, I commend Alexander on that score as well.[45]

Alexander's victory at Issus not only struck a major blow at the heart of Persian power but, unbeknownst to him, had further consequences back home in Europe. A Spartan king, Agis, had begun conspiring with Persian agents to foment a Greek revolt from Macedonian rule; if successful, such a rebellion would almost certainly have forced Alexander to return home with his conquest of Asia still incomplete. But during a crucial meeting between Agis and the Persians, news arrived that Darius had lost the battle of Issus. The Persian agents hurriedly departed to try to safeguard Persia's few remaining Aegean outposts, leaving Agis with only a small fraction of the money and ships he had been expecting to receive. Here, as in the earlier circumstance of Memnon's death, a potential threat to Alexander's Aegean power base had suddenly lost its vigor, sparing him from having to fight a two-front war.

Meanwhile, Darius, shaken by his narrow escape at the battle of Issus, decided to try to negotiate a settlement with Alexander, as related below.

[II.14] While Alexander was still at Marathus, envoys arrived bringing a letter from Darius and intending to appeal personally to Alexander to release Darius' mother, wife, and children. The letter declared that a friendship and an alliance had existed between Philip and Artaxerxes,[46] but when Arses, Artaxerxes' son, became king,[47] Philip had set about injuring him,[48] though the Persians had done Philip no

---

45. The first of many places in which Arrian steps back to pass moral judgment on the behavior of Alexander. It bears recalling that in his youth, Arrian had attended the lectures of the Stoic sage Epictetus and had an intense interest in ethical and characterological issues.

46. Philip and Artaxerxes III came to the thrones of their respective kingdoms at about the same time (359–358 B.C.E.), and both died at the hands of assassins, Artaxerxes in 338 and Philip two years later. The terms of their relationship are certainly distorted here in the letter attributed to Darius; Persia and Macedonia were already wrestling one another for control of the eastern Aegean in the 340s, well before Artaxerxes' death.

47. In 338 B.C.E.; Arses, who took the name Artaxerxes (IV) when he ascended the throne, ruled only two years.

48. The reference is to the advance force under Parmenio Philip had sent into Asia Minor after the battle of Chaeronea.

harm. And since Darius' accession Alexander had sent no one to his court to confirm their past friendship and alliance but had crossed with an army into Asia and done the Persians great harm. Accordingly, Darius had journeyed down in person to defend his country and rescue the empire he had inherited. Their battle's outcome had doubtless accorded with the will of some god, and as a king he was now asking a king for his wife, mother, and captured children, and was also ready to form a friendship and an alliance with Alexander. To this end, Darius recommended that Alexander send representatives along with Meniscus and Arsimas (the envoys who had come from Persia) who could exchange pledges on Alexander's behalf. Alexander wrote a reply and sent Thersippus along with Darius' envoys, having instructed him to give Darius the letter but not to discuss its contents.[49] Alexander's letter runs as follows: "Your ancestors came to Macedonia and the rest of Greece and did us great harm,[50] though you had suffered no prior injury. I, appointed as leader of the Greeks, and wishing to punish the Persians, crossed into Asia, but *you* began the quarrel. For you went in aid to the Perinthians, who had wronged my father,[51] and Ochus[52] sent a force to Thrace, over which we held sway. When my father died at the hands of conspirators whom you had organized (as you yourself boasted in letters to one and all), and you killed Arses with Bagoas' help,[53] and usurped the sovereign power, in violation of Persian custom and to the Persians' detriment, and sent the Greeks unfriendly letters about me, inciting them to war against

49. An interesting prohibition. Perhaps Alexander felt that any discussion would amount to a negotiation, which would be taken by Darius as a sign of weakness.
50. The reference is to the Persian incursions into Thrace and Macedonia under Darius I, beginning in the late sixth century B.C.E., more than 170 years before this time.
51. In 340 B.C.E., the Persians had given money and mercenary soldiers to help Perinthus withstand a Macedonian siege.
52. Ochus is another name for Artaxerxes III.
53. This charge is not supported by any known evidence, though it is not inconceivable. Bagoas was a power-hungry palace eunuch who contrived the poisoning first of Artaxerxes and then of Arses; after Darius took the throne Bagoas tried to poison him as well, but he was killed by a dose of his own poison. There is some irony here in Alexander's accusation that Darius had reached the throne by conspiring at the murder of his predecessor, since many of Alexander's contemporaries thought the same was true of him.

me, and sent money to the Spartans and some of the other Greeks (which no other city accepted but the Spartans), and sent your agents to destroy my friends and try to destroy the peace that I had arranged for the Greeks[54]—when you did all this, I marched against you, as you had begun hostilities.

"Since I have prevailed in battle—over your generals and satraps earlier, and now over you and your own forces—and am in possession of the country, the gods having granted it to me, I am also responsible for all the men who fought on your side, survived the battle and fled to me, and who remain with me not unwillingly, but have joined my campaign voluntarily. Come to me, therefore, on the understanding that I am master of all of Asia. If you fear you may suffer some unpleasantness at my hands, send some of your friends to receive pledges. Approach me and ask for your mother, wife, children, and anything else you like, and receive them. Anything you persuade me to give will be yours. And in the future, whenever you send word to me, address yourself to me as King of Asia[55] and not as an equal, and let me know, as the master of all that belonged to you, if you have need of anything. Otherwise, I plan to deal with you as a criminal. But if you dispute me about the sovereignty, hold your ground, fight for it, and do not flee, as I am coming after you wherever you are." This was the letter Alexander sent to Darius.

d. The siege of Tyre

As Alexander proceeded down the Levantine coast, most of the Phoenician cities came over to his side, largely because they had no way to defend themselves had they chosen to resist. At Tyre, however, things promised to be more complicated: the site of the city, an island a half mile from shore fortified by high walls, was thought to be safe from any attack except a prolonged naval blockade, and Alexander no longer had a navy at his disposal.

54. All the foregoing—the unfriendly letters, the use of bribe money to oppose Macedonian interests, the attempts to fragment the Greek alliance (for example, by support of the Theban revolt)—are attested by evidence; but Darius might have responded that Macedonian troops were already on his soil at that time, and so the war had already begun.
55. The first occurrence of the peculiar title Alexander seems to have invented for himself, in part to avoid becoming King of Persia, an office the Greek world had learned to detest.

With control of the sea firmly in their own hands and those of their Persian
masters, with additional aid promised by their sister city Carthage, and with
their storerooms well stocked with armaments and food supplies, the Tyri-
ans felt they could afford to give Alexander only perfunctory obeisance and
send him on his way. Tyrian envoys met Alexander on the march and offered
some superficial benefactions, but Alexander tested their goodwill: he asked
to enter the city and lead a sacrifice to its patron deity, whom the Greeks
called Tyrian Heracles (actually the Phoenician god Melqart). The Tyrians
recognized that granting this request would effectively mean yielding a kind
of symbolic sovereignty to Alexander. When they refused—perhaps even (as
one source reports) killing the Macedonian envoys who had brought the re-
quest—the stage was set for an intense struggle that would summon forth
the utmost ingenuity and determination from both sides.

[II.16] At Tyre there is a temple of Heracles, the most ancient of
those retained in human memory. This was not the Argive Heracles,
son of Alcmene. For Heracles was honored in Tyre for many generations before Cadmus set out from Phoenicia, took possession of
Thebes, and had a daughter, Semele, who gave birth to Dionysus, son
of Zeus. . . .

Alexander said he wished to sacrifice to this Tyrian Heracles.
When the envoys reported this in Tyre, the Tyrians decided to do
everything else Alexander commanded, but to receive no Persian or
Macedonian in their city, recognizing that this was the most appropriate course of action given their present policy, and the safest with
regard to the war's outcome, which was still unknown. When the Tyrians' response was reported to Alexander, he angrily sent back the envoys, assembled the Companions, generals, squadron leaders, and
cavalry commanders, and spoke as follows:

[II.17] "Friends and allies, I see it will not be safe for us to march
against Egypt while the Persians control the sea. And for us to leave
Tyre behind, its loyalty dubious, to pursue Darius while Egypt and
Cyprus remain in the hands of the Persians would be unsafe for any
number of reasons, but particularly when one considers the state of
affairs in Greece. For if the Persians regain control of the coast while
we proceed with our forces against Babylon and Darius, they might,
with a larger army, shift the war to Greece, where the Spartans are
openly at war with us, and our control of Athens is currently founded
more on fear than on goodwill. But with Tyre demolished, all
of Phoenicia would be in our hands, and the largest and strongest

contingent of the Persian navy, namely the Phoenician, would likely come over to us. For while their cities are under our control, the Phoenician oarsmen and marines will not consent to run risks at sea on others' behalf.[56] Then Cyprus will either join us willingly or be taken easily in a naval attack. And if we maintain a naval presence with the fleets from Macedonia and Phoenicia, and Cyprus joins us as well, our mastery of the sea would be secure, and hence our expedition to Egypt would be easy. And once we have won control of Egypt, we will have no reason to be concerned about Greece or our own home. Secure at home, our renown increased, we will march against Babylon, having cut the Persians off from the sea completely and from all the territory this side of the Euphrates."

[II.18] So saying, Alexander had no difficulty persuading his officers to make an attempt on Tyre. And to some extent an omen persuaded him, since on that very night Alexander dreamed he was approaching the wall of Tyre, and Heracles grasped his right hand and brought him into the city. Aristander interpreted this to mean that with hard toil Tyre would be captured, as Heracles' feats had also been the fruit of hard toil.

For it was obvious that the siege of Tyre would be an enormous task. The city was an island, fortified on all sides with high walls, and at that time Tyre's naval power seemed superior, as the Persians still controlled the sea and the Tyrians themselves were still in possession of a large fleet. When, despite the difficulties, Alexander won support for his plan, he decided to build a mole extending from the mainland to the city. The proposed site for the mole was a strait covered with shoal water: the section near the mainland consisted of shallows and muddy spots; near the city itself, where the channel was deepest, the water was nearly three fathoms deep. But there were plenty of stones and an abundance of wood, which Alexander's men laid over the stones. Stakes were easily fixed in the mud, and the mud itself served to hold the stones in place.

The Macedonians showed great eagerness for the task, as did Alexander. Present himself, he directed their every move, offered encouraging words, and lightened the labor by presenting gifts to those whose efforts were outstanding. As long as they were at work on the

---

56. A shrewd judgment regarding the loyalty of the Phoenician sailors who manned Persia's fleet. Subsequent events proved Alexander right.

section near the mainland, the project went forward with no difficulty, as they were working in shallow water and no one hindered them. But by the time they neared the deeper section and approached the city itself, they were bombarded from the high walls and were coming to grief, as they were dressed for work, not combat; and when the Tyrians, who still had control of the sea, sailed out in triremes here and there near the mole, they often made it impossible for the Macedonians to build it up. The Macedonians set two towers at the edge of the mole (which eventually extended far out to sea) and placed siege engines on the towers. These were covered with screens made of skins and hides, in case they were hit from the wall with fire-bearing projectiles, and to shield the men working on them from bow shots. And meanwhile, all the Tyrians who sailed up close to injure the builders were likely to be repulsed with no difficulty, as they could now be bombarded from the towers.

[II.19] But the Tyrians devised the following countermeasure. Filling a cavalry transport-ship with dry vine twigs and other kindling, they fixed two masts at the bow and built a circular fence large enough to accommodate the greatest possible quantity of refuse and firewood as well as pitch, sulfur, and every other substance that stokes up a blaze, all of which they heaped up. Over both masts they stretched a double yardarm from which they hung basins containing all the flammable material they could find. They also put ballast in the stern to weigh it down and lift the bow. Then, keeping watch for a breeze wafting over the mole, they fastened ropes to the ship and towed it from the stern with triremes. When they had drawn near the mole and its towers, they kindled the wood, hauled the ship as forcefully as they could with the triremes, and drove it onto the edge of the mole. The men in the burning ship then swam away with no difficulty. At that point the conflagration fell on the towers, and the yardarms, when they broke, poured out all the stuff that had been prepared for fueling the fire. The men from the triremes, riding at anchor near the mole, shot arrows at the towers, making it unsafe to approach them with material to quench the fire. And while the towers were burning, many men, rushing out from the city and boarding light vessels, ran their ships ashore here and there at the mole, tore down the palisade that had been built to shield it, and burned down all the siege engines that the fire from the ship had not reached.

Alexander ordered his men to widen the mole,[57] starting from the shore, so it could accommodate more towers, and he instructed the engineers to furnish new siege engines. When these had been prepared, he set out for Sidon, taking the shield-bearers and the Agrianians, to collect all the triremes that lay ready for him there. For the siege appeared impracticable while the Tyrians retained the upper hand at sea.

[II.20] Meanwhile, Gerostratus, the king of Aradus, and Enylus of Byblus had learned that their cities were in Alexander's hands.[58] After leaving Autophradates and his ships, they went to Alexander with their own fleet and the Sidonians' triremes. And thus Alexander was joined by some eighty Phoenician ships. In the same days there arrived ten triremes from Rhodes, including their so-called patrol ship, three from Soli and Mallus, ten from Lycia, and a fifty-oared ship from Macedonia in which Proteas, son of Andronicus, was serving. Not much later the kings of Cyprus also touched at Sidon with nearly 120 ships. For they had heard of Darius' defeat at Issus and were alarmed to learn that all of Phoenicia was now in Alexander's power.[59] Alexander granted all of these men an amnesty for past offenses, on the assumption that they had joined the Persian fleet more under duress than by choice.

While his war engines were being built and the ships were being equipped for attack and for service in a naval engagement, Alexander set out for Arabia, to the Antilibanus range, taking some of the cavalry squadrons, the shield-bearers, the Agrianians, and the archers.[60] Capturing a number of places there (occupying some by force and bringing others to terms), he returned to Sidon ten days later and came upon Cleander, son of Polemocrates, who had arrived from the Peloponnese with nearly four thousand Greek mercenaries.

57. In typical fashion Arrian declines to give Alexander any emotional reaction to the stunning setback he had just experienced but imagines him proceeding in cool-headed detachment to the next phase of his project.

58. These two Phoenician kings had been at sea with their fleets when Alexander had received the surrender of their cities.

59. This last sentence helps explain all the various defections mentioned in this paragraph. As Alexander had predicted (see II.17 above, page 60), the Phoenician sea captains felt no great loyalty to Persia and mostly wanted to join whichever side appeared likely to be the future masters of their coastline.

60. This brief foray into the foothills was designed to put down the hostile tribesmen who were threatening the Macedonian supply routes.

When his fleet had been organized, Alexander embarked as many shield-bearers on his decks as seemed to him sufficient for the action, in case the battle's outcome should hinge less on breaking the enemy's line than on fighting at close quarters. Starting from Sidon, he sailed against Tyre, his fleet drawn up in battle array. He himself commanded the right wing (on the ocean side) in company with the kings of the Cyprians and all the Phoenicians except Pnytagoras, who with Craterus commanded the left wing of the entire line.

The Tyrians had previously decided to accept a battle at sea if Alexander brought his ships against them. But now, having unexpectedly caught sight of a vast number of ships (they had not learned before this that Alexander held all the Cyprian and Phoenician ships) and finding themselves faced with an organized attack (for just before touching at the city, Alexander's fleet had ridden at anchor, hoping to provoke the Tyrians to fight at sea; and when the latter did not put to sea against them, the fleet had surged forward with a great plashing of oars), the Tyrians decided not to give battle. Having tightly blocked their harbors' entrances with as many triremes as the harbors' mouths could accommodate, they were standing guard to prevent an enemy fleet coming to anchor in any of their harbors.

When the Tyrians did not put to sea against him, Alexander sailed against the city. He decided not to force his way into the harbor facing Sidon, as its mouth was narrow and he saw that many triremes were blocking its entrance, their prows facing seaward. (The Phoenicians, however, falling on the three Tyrian triremes moored farthest out, attacked them prow to prow and sank them. The shipwrecked crews had no trouble swimming to the friendly shore.) For the time being Alexander's ships anchored not far from the newly built mole along the shore, where there appeared to be a shelter from the winds.

The next day, he ordered the Cyprians and Andromachus, the admiral, to blockade the city at the harbor facing Sidon, and the Phoenicians to do the same at the harbor beyond the mole, where his own tent was pitched.[61]

[II.21] By that time Alexander had brought many engineers from Cyprus and from all over Phoenicia,[62] and several war engines

---

61. That is, having failed to draw the Tyrian ships out into open water to fight a sea battle, Alexander chose instead to seal them up inside the city's two harbors so they could no longer impede his siege operations.

62. The Phoenicians had long been famous for their cleverness and techni-

had been built—some on the mole, others on the horse transports he had brought from Sidon, and still others on some of the slower-sailing triremes. When everything was ready, they brought the engines forward down the newly built mole and from the ships anchored here and there near the wall, and set about putting its strength to the test. The Tyrians, meanwhile, set wooden towers on the battlements facing the mole, from which they meant to fight off the enemy. And whenever the engines came within range, the Tyrians defended themselves with missiles and shot fire-bearing arrows at the enemy ships, making it dangerous for the Macedonians to approach the wall. (The Tyrian walls that faced the mole were about 150 feet high[63] and proportionately thick and were built of huge stones embedded in cement.) The Macedonian horse transports and the triremes bringing engines to the wall also encountered another difficulty: a great many rocks had been cast into the sea, and these prevented the Macedonians from attacking at close range. Alexander decided to pull these rocks from the water. This was achieved with difficulty, as the work had to be undertaken from ships, not from firm ground; and further trouble was given by the Tyrians, who had covered some of their own ships with armor and regularly sailed past the triremes' anchors and severed their cords, making it hard for the Macedonian ships to remain in place.[64] Alexander armored several thirty-oared ships in the same way and stationed them at an oblique angle in front of the triremes to protect their anchors. The Tyrians responded by sending out divers to cut the cords, but the Macedonians foiled the divers by lowering anchors secured with chains instead of cords. From the mole Alexander's men now fastened nooses to the rocks and pulled them from the sea; then, raising them aloft with the engines, the men discharged them into the deep water where they were unlikely to cause harm. Wherever the approach to the wall had been cleared of rocks, the ships could now be brought near with no difficulty.

Sorely pressed in every way, the Tyrians decided to launch an attack on the Cyprian ships blockading the harbor facing Sidon. For a

---

cal skill (see, for example, Herodotus VII.23). Engineering was coming to play a large part in warfare in the late fourth century B.C.E., and Alexander was very much at the forefront of the developing military technologies.

63. This figure must be a gross exaggeration.

64. How these Tyrian ships evaded the Macedonian blockade of their harbors is not explained.

long time they stretched out sails across the mouth of the harbor so they might man their triremes without attracting attention. About midday, when Alexander's sailors had dispersed on necessary errands, and he himself, having left the fleet at the other side of the city, had withdrawn to his tent, the Tyrians, manning three quinquiremes, three quadriremes, and seven triremes with their sharpest crews (the ones who were most courageous in a sea battle and best equipped to fight from the decks), rowed out quietly in single file without a signalman. Then, as they were turning toward the Cyprians and were almost in sight, they raised a great shout, urging one another on, and bore down on the enemy, straining eagerly at their oars.

[II.22] On that day it happened that when Alexander withdrew to his tent he did not stay there as usual, but returned after a short time to the ships. The Tyrians, falling unexpectedly upon the moored ships, found some of them quite empty; others, in the uproar of the attack, were being manned with difficulty by those who happened to be at hand. In the first charge, the Tyrians quickly sank the quinquiremes of King Pnytagoras, Androcles the Amathusian, and Pasicrates of Curium. Driving all the others out onto the beach, they broke them apart. When Alexander saw the Tyrians' triremes making a breakout, he gave orders for most of his ships, once each was manned, to ride at anchor at the mouth of the harbor and thereby prevent the other Tyrian ships from sailing out. He himself, taking the quinquiremes he had with him and about five triremes (those that had got their crews aboard first), sailed around the city against the Tyrians who had broken out of the harbor. The Tyrians atop the wall, catching sight of the enemy attack and seeing Alexander himself on board, shouted to the men on their own ships, urging them to return; and when their shouts went unheard in the hubbub made by those engaged in combat, they resorted to a variety of other methods to signal a retreat. When at long last the Tyrian ships became aware of Alexander's attack, they turned back and tried to flee to the harbor.[65] A few Tyrian ships managed to escape, but most were assaulted by Alexander's ships. Some were disabled, and a quinquireme and quadrireme were seized at the mouth of the harbor. The crews

---

65. The pattern of the battle of Issus, and many other land engagements, repeats here on the sea: the sight of Alexander himself charging forward puts his opponents to flight.

suffered few casualties, as they swam to the harbor with no difficulty when they saw their ships in enemy hands.

Once the Tyrians could no longer look to their ships for help, the Macedonians brought their siege engines up to the wall. Those that they moved up along the mole proved ineffectual, due to the thickness of the wall; so some of their ships, carrying similar machines, were brought to the side of the city facing Sidon. But when nothing was achieved there either, Alexander moved southward to the wall facing Egypt and tested its strength at every point. And there, after a lengthy battering, the wall crumbled and was even breached with a small crack. After bridging the opening with gangways, Alexander attempted a brief assault, but the Tyrians had no trouble beating back the Macedonians.

[II.23] Two days later, having waited for a calm, Alexander called his battalion commanders into action and brought the engines aboard his ships. He first pounded at the wall for a considerable time, and when the breach seemed wide enough, he ordered the ships carrying the siege engines to withdraw; he then brought up two other ships, carrying the gangways he intended to throw across the breach in the wall. The shield-bearers took one of the ships (the one in which Admetus was serving); Coenus' battalion, the so-called *astheteroi*,[66] took the other. Alexander himself intended to mount the wall with his shield-bearers wherever this was practicable. He ordered some of the triremes to patrol both harbors in the event they could force an entrance while the Tyrians were occupied in resisting his own party. The ships that had projectiles to be fired from engines and those carrying archers on their decks were ordered to sail around the wall and come ashore wherever this could be managed, or to ride at anchor within range until they had an opportunity to land, so that the Tyrians, assailed from all sides, would not know which way to turn in the heat of the moment.

When the ships with Alexander touched at the city, and the gangways were thrown over the breach, the shield-bearers climbed them boldly to the top of the wall. Admetus proved a brave man on that occasion. Alexander accompanied them, taking an energetic part in the action and serving as a witness of any glorious exploit undertaken by his men in their danger. The wall was captured first at the point where Alexander had stationed himself—the Tyrians were beaten back from

66. No one is quite sure of the nature of this Macedonian contingent.

it with no difficulty—since for the first time the Macedonians had a means of approach that was sturdy and not too steep. Admetus mounted the wall first, and as he cheered his men onward he was hit by a spear and died on the spot. Coming up after him, Alexander and the Companions took possession of the wall. When some of the towers and their curtain walls were under his control, Alexander proceeded across the battlements to the palace, as the descent into the city appeared easier from there.

[II.24] As for the men on the ships, the Phoenicians, who were moored at the harbor facing Egypt, forced their way in, having torn apart the booms, and set about disabling the Tyrian ships, attacking some in the open water, driving others out onto the shore;[67] meanwhile, the Cyprians at the harbor facing Sidon (which did not have a protecting boom) sailed in and immediately captured that part of the town. Most of the Tyrians, when they saw the wall occupied, abandoned it. Having rallied at the so-called Shrine of Agenor, they turned upon the Macedonians, at which point Alexander, advancing against them with his shield-bearers, slaughtered some of them there and pursued those who fled. The slaughter was great, now that those from the harbor were already in control of the town and Coenus' battalion had entered it as well. The Macedonians advanced, most of them in a rage, as they were vexed at the delay occasioned by the siege[68] and because the Tyrians had seized some of their men sailing from Sidon, had made them mount the wall so that they might be seen from the camp, and had cut their throats and flung their bodies into the sea. Nearly eight thousand Tyrians perished. As for the Macedonians, in the actual assault they lost Admetus, who had proved his bravery as the first man to capture the wall, and twenty shield-bearers. In the course of the entire siege, about four hundred Macedonians died.[69] Alexander granted an amnesty to all who had fled to the shrine of Heracles—a group that included a number of Tyrians who held high

67. It is interesting to note the willingness of these pro-Alexander Phoenicians to attack and kill fellow Phoenicians who opposed Alexander. A similar phenomenon occurred at the sack of Thebes, where the Greeks fighting on Alexander's side had zealously butchered their fellow Greeks.
68. The operation had lasted seven months, an eternity compared with the speed of the Macedonian advance up to that point.
69. Bosworth comments, "It is inconceivable that such fierce and protracted fighting could have taken so small a toll" (*Commentary* I.254).

office, King Azemilcus, and some ambassadors from Carthage who had come to the mother city to pay homage to Heracles according to an ancient custom.[70] He enslaved all the others: some thirty thousand Tyrians and foreigners were caught and sold.

Alexander sacrificed to Heracles and in honor of that god held a parade of the armed forces and a review of the fleet. He also held athletic games and a torch race in the sacred precinct. As for the siege engine with which the wall had been breached, he dedicated it in the temple. He also dedicated the Tyrian ship sacred to Heracles (which he had seized in the naval attack) and included an inscription, composed either by himself or another, not worth recording (which is why I have not taken the trouble to record it).

Tyre was captured in the month of Hecatombaeon during Nicetus' archonship at Athens.[71]

[II.25] While Alexander was still engaged in the siege of Tyre, envoys arrived from Darius to report that their king was prepared to give Alexander ten thousand talents in return for his mother, wife, and children; he also proposed that the entire territory between the Euphrates and the Mediterranean be Alexander's and that Alexander marry Darius' daughter and become his friend and ally.[72] When these proposals were announced in an assembly of the Companions, Parmenio reportedly said to Alexander that if he were Alexander he would be content, on those terms, to end the war and run no further risks. Alexander replied that if he were Parmenio, that is what he would do, but since he was Alexander, he would answer Darius as he did in fact answer him. For he said he had no need of Darius' money

70. Alexander's deference to the Carthaginian ambassadors is partly explained by the fact that Carthage had in the end declined to send military aid to the besieged Tyrians, despite their initial promise to do so. At the end of his life Alexander was planning a naval expedition against Carthage, to eliminate his one remaining threat on the seas.

71. August 332 B.C.E.

72. The various letters sent by Darius to Alexander with offers of appeasement form a tangled tale in our extant sources. According to Diodorus and Curtius, Darius made a much more modest offer after the fall of Tyre—all territory west of the Halys, plus alliance by marriage—and reserved the above offer (or something like it) for a later, more desperate occasion, before the battle of Gaugamela. In Arrian, Darius' offer following Tyre is his last; clearly there would be no point in future negotiations once Alexander had declined an enormous sum of money, plus sovereignty over nearly half the empire.

nor of any part of the country instead of the whole, as the money and the entire country were his. And he would marry Darius' daughter if he wished to;[73] he would marry her even if Darius failed to offer her. He urged Darius to come to him if he wanted to be treated generously. When Darius heard this, he gave up hope of coming to terms with Alexander and again set about preparing for war.

Alexander now decided to launch his expedition to Egypt.

73. Alexander indeed married Stateira (Barsine), Darius' eldest daughter, just before his death.

IV

The Egyptian Interlude

(Autumn 332–Spring 331 B.C.E.)

The conquest of the Levantine coast was not completed by the fall of Tyre; one more siege awaited Alexander as he moved south, at the port city of Gaza. Here Alexander's engineers confronted another seemingly insoluble problem, a strongly fortified city atop a plateau said to be 250 feet high (though this figure is doubtless exaggerated). As at Tyre, the army was put to work carrying landfill to build a great mound so that siege machinery could be wheeled into place beside Gaza's walls. Once again the work progressed slowly and perilously, under constant missile fire from Gaza's defenders; on one occasion Alexander himself was seriously wounded by a catapult-fired bolt that passed through his armor and into his shoulder. Finally, after two months of siege operations and three unsuccessful assaults, the Macedonians overwhelmed Gaza's defenses and captured the "impregnable" city. A mass slaughter resulted as the still-defiant Gazans refused to submit and the Macedonians vented the anger built up during nearly a year of continuous siegecraft.

One ancient source, Quintus Curtius, mentions a particularly nasty form of revenge taken at Gaza, supposedly ordered by Alexander himself: the dragging of the city's king, Batis, behind a chariot while still (briefly) alive, an even crueler act than the dragging of Hector's body by Achilles in Homer's Iliad. One other ancient writer, Hegesias, records something similar, but Plutarch, Diodorus, and Arrian show no knowledge of the incident. The discrepancy presents modern scholars with a problem typical of Alexander studies, requiring a general assessment of Alexander's nature for a solution. Does one assume that Alexander was capable of wanton cruelty and explain the absence of this episode from some accounts as an attempt by his supporters at a whitewash? Or does one assume that he had no such propensities, at least in this stage of his life, and assume that the story was invented by detractors seeking to demonize him? Both approaches have their partisans among recent historians of the period.

After the conquest of Gaza, Alexander could feel that his grand strategy in Asia Minor, neutralizing the Persian fleet by depriving it of safe anchorage, had been enacted. Now he could move on to his next target, Egypt.

[Arrian III.1] Alexander now started for Egypt,[1] and after a six days' march from Gaza reached Egyptian Pelusium. His navy had been voyaging along the coast from Phoenicia to Egypt, and he found it moored at Pelusium. Mazaces the Persian, who had been appointed satrap of Egypt by Darius, had been informed about the battle at Issus and about Darius' disgraceful flight and the fact that Phoenicia, Syria, and the greater part of Arabia were in Alexander's power. Possessing no Persian force himself, Mazaces received Alexander hospitably in the cities and the country. Alexander established a garrison at Pelusium, and after commanding his officers to sail up the river as far as Memphis, he himself proceeded to Heliopolis, keeping the Nile on his right.

After taking control of all the places along his route (they were all surrendered by their inhabitants), he crossed the desert and arrived in Heliopolis. From there he crossed the river and visited Memphis, where he sacrificed to Apis[2] and all the other gods and held a competition in athletics and the arts. The most distinguished experts in these fields came from Greece to compete. From Memphis he sailed down to the sea, taking the shield-bearers aboard as well as the archers, the Agrianians, and the royal squadron of the Companion Cavalry. On reaching Canobus he sailed around Lake Mareotis and disembarked at the site of present-day Alexandria, the city named after him. The site struck him as very beautiful for a new settlement, and he imagined that a city founded there would prosper.[3] A sudden passion for the project seized him, and he himself marked out where the agora was to be built and decided how many temples were to be erected and to which gods they were to be dedicated—the Greek gods

1. Egypt was a target of conquest for Alexander in that it ostensibly belonged to the Persian empire, though by way of numerous revolts over the preceding century it had largely regained its autonomy. Egyptians had detested Persian rule, so Alexander knew that his conquering army would be welcomed by them as liberators.
2. Apis was a divine calf worshiped by the Egyptians. Alexander was careful to show great reverence to Apis and other local deities, since dishonor of Egyptian religion by the Persians had led to widespread unrest.
3. There is some dispute among the sources as to whether the foundation of the city of Alexandria took place upon Alexander's entry into Egypt (as Arrian says here) or on his return from the oracle at Siwah, some months later (as Diodorus and Curtius have it).

and Egyptian Isis—and where the wall was to be built around the city. With these plans in mind he offered sacrifices, and the omens proved favorable.

[III.2] The following story is also told, and I, for one, find it credible. Alexander is said to have wanted to leave the builders with an outline of the proposed wall, but had nothing with which to mark the surface of the ground. It occurred to one of the builders to gather the barley meal the soldiers carried in their mess kits and to lay it down where the king indicated. In this way the circuit wall designed for the city was outlined. The seers pondered this incident, particularly Aristander of Telmissus, many of whose other predictions are said to have come true. Aristander predicted that the city would be prosperous in every way, especially with respect to the fruits of the earth.

[III.3] A sudden desire now seized Alexander to visit and consult Ammon in Libya,[4] both because the oracle of Ammon was said to be truthful and because Perseus and Heracles had consulted it: the former when he was sent against the Gorgon by Polydectes, the latter when he was seeking Antaeus in Libya and Busiris in Egypt. Alexander was engaged in a rivalry with Perseus and Heracles, as both heroes were his kinsmen. Moreover, he traced his own birth to Ammon, just as the myths trace the births of Perseus and Heracles to Zeus. In any case, he set out with this in mind and imagined that he would obtain more precise knowledge of his own affairs, or at least would say he had obtained it.

4. The oracle of the Egyptian god Ammon, whom the Greeks roughly equated with Zeus, was one of the most important shrines in the ancient world, despite its obscure location: at the oasis of Siwah in the midst of the Sahara desert. Alexander's journey to this site, a perilous and lengthy one, must have had some powerful objective; the primary one reported by Arrian, that he was engaged in a rivalry with Perseus and Heracles, is given less credence by historians than the secondary one, that he sought confirmation of the divine lineage he had already begun to believe in. But just what Arrian means when he says that Alexander "traced his own birth to Ammon" is unclear; it might refer either to parentage or to more remote ancestry, such as the connection to Ammon-Zeus that Alexander naturally had through his paternal line, descended from Heracles. Nor is it clear what Arrian means when he says that Alexander sought "precise knowledge of his own affairs." Our author leaves much about the visit to Siwah an open question, and so it has remained.

Taking the coastal route to Paraetonium, he traveled two hundred miles (according to Aristobulus) across a land not wholly without water but deserted. From Paraetonium he headed into the interior, to the oracle of Ammon. The route is deserted and for the most part sandy and waterless. There was considerable rainfall, however, and this was attributed to divine influences.

A divine influence was also felt to be at work in the following incident. Whenever the south wind blows in that country, it buries the road in sand. The road's landmarks disappear, and it is impossible to find one's way, just as in an ocean of sand. No mountain, tree, or unshifting mound rises up by which wayfarers may judge their course, as sailors do by the stars. Accordingly, Alexander's army was wandering, and his guides were in doubt about the route. Ptolemy says that two serpents, giving voice, advanced in front of the army. Alexander ordered his officers to follow them and to put their trust in god, and the serpents led the way to the oracle and back again. But according to Aristobulus, whose version of the story is more widely accepted, two ravens flew ahead of the army and became Alexander's guides. And I can confidently declare that he met with divine aid, as probability also favors such a view,[5] though the exact truth of the story has been lost in the welter of conflicting accounts.

[III.4] The temple of Ammon lies in a sandy and waterless desert. At the desert's center there is a small area, forty stades wide at most, full of cultivated trees, olive trees, and palms. It is the only place thereabouts where dew forms. The place boasts a spring unlike any other on earth: at midday the water is cold to the taste and still more to the touch—as cold as water can be. As the sun declines toward evening, the water grows warmer, and from evening until midnight it grows warmer still, reaching its warmest at midnight. Past midnight it gradually cools, and early in the morning is cold, though it is coldest at midday. This cycle is repeated every day. Salts form there naturally and are excavated and brought to Egypt by the priests of Ammon. For whenever these priests journey to Egypt, they place the salt in baskets woven from palm leaves and present it as a gift to the king of Egypt or to someone else. The grains of this salt are large (some of them larger than three finger breadths) and are clear as crystal. As it is more pure than sea salt, it is used in sacrifices by the Egyptians and by all who are not careless in their religious observances.

---

5. In that it is unlikely that the expedition could have found its way unaided.

Alexander marveled at the place and consulted Ammon. When he had heard all that could satisfy his heart's desire (as he said),[6] he led the army back to Egypt, returning by the same road, according to Aristobulus, though Ptolemy says they took another, a road that led straight to Memphis.

6. Again Arrian leaves the questions surrounding the Siwah visit unanswered, seemingly agreeing with the account of Callisthenes that Alexander consulted the priests of the shrine in private, leaving no record of what transpired. Other sources, however, give various versions of the questions Alexander asked and the replies he received. Most say that he inquired whether the murderers of his father, Philip, had all been punished and received an affirmative answer. Diodorus also reports that he asked whether he would rule the whole world and was told that he would.

V

The War with Darius— Phase II

(Summer 331–Summer 330 B.C.E.)

a. The battle of Gaugamela

In the summer of 331 Alexander led his army out of Egypt and back through Phoenicia, then eastward toward the Persian heartlands. Darius, as he knew, was mustering a huge army in the vicinity of Babylon, preparing for a decisive showdown. Alexander now turned all his energies toward this match with Darius, virtually ignoring the Spartan-led rebellion brewing back home in the Aegean: King Agis of Sparta, though short of Persian aid (see page 56 above) and lacking the crucial support of Athens, had gathered a formidable army and had inflicted a defeat on Macedonian forces in the Peloponnese. Though he had likely received word of these events during his march out of Egypt, Alexander gambled that his appointed steward of Macedonia, Antipater, could put down the revolt without additional land forces and sent back only the navy, which he himself would no longer need. All other resources he kept in Asia in preparation for the next phase of the war with Darius, now about to begin.

[Arrian III.7] Alexander reached Thapsacus in the month of Hecatombaeon, during Aristophanes' archonship at Athens,[1] and found the river yoked with two bridges. For Darius had entrusted the guardianship of the river[2] to Mazaeus, who had been guarding it with roughly three thousand horsemen and [ ][3] foot soldiers, two thousand of whom were Greek mercenaries. The Macedonians had not

---

1. August 331 B.C.E.
2. The Euphrates.
3. A numeral here has fallen out of the text.

connected the bridge to the opposite bank, as they feared that Mazaeus' men might attack the bridge where it ended. But as soon as Mazaeus heard that Alexander was approaching, he fled with the entire army. And once Mazaeus had fled, the bridges were carried across to the opposite bank, and Alexander crossed them with his army.

He then advanced inland, keeping the Euphrates and the mountains of Armenia on his left, through the country known as Mesopotamia. When he set out from the Euphrates, he did not take the road that led directly to Babylon, since everything was more practicable for the army on the other road: it was easier to obtain green fodder for the horses and provisions for the men, and the heat was not so intense. Some of the Persians from Darius' army who had dispersed along the road to reconnoiter were caught, and these men reported that Darius had taken up a position at the Tigris and was determined to bar Alexander's way should he try to cross. They reported that the army with Darius was much larger than the force that had fought in Cilicia. On hearing this, Alexander hastened to the Tigris. When he arrived he found neither Darius nor the guard Darius had left behind.[4] He crossed the river—a difficult task only because the current was swift; for no one barred his way.

Alexander now gave the army a rest. When an almost total eclipse of the moon occurred,[5] Alexander sacrificed to the moon, the sun, and the earth, which are said to be responsible for this phenomenon. Aristander thought the eclipse was a favorable omen for the Macedonians and Alexander, and that their battle would take place that month. He said that the sacrifices foreshadowed a victory for Alexander. Starting from the Tigris, Alexander marched across Assyria, keeping the Gordyenian Mountains on his left, the Tigris on his right. Four days after he had crossed the river, his guides reported that enemy horsemen could be seen in the plain, though they could not estimate their number. Arraying the army, Alexander advanced as for battle, whereupon other guides, who had made a more exact observation, rode up to report that there seemed to be no more than a thousand horsemen.

---

4. It is hard to explain Darius' decision not to defend the Tigris crossing, especially since Persian strategy at both the battles of the Granicus and Issus had relied on preventing the Macedonians from fording a river.
5. Dated by astronomers to September 20, 331 B.C.E.

[III.8] Taking the royal squadron, one squadron of Companion Cavalry, and the Paeonian guides, Alexander hastened ahead, having ordered the rest of the army to follow at a marching pace. When the Persian horsemen beheld the swift approach of Alexander's troops, they fled as fast as they could. Alexander, in pursuit, pressed them hard. Most of them escaped, though Alexander's men killed those whose horses were exhausted in the flight, and took others alive with their horses. From these men the Macedonians learned that Darius was not far off with a large force.

For all the Indians[6] who dwelt near the Bactrians had rushed to Darius' aid along with the Bactrians themselves and the Sogdianians. These contingents were all under the command of Bessus, the satrap of Bactria. The Sacae, a Scythian tribe related to the Scythians who dwell in Asia, were also accompanying them, not as Bessus' subjects but in fulfillment of the terms of their alliance with Darius. Their commander was Mauaces, and they were mounted bowmen. Barsaentes, the satrap of the Arachosians, was leading the Arachosians and the so-called mountain Indians. Satibarzanes, the satrap of Areia, was leading the Areians. Phrataphernes was leading the Parthyaeans, Hyrcanians, and Topeirians, all of whom were horsemen. Atropates led the Medes, with whom the Cadusians, Albanians, and Sacesinae had been posted. Orontobates, Ariobarzanes, and Orxines were leading the Red Sea tribes. The Uxians and Susians were commanded by Oxathres, son of Abulites. Bupares was leading the Babylonians. The displaced Carians and the Sittacenians had been posted with the Babylonians. Orontes and Mithraustes led the Armenians, Ariaces the Cappadocians. Mazaeus was leading the contingent from Hollow Syria and all the Mesopotamians. Darius' entire army was said to include nearly forty thousand horsemen, a million foot soldiers, two hundred scythe-bearing chariots, and a modest number of elephants (the Indians dwelling west of the Indus had about fifteen).[7]

6. The term "Indians" is used very loosely in Greek literature to denote various peoples dwelling east of the Hindu Kush mountain range. Those "near the Bactrians" would have lived in what is now eastern Afghanistan or western Pakistan.
7. The numbers of these forces are no doubt exaggerated (with the exception of the elephants), but Darius' army certainly exceeded that of Alexander several times over, especially in the crucial cavalry divisions.

With this force Darius had encamped at Gaugamela, near the river Bumelus, roughly seventy miles from the city of Arbela, on completely level ground. The Persians had long since leveled the uneven ground thereabouts, making it fit for chariot driving and for use by the cavalry. For some were trying to persuade Darius that he had fallen short in the battle at Issus owing to the narrowness of the battlefield, and Darius was easily persuaded.

[III.9] When the captured Persian spies reported this to Alexander, he remained where he was for four days. He gave the army a rest after its march and fortified the camp with a ditch and a palisade, as he had decided to leave behind the baggage train and all the soldiers unfit for fighting and to proceed to the battlefield with troops carrying only their arms. Taking his forces at night, he set out near the second watch, intending to join battle with the barbarians at daybreak. When it was reported to Darius that Alexander was drawing near, he marshaled his army for battle, and Alexander led his own men forward, likewise drawn up in battle array. The armies were about seven miles apart, not yet within sight of one another, as the terrain that separated them was hilly.

When Alexander was about three miles away and his army was descending the intervening hills, he caught sight of the barbarians and halted the phalanx. Again calling together the Companions, generals, squadron leaders, and the commanders of the allies and the foreign mercenaries, he asked them whether he should immediately advance the phalanx from its present position, as the majority urged, or follow Parmenio's advice and encamp where they were, reconnoiter the entire area to find out if there was anything suspicious or difficult, or any concealed ditches or stakes fixed in the ground, and inspect the enemy's arrangements more carefully. Parmenio's view prevailed, and they encamped where they were, in the order in which they were going to advance into battle.

Taking the light-armed troops and the Companion Cavalry, Alexander rode all around, inspecting the entire ground where his action would be fought. After returning to camp and again convening the same officers, he said that there was no need for him to inspire them for battle, as they had long been inspired by their own bravery and their excellent record. He expected each of them to urge his own men on, each captain to encourage his company, each squadron leader his own squadron, each taxiarch his battalion, and each infantry commander the phalanx that had been entrusted to him, since in this battle they were fighting not for Hollow Syria, as previously, or for Phoenicia, or even for Egypt; on *this* occasion, the sovereignty of all of Asia would be decided. Accordingly, there was no need to make long speeches heartening men who were naturally disposed to fight nobly. Instead, they should urge each man to look to his own orderly conduct at the moment of danger, and to keep a strict silence whenever it was necessary to advance in silence, and to send up a glorious shout where it was appropriate to shout, and to raise a terrifying howl when the time was ripe for howling. They themselves should obey instructions swiftly, and swiftly pass them on to their units, and everyone should bear in mind that the entire outcome depended on each man's conduct: negligence on anyone's part endangered them all, while every man's diligent effort contributed to their common success.

[III.10] When Alexander had encouraged the men with these words and a few others in the same vein, and his officers had in turn urged him to rely on them, he ordered the army to dine and rest. Parmenio, they say, went to him in his tent and advised him to attack the Persians at night, as they would be surprised and confused, and a night attack would be more terrifying. But Alexander replied, because others were listening, that it would be disgraceful to steal the victory; instead, Alexander must win openly and without trickery. His high-flown rhetoric seemed less an expression of arrogance than of self-confidence in the face of danger, and I think he was calculating accurately in this regard:[8] at night, whether or not men have been sufficiently prepared for battle, it often happens, when many things turn out contrary to calculation, that the stronger are foiled and the victory goes to the weaker, against the expectations of both. Though Alexander took many chances in his battles, he recognized that the night posed dangers. Furthermore, if Darius were again defeated, the fact that the attack was made secretly and at night would forestall any concession on his part that he and the men he led were inferior, while if Alexander's men should meet with an unexpected reverse in a country friendly to his enemies (who were themselves familiar with the region, whereas *his* men were not and were surrounded by enemies, including their own prisoners of war), those enemies might join in attacking them at night even if the Macedonians' victory were not

8. Arrian speaks here from the experience of his own military career.

decisive, let alone if they were defeated. I commend Alexander for these calculations no less than for his bravado.

[III.13] As the armies were now drawing near one another, Darius could be seen, along with his troops: the Persian apple-bearers,[9] the Indians, the Albanians, the displaced Carians, and the Mardian archers, all of whom were posted opposite Alexander and the royal squadron. But Alexander was heading more to his right, and the Persians, shifting in response to this move, were far outflanking his army with their left wing. The Scythian horsemen, riding alongside, had already attacked the troops posted in front of Alexander's line, but Alexander continued to move to the right and was about to leave the ground the Persians had leveled.[10] Fearing that if the Macedonians advanced to the unlevel ground the Persians' chariots would be of no use, Darius commanded the men posted in front of his left wing to ride around the Macedonians' right, where Alexander was leading, so that they would not extend their wing any farther. When this happened, Alexander commanded Menidas' mercenary cavalry to charge them. Sallying out to meet this force, the Scythian horsemen and the Bactrians posted with them routed Menidas' cavalry, as the barbarians far outnumbered them. Alexander then ordered Ariston's Paeonians and the mercenaries to attack the Scythians, and the barbarians gave way. But the rest of the Bactrians, having drawn near the Paeonians and the mercenaries, rallied their own fleeing troops and made the cavalry engagement a close contest. Alexander's men were falling in greater numbers. They were pressed hard on account of the barbarians' superior numbers and because the Scythians and their horses had been better equipped for defense. But even so, the Macedonians withstood their attacks; assaulting one squadron after another, they were driving them from the line.

9. So called because of the fruit-shaped ornaments on the butt end of their spears.
10. This initial move rightward reveals much about Alexander's daring, self-confident strategy for the overall battle. Knowing that, in a head-to-head collision, his line would inevitably be outflanked by the Persians, he chose to stretch his right wing even farther right and threaten to outflank *them*. The result, as he well knew, would be that his left wing, under Parmenio, would be nearly surrounded by enemy forces, but he wagered that their superior fighting skills would allow them to hold their own long enough for his right wing to find an opening and win the battle.

At that point the barbarians sent their scythe-bearing chariots out against Alexander himself,[11] intending to throw his phalanx into disarray. Here they were particularly disappointed. For just as they were approaching, the Agrianians and Balacrus' javelin men (both contingents were posted in front of the Companion Cavalry) hurled their javelins. Then, seizing the chariots' reins, they pulled down the drivers, stood around the horses, and cut them to pieces. Some of the chariots also went right through the lines: for the Macedonian infantrymen broke ranks, as they had been instructed to do, wherever the chariots charged. This was the chief reason the chariots themselves and those against whom they were driven escaped unharmed. These chariots, too, were seized by the grooms of Alexander's army and the royal shield-bearers.

[III.14] Now that Darius was leading his army against the entire phalanx, Alexander ordered Aretes to attack the cavalry trying to surround their right wing. For a time Alexander himself led his men in column, but when the horsemen, who had sallied out against the Persian cavalry trying to surround the right wing, first breached the barbarian phalanx, Alexander wheeled about opposite the gap, arrayed the Companion Cavalry and the nearby portion of the phalanx in a wedge formation, and led them at full speed and with a war cry against Darius himself. For a brief period the fighting was hand to hand, but when Alexander and his horsemen pressed the enemy hard, shoving the Persians and striking their faces with spears, and the Macedonian phalanx, tightly arrayed and bristling with pikes, was already upon them, Darius, who had long been in a state of dread, now saw terrors all around him; he wheeled about—the first to do so—and fled.[12] The Persians who were trying to surround the Macedonian wing also took fright when Aretes and his men attacked them in force.

Here, then, the Persians' flight was desperate, and the Macedonians, in pursuit, were slaughtering their enemies as they fled. But elsewhere, Simmias and his battalion were unable to join Alexander in the pursuit; having halted the phalanx, they fought where they

11. It is not clear why Arrian says "against Alexander himself," since the king was on the far right of the battlefield, not in the center where the scythed chariots encountered the phalanx.
12. As at Issus, the flight of Darius became the turning point in the battle, though our other sources give the Persian king more credit for putting up a brave fight. Arrian makes him a weak and pathetic figure.

were, as the Macedonians' left was reported to be in trouble. On this side the Macedonians broke formation, and some Indians and Persian horsemen burst through the gap toward their baggage train. A desperate action ensued. For the Persians boldly attacked many unarmed men who had not expected anyone to cut through the double phalanx, and the barbarian prisoners of war joined in the action against the Macedonians when the Persians attacked. But the commanders of the reserves for the Macedonians' first phalanx soon learned what was happening; facing about as they had been instructed to do, they assaulted the Persians' rear and killed many who were crowded around the baggage train, though some wheeled around and fled. Meanwhile, the Persians at the right wing, not yet aware that Darius had fled, rode around Alexander's left wing and assaulted Parmenio's troops.

[III.15] At that point, when for the first time the Macedonians found themselves attacked on both sides, Parmenio quickly sent a messenger to Alexander to report that their men were in trouble and needed help.[13] When this was reported to Alexander, he turned back from further pursuit. Wheeling about with the Companion Cavalry, he hastened toward the barbarians' right. First he attacked the largest and strongest contingents of the fleeing enemy cavalry—the Parthyaeans, some Indians, and the Persians. This cavalry engagement was the most desperate of the entire battle. For the barbarians, posted many rows deep (as they had been arrayed in squadrons), encountered Alexander's troops face to face and resorted neither to javelin throwing nor to countermarching of horses, which are common in cavalry actions. Instead, each man strove on his own to burst through, as this was their only hope of rescue. They eagerly struck their enemies (and were themselves being struck without mercy), as they were no longer contending for another's victory but for their own

13. There has been much discussion among historians of Parmenio's purported message. It seems unlikely that such a message, if it was even sent, could have caught up with Alexander, who was pursuing Darius at full speed. More likely, Alexander turned back on his own initiative, realizing that he had left the field with much of his forces still in difficulty and that the pursuit of Darius simply had to be postponed. Later traditions hostile to Parmenio may have sought to emphasize the old general's helplessness and reliance on Alexander.

survival. Some sixty of Alexander's Companions fell in that action, and Hephaestion himself was wounded, as were Coenus and Menidas. Yet here, too, Alexander prevailed.

All the Persians who managed to break through Alexander's phalanx fled for their lives. Alexander himself now approached to engage the enemy's right wing. At that point the Thessalian horsemen, who had fought gloriously, did not prove inferior to Alexander in the action. But the barbarians' right wing was already fleeing when Alexander encountered them. He therefore turned back to pursue Darius, and pursued him as long as there was daylight. Parmenio and his men followed, pursuing their opponents. But when Alexander had crossed the river Lycus, he encamped to give his men and horses a brief rest. Parmenio, meanwhile, captured the barbarians' camp, its baggage train, elephants,[14] and camels.

Having rested his horsemen until midnight, Alexander hastened toward Arbela, intending to capture Darius there with all his treasure and all the royal furniture. He reached Arbela the next day, having covered nearly seventy miles since the battle. Alexander did not find Darius at Arbela, as Darius, having taken no rest, was still fleeing. But his treasure and all his furniture were seized. His chariot and shield were captured for the second time; his bow and arrows were also taken.

Nearly a hundred of Alexander's men died, and more than a thousand horses died from wounds and the stress of the pursuit. Almost half of these horses belonged to the Companion Cavalry. There were said to be nearly three hundred thousand barbarian corpses, but far more barbarians were captured than killed, and the elephants were captured as were all the chariots that had not been cut to pieces.

So ended the battle, which took place in the month of Pyanepsion, during Aristophanes' archonship at Athens.[15] And Aristander's prophecy, that the battle would take place in the same month as the lunar eclipse and would be a victory, came true.

14. The aftermath of the battle of Gaugamela brought Europeans into contact with the Indian elephant for the first time. The men of Alexander's army would have many more encounters with this much-dreaded war machine in the years ahead.
15. A slight error in chronology on Arrian's part. The exact date of the battle of Gaugamela was October 1, 331 B.C.E.

b. The capture of the spoils

[III.16] Immediately after the battle, Darius hastened past the Armenian Mountains toward Media. As the Bactrian horsemen had been posted with him in the battle, they joined him in the flight. The Persians who accompanied him included the King's kinsmen and a few of the so-called apple-bearers. He was also joined by some two thousand foreign mercenaries under the command of Patron the Phocian and Glaucus the Aetolian.[16] He had chosen to flee to Media as he supposed that after the battle Alexander would advance toward Susa and Babylon. For the road to Babylon was inhabited from beginning to end and was not impassable for baggage animals, and furthermore, Babylon and Susa seemed to be the prize of the war. The road to Media, on the other hand, would not easily accommodate a large army. Darius was not mistaken. Setting out from Arbela, Alexander advanced directly toward Babylon, and when he was not far from the city, leading his forces in battle array, the Babylonians met him with their whole people, including their priests and rulers, each bearing gifts and surrendering the city, the citadel, and their treasure.

On entering Babylon, Alexander ordered the Babylonians to rebuild all the temples Xerxes had destroyed, including the temple of Bel, a god the Babylonians especially esteem. He appointed Mazaeus as satrap of Babylon and named Apollodorus, son of Amphipolites, as commander of the soldiers left behind with Mazaeus, and Asclepiodorus, son of Philon, as collector of the taxes.[17] He also sent Mithrenes to Armenia as satrap, since the latter had surrendered the

---

16. The loyalty of these Greek mercenaries to their Persian paymasters, even after the decisive defeat at Gaugamela, is remarkable. Alexander had assured his troops that it would be otherwise (see page 50 above).

17. The administrative arrangements Alexander made for Babylon follow the tripartite scheme first used in Asia Minor (see page 43 above), with separate officers for governance, tax collection, and military command—the last post inevitably placed in the hands of a Macedonian. What is striking and new in this case is that a Persian official, Mazaeus, who had served under Darius as satrap at Babylon, was retained by Alexander as head of the local government under the new regime, the first step in a "Persification" policy that would later become one of the most controversial aspects of Alexander's career. Mazaeus had presumably impressed Alexander both with his abilities and his willingness to endorse the new Macedonian order, even after fighting fiercely on Darius' side at Gaugamela.

citadel at Sardis. In Babylon Alexander also met with the Chaldaeans and did everything they advised with regard to the Babylonian temples. He even sacrificed to Bel in the manner they prescribed.[18]

Alexander started for Susa and was met on the road by the son of Susa's satrap and a courier from Philoxenus. (Alexander had dispatched Philoxenus to Susa right after the battle.) The letter from Philoxenus related that the Susians had surrendered their city and that all the treasure was being kept safe for Alexander. Twenty days after leaving Babylon, Alexander reached Susa. On entering the city, he received the treasure—nearly fifty thousand talents of silver[19]—and the other royal property. Many other objects were captured there, including everything Xerxes had brought back with him from Greece. The treasure from Greece included bronze statues of Harmodius and Aristogeiton.[20] These Alexander sent back to Athens, and today they stand in the Athenian Cerameicus. . . .

Alexander then sacrificed in the traditional manner and held a torch race and an athletic competition. After appointing Abulites the Persian as satrap of Susiana, Mazarus, one of the Companions, as commander of the fortress at Susa, and Archelaus, son of Theodorus, as general, he proceeded against the Persians. He sent Menes down to the coast as governor of Syria, Phoenicia, and Cilicia, having given him nearly three thousand talents of silver to carry to the coast, from which he was instructed to send Antipater as much as he needed for

18. Another instance, like the sacrifice to Apis in Egypt, of Alexander's eagerness to cross cultural boundaries by participating in foreign religious rites, especially when they reinforced his own political legitimacy. The annual festival of Bel-Marduk at Babylon included a solemn rite in which Bel symbolically affirmed the power of the reigning king.

19. A fantastic amount of wealth, unimaginable by any European power up to this point. Susa was one of the imperial capitals of the Persian state, which (along with Persepolis and Pasargadae) contained the treasury stocks built up from the tribute payments of all twenty satrapies.

20. King Xerxes had sacked Athens in 480 B.C.E., 150 years before the events described here. The return of these treasures was highly symbolic, given that the ostensible goal of the invasion of Asia was retribution for Xerxes' invasion of Europe. In particular, the restoration to Athens of the statues of Harmodius and Aristogeiton served to reinforce Alexander's professed political ideology: these were the "tyrant-slayers" celebrated by Athens for their assassination of a member of the city's ruling family, an event that helped accelerate the eventual move toward a democratic regime.

the war with the Spartans.[21] Amyntas, son of Andromenes, also reached Susa with the troops he had brought from Macedonia.[22]

[III.18] Alexander now sent the baggage train, the Thessalian horsemen, the allies, the foreign mercenaries, and all his army's other more heavily armed troops with Parmenio, who was to lead them to Persia by way of the high road. He himself took the Macedonian infantry, the Companion Cavalry, the mounted guides, the Agrianians, and the archers and hastened along the route through the mountains. When he reached the Persian gates, he came upon Ariobarzanes, the satrap of Persia, with some forty thousand foot soldiers and seven hundred horsemen. Ariobarzanes had walled off the gates and encamped near the wall in order to bar Alexander's way.

For the time being Alexander encamped nearby; on the following day he arrayed his troops and led them up to the wall. But as the place appeared hard to capture owing to the rough terrain, and as his men, assailed from higher ground and from volleys fired by siege engines, were sustaining many casualties, he withdrew for a time to the camp. But then some of his prisoners told him of another path that would lead him around to the gates, one that was rugged and narrow; so he left Craterus in camp with his own battalion and Meleager's, a few archers, and nearly five hundred horsemen, with orders to assault the wall as soon as he noticed that Alexander himself had made his way around and was approaching the Persians' camp. (It would be easy to determine this, as Alexander's trumpets would sound the signal.) Alexander set out at night, and after covering about a mile took the shield-bearers, Perdiccas' battalion, the nimblest of the archers, the Agrianians, the royal squadron of the Companion Cavalry, and one additional cavalry tetrarchy; with the prisoners showing the way, they advanced at an angle toward the gates. Alexander ordered Amyntas, Philotas, and Coenus to lead the rest of the army to the plain and

---

21. The war would already be decided by the time this aid reached Antipater. Agis was crushed by a vast Greco-Macedonian army at the end of 331 or the beginning of 330. Alexander, when later told the news of Agis' defeat, is reported to have called the whole affair "a war of mice," implying that it was but a footnote to his own heroic endeavor.

22. Reinforcements recruited from Macedonia and its Balkan neighbors and from the allied Greek states. Curtius reports their numbers as 13,500 infantry and almost 1,500 cavalry.

to bridge the river that had to be crossed to enter Persia.[23] He himself took a difficult and rugged road and led his men along it, mostly on the run. Falling on the first barbarian guard before daylight, he destroyed it, and most of the second guard as well; most of the third guard fled, just as they were, and such was their fear that they fled not to Ariobarzanes' camp but to the mountains. Consequently, Alexander's attack, near dawn, took the enemy by surprise. And just as he was assaulting the ditch, the trumpets sounded the signal, and Craterus led his men against the fortification. Their enemies, attacked from all sides, fled without even attempting to fight; but as they were hemmed in on all sides, both where Alexander was pressing them hard and where Craterus' men were running to the scene, most of them were forced to turn back and flee to the walls. But the walls were already occupied by the Macedonians; for Alexander, having foreseen what would happen, had left Ptolemy there with nearly three thousand foot soldiers, and as a result most of the barbarians were cut to pieces by the Macedonians in hand-to-hand combat, while others, in a flight that proved desperate, flung themselves from the cliffs and perished. Ariobarzanes himself fled to the mountains with a few horsemen.

Alexander now hastened with his men to the river, found the bridge already in place, and crossed easily with the army. He then pressed on to Persepolis and arrived before the guards had plundered the treasure. He also seized the treasure in the coffers of Cyrus I in Pasargadae. He appointed Phrasaortes, son of Rheomithras, as satrap of Persia. He also set the Persian palace on fire[24] against the advice of

23. "Persia" here refers to the satrapy of Persis, the homeland of the Persian people, as opposed to the vastly larger Persian empire.

24. Arrian here deals in very abbreviated fashion with one of the most controversial, and variously reported, of Alexander's actions: the burning of the palace at Persepolis. Arrian is alone among our extant sources in explaining this act as the result of a deliberate policy. The version given (with slight variations) by Plutarch, Diodorus, and Curtius portrays Alexander in a very different light. Here, for purposes of comparison, is how Curtius tells the story: "Alexander took part in banquets that started early in the day and included women whom it was permissible to rape—courtesans who had grown used to living in a military camp and behaving with less propriety than they ought. One of these women was Thais. In a drunken state, she declared that Alexander would gain very great esteem among the Greeks if he were to order the palace of the Persians to be burned, and that indeed those whose cities had

Parmenio, who argued that it was ignoble to destroy what was now his own property, and that the peoples of Asia would not pay heed to him in the same way if they assumed he had no intention of governing Asia but would merely conquer and move on. But Alexander declared that he wanted to take vengeance on the Persians (who, when they invaded Greece, had razed Athens and burned the temples) and to exact retribution for all the other iniquities they had committed against the Greeks. It seems to me, however, that in this instance Alexander was not acting sensibly, nor do I think there *could* be any punishment for Persians of a bygone era.[25]

c. The pursuit of the King

Alexander conveyed the immense wealth he had amassed from the three Persian capitals to the city of Ecbatana in Media, which he now made a major headquarters of his new regime. He installed Harpalus, an old boyhood friend, to take charge of the burgeoning imperial treasury, and—in a surprising move—he also stationed Parmenio, his former right-hand man, as regional commander. The old general, now seventy and the veteran of thirty years' fighting, was not to go on with Alexander in his further push to the east. Either Alexander no longer thought Parmenio's advice useful (indeed, he had disregarded that advice on several recent occasions), or he mistrusted the man as a rival for power, or both. In Ecbatana, Parmenio would meet the gruesome end described further on in Chapter VI (page 97).

---

been burned by the barbarians expected no less. First one man, then another, though they, too, were fogged with wine, seconded the drunken tramp who had professed such a weighty opinion. The king, too, who by then was more thirsty for drink than able to hold it, said: 'Why not, indeed, avenge Greece and put the city to the torch?' All present were fired up by drink, and so they rushed, drunk as they were, to burn down the city the soldiers had spared while under arms. The king threw the first torch into the palace. . . ." (Quintus Curtius V.7.3–5). In neither Arrian's nor Curtius' version does the burning of Persepolis reflect well on Alexander, but the idea that it was the result of a courtesan's whim during a drunken debauch certainly puts it in a more disturbing light than what Arrian reports here. On this matter, as on so many that concern Alexander's character and political morality, modern historians are deeply divided.

25. A comment that casts a rather troubling light on the primary justification both Philip and Alexander had used for their attack on Persia. Arrian is essentially saying that after almost a century and a half, the statute of limitations on Persia's war crimes under King Xerxes had long expired.

Also at Ecbatana, Alexander dismissed the allied Greek troops he had requisitioned thus far under the powers granted him by the Greek League. The official goal of the invasion, the destruction of the Persian empire in revenge for its attack on Greece, had now been achieved, so the official duties of these troops were fulfilled. However, Alexander also invited all who so desired to reenlist with him for the next mission he had taken on: the pursuit and capture of Darius, who, though in exile, could still lay claim to the title of Great King.

[III.19] Alexander now headed for Media, as he kept hearing that Darius was there. Darius had decided that if Alexander remained at Susa and Babylon, he would himself remain in Media in case there was any sedition among the partisans of Alexander; but if Alexander should march against him, he would go up to the Parthyaeans and Hyrcania as far as Bactra, laying waste the entire countryside and hampering Alexander's progress. He sent the women, his remaining furniture, and the covered carriages to the so-called Caspian Gates. He himself remained in Ecbatana with the forces he had selected from those at hand. On hearing this, Alexander advanced toward Media. Attacking the Paraetacae in their country, he subjugated them and appointed Oxathres, son of Abulites, the satrap of Susa, as their satrap. When it was reported to him on the road that Darius had decided to meet him in battle and again risk his all, and that he had been joined by his Scythian and Cadusian allies, Alexander gave orders for the pack animals, their keepers, and the rest of the gear to follow, while he led the rest of the army forward, armed for battle. In twelve days he reached Media. There he learned that Darius lacked sufficient forces to do battle, that his Cadusian and Scythian allies had not come, and that Darius had decided to flee. Alexander now increased his pace. When he was roughly a three days' journey from Ecbatana, he was met by Bisthanes, son of Ochus. (Ochus had been king of the Persians before Darius.) Bisthanes reported that Darius had fled four days earlier with the treasure from Media (about seven thousand talents) and an army of nearly three thousand horsemen and six thousand foot soldiers.

On his arrival in Ecbatana, Alexander sent the Thessalian cavalry and the other allies back to the coast, having paid them their full wages and given them an additional two thousand talents out of his own pocket.[26] Any individual who wished to continue to serve with him as

26. The dismissal of the Greek allies marks the end of the retributive phase

a mercenary was ordered to put down his name. It turned out that a considerable number of them enlisted. Alexander appointed Epocillus, son of Polyides, to lead the departing troops to the coast, taking other horsemen to guard them (for the Thessalians sold their horses there). Alexander also ordered Menes to see to it, when they reached the coast, that these men were conveyed in triremes to Euboea. He assigned Parmenio to deposit the Persian treasure in the citadel at Ecbatana and hand it over to Harpalus. For he left Harpalus in charge of the treasure[27] and posted some six thousand Macedonians, both horsemen and a few light-armed troops, to guard it.

[III.20] Taking the Companion Cavalry, the guides, the mercenary horsemen (under Erigyius' command), the Macedonian phalanx (except for the men assigned to guard the treasure), the archers, and the Agrianians, Alexander went after Darius. Owing to the urgent pace of the march, many of his soldiers were left behind exhausted, and the horses were dying. Undeterred, he hastened onward and reached Rhagae on the eleventh day. (For anyone traveling at Alexander's pace the place lies a day's journey from the Caspian Gates.) But Darius, anticipating him, had already passed the gates. Many of those who fled with Darius deserted him in the course of the flight and withdrew, each man to his own country, and no small number gave themselves up to Alexander. Having given up hope of overtaking Darius by a close pursuit, Alexander remained in Rhagae for five days and gave his army a rest. He appointed Oxydates, a Persian, as satrap of Media. (Oxydates happened to have been arrested by Darius and confined at Susa, a circumstance that encouraged Alexander to trust him.) Alexander then proceeded to Parthyaea. The first day, he encamped near the Caspian Gates; on the second, he passed beyond them and advanced until he reached settled country. In order to obtain provisions there (as he heard that the country ahead was uninhabited), he

---

of the war, when the army was, officially at least, engaged in avenging the Persian invasion of Europe in 480. After the fall of Susa and Persepolis, any further actions against the Persians could no longer be couched as retribution.
27. An unwise move, as later events would demonstrate (see pages 149–50 below). Harpalus was a childhood friend of Alexander who had already once deserted the Macedonian cause in 333, before the battle of Issus, by fleeing to Greece with purloined treasure. Remarkably, Alexander seems to have taken him back thereafter and restored him to his old position of chief treasurer to the expedition.

sent Coenus on a foraging expedition with some horsemen and a few foot soldiers.

[III.21] At that point Bagistanes, a distinguished Babylonian, reached Alexander from Darius' camp with Antibelus, one of Mazaeus' sons. These men reported that Darius had been arrested by Nabarzanes, the commander of the horsemen who had fled with him; by Bessus, the satrap of Bactria; and by Barsaentes, the satrap of the Arachosians and Drangians. On hearing this, Alexander advanced even faster, accompanied only by the Companions, the mounted guides, and the strongest and nimblest foot soldiers. He did not even wait for Coenus' party to return from their foraging expedition. Putting Craterus in charge of the men left behind, he ordered him to follow, but not to lead the men on long marches. The men with Alexander carried only their weapons and two days' rations. Having marched throughout the night until noon the next day, he gave the army a brief rest and again marched all night long. At daybreak he reached the camp from which Bagistanes had started, but encountered none of the enemy. As for Darius, Alexander learned that he had been arrested and was being transported in a covered carriage, and that Bessus held power in Darius' place and had been named commander by the Bactrian horsemen and all the other barbarians who had fled with Darius, with the exception of Artabazus and his sons and the Greek mercenaries. These men had remained loyal to Darius but had been unable to prevent what was happening; they had left the high road and were on their way to the mountains by themselves, taking no part in the acts of Bessus and his followers. The men who had seized Darius had decided that if they learned that Alexander was pursuing them, they would surrender Darius to him and get something out of it for themselves; but if they learned that he had turned back, they would assemble as large an army as they could and preserve their power in common. Finally, Alexander learned that Bessus, because of his relationship with Darius and because the action was occurring in his satrapy,[28] was for the moment in command.

It was plain to Alexander, when he heard this report, that he must pursue these men with all possible speed. His own men and horses were already exhausted by the constant strain, but he nevertheless pressed on. After traveling a great distance, marching through the

---

28. Actually the royal party was at that point in a different province than Bessus' own, Bactria.

night until noon the next day, he reached a village where the party traveling with Darius had encamped the day before. On hearing that the barbarians had decided to travel at night, he asked the inhabitants if they knew of any shortcut to the fugitives. They said they did know of one, but the road was deserted as it lacked water. Alexander ordered them to lead him to that road. As he realized that the foot soldiers would not follow him at his rapid pace, he dismounted some five hundred horsemen, selected the fittest officers of the infantry and the other units, and ordered them to mount the horses, carrying their regular infantry weapons.[29] He ordered Nicanor, the commander of the shield-bearers, and Attalus, who led the Agrianians, to take the men who were being left behind and lead them along the road Bessus' party had taken, equipping them as lightly as possible. The rest of the infantry was ordered to follow in regular formation. Alexander himself, starting in the afternoon, led his men at full speed. At dawn, after traveling nearly forty-five miles overnight, he caught up with the barbarians marching in disorder and without armor. A few of them tried to defend themselves, but the majority, as soon as they caught sight of Alexander himself, fled without even coming to blows. Those who turned and resisted also fled after a few had fallen. For a time Bessus and his confederates had kept Darius with them in a covered carriage; but when Alexander drew near, Satibarzanes and Barsaentes wounded Darius, left him there, and fled with six hundred horsemen. Darius died from his wounds shortly thereafter, before Alexander had seen him.[30]

[III.22] Alexander sent Darius' body back to Persepolis and ordered that he be buried, like all his royal predecessors, in the royal tombs. He appointed Amminapes the Parthyaean as satrap of Parthyaea and Hyrcania. (A member of Mazaces' party, Amminapes

---

29. The complex arrangements Alexander made during the pursuit of Darius, designed to maximize the mobility of his advance guard while still keeping slower units in contact with one another, adequately provisioned and equipped, and moving along the same route as himself, is one of the clearest examples of his well-known logistical brilliance. It should be noted that all these arrangements were made in great haste under the pressures of an all-out pursuit.

30. Arrian's account of this dramatic encounter differs from that of the "vulgate" sources, which depict a still-breathing Darius delivering his last words—not surprisingly, a benediction—before expiring in Alexander's arms.

had been among those who surrendered Egypt to Alexander.) One of the Companions—Tlepolemus, son of Pythophanes—was assigned to help Amminapes oversee Parthyaean and Hyrcanian affairs.

This was the end of Darius, who died in the month of Hecatombaeon, during Aristophon's archonship at Athens. He was a man who, with respect to military matters, could scarcely have been more cowardly or misguided. In other areas he did nothing amiss, though he lacked the opportunity to make any kind of showing, since as soon as he ascended the throne he found himself at war with the Macedonians and Greeks. Accordingly, even if he had wanted to persecute his subjects he would have found it impossible to do so, as *his* danger was graver than theirs. Throughout his life he was afflicted by one disaster after another, nor was there any respite after his accession. His misfortunes began with the satraps' cavalry defeat at the Granicus. Almost immediately thereafter, Ionia and Aeolia were in enemy hands along with both Phrygias, Lydia, and all the Carians except for the Halicarnassians. Soon Halicarnassus was also captured and shortly afterward the entire coast as far as Cilicia. Then came his defeat at Issus, where he saw his mother, wife, and children taken prisoner. Then Phoenicia and all of Egypt were lost. He then disgraced himself at Arbela, where he was among the first to flee, and lost the largest army of the entire barbarian race. A fugitive from his own empire, a wanderer finally betrayed to the utmost by his own party, he became, at one and the same time, a king and a prisoner carried off in dishonor. At last, plotted against by his closest associates, he died. Such was Darius' fate while he lived, but when he died he met with a royal burial, his children were raised and educated by Alexander as if he were still on the throne, and Alexander became his son-in-law.[31] Darius was about fifty years old when he died.

---

31. By marrying Darius' eldest daughter in 324 B.C.E.

VI

The Central Asian Campaigns

(Summer 330–Spring 327 B.C.E.)

a. The Philotas affair and the killing of Parmenio

With the death of Darius, Alexander could legitimately claim rulership of all the lands that comprised the former Persian empire, and he might well have ended his campaign then and there. But such a resolution did not square with the king's restless and indomitable nature. He immediately undertook a quest to capture the murderers of Darius, chief among them Bessus of Bactria, who had assumed the title and insignia of the Persian king and had fled into the hinterlands to organize an anti-Macedonian resistance. The hunt for Bessus took Alexander into the rugged, dry, inhospitable northeastern quadrant of the Persian realm, the provinces of Drangiana and Areia (making up parts of today's Afghanistan and Iran). The landscape was harsher here than what the Macedonians had met with thus far, and the local politics more treacherous: twice in the year 330 the Persian satraps appointed by Alexander to govern this region revolted against him. Both rebellions were successfully put down but only at considerable cost to the morale of the army and the pace of the pursuit of Bessus. Small wonder that, in the midst of this parched and unfriendly environment, tensions began to build among the troops, leading to the first of a series of conspiracy trials in the autumn of 330: the so-called Philotas affair.

Philotas was the last surviving son of Parmenio, the great senior general who had served first as Philip's and then Alexander's second in command. Philotas, unlike his father, was not well-liked by his countrymen, and thus far in the campaign he had not received any significant commands, though due to his lineage he was of course included among the Companions who made up Alexander's inner circle. Because he had direct access to the king, a lower-ranking Macedonian named Cebalinus came to him one day and reported that a fellow soldier, Dymnus, had invited him to join a conspiracy against Alexander's life. Cebalinus intended that the report be passed on by

Philotas to Alexander, but, for whatever reason, Philotas said nothing. A few days later Cebalinus anxiously brought the plot to someone else's attention, and Alexander was thereby informed; Dymnus was summoned for questioning but promptly wounded himself so severely with his sword that nothing could be learned from him.

Suspicion of involvement now fell on Philotas, who had failed to pass on Cebalinus' information at the first opportunity. (Evidently it was not the first time Alexander had questioned the loyalty of this natural rival: some sources claim that Philotas' Greek courtesan had been recruited as an informant during the sojourn in Egypt two years earlier.) Some sort of trial was held, though the outcome was hardly in doubt, and Philotas was also apparently interrogated under torture (though Arrian is silent on this point) and made to admit some role in the plot, as well as to implicate his father, Parmenio. He was summarily executed along with a number of other perceived enemies of Alexander, including the hapless Alexander of Lyncestis, who had been dragged about in chains for three years after first falling under suspicion (see page 47 above). Afterward an assassin was dispatched to murder Parmenio, Philotas' father and Alexander's most senior officer, then stationed in Ecbatana, capital of Media.

Arrian's brief treatment of the Philotas affair and the slaying of Parmenio reveals the reluctance of his main sources, Ptolemy and Aristobulus, to go into detail on topics that reflected poorly on Alexander. Other versions of the Alexander story give much more information about this episode and its bloody aftermath. One of these, that of Quintus Curtius, forms the perfect contrast to Arrian's version: where Arrian provides only a bare-bones outline of events, Curtius gives a luridly detailed melodrama, complete with long, elaborate speeches that are, in large part at least, his own inventions. To complement Arrian's toneless summary, therefore, a brief selection from Curtius' account, describing the assassination of Parmenio, is also included.

[Arrian III.26] Alexander now learned of Philotas' plot. Ptolemy and Aristobulus both say that it had been reported to him earlier, in Egypt, but had not seemed credible to him given his long-standing friendship with Philotas, the honor he had bestowed on Philotas' father, Parmenio, and the faith he had in Philotas himself. Ptolemy relates that Philotas was tried before the Macedonians, that Alexander accused him aggressively, and that Philotas defended himself. The informers who testified brought clear proof against Philotas and his associates. Laying particular stress on Philotas' admission that he had been aware that some plot had been laid for Alexander, they convicted him of having said nothing to the king though he visited his tent twice a day. The Macedonians executed Philotas and his fellow conspirators with a volley of javelins.[1]

Alexander dealt with Parmenio by sending Polydamas, one of the Companions, with a letter to Cleander, Sitalces, and Menidas, the commanders in Media, as these men had been posted with the army under Parmenio's command. These were the men by whom Parmenio was put to death, perhaps because Alexander could not believe that Parmenio had taken no part in his own son's plot, or perhaps because, even had he not taken part, there was a danger in Parmenio's surviving his son's execution, given the high rank he held with Alexander himself and his popularity with the troops (Macedonians and foreigners alike), whom he had often led, both in and out of turn, at Alexander's command.

[Quintus Curtius VII.2.11–27] Alexander ordered Polydamas to be brought before him, a man who had long been a close friend of Parmenio and had often stood beside him in battle. And, though he had come into the royal palace with a clear conscience, Polydamas began to be afraid when he was ordered to produce his brothers, who were still youths and therefore unknown to Alexander. . . . The guards to whom the orders had been given brought these men in, and the king ordered Polydamas, now pale with fear, to draw nearer. Having ordered all others out of the room, the king said: "We were all the targets of this crime of Parmenio's, especially myself and you who were tricked by his pretense of friendship. So I have chosen to draft you into my service to pursue and punish him—that's how much I trust in your loyalty. Your brothers will be hostages while you carry this out. . . ." Polydamas, freed from his great terror, promised his help even more eagerly than the king had demanded. . . .

He took off the clothes he wore and put on Arab dress.[2] Two Arabs were given to him as guides, their own wives and children held as hostages by the king. They crossed a region that was waterless and uninhabited[3] and reached the appointed spot on the eleventh day. And

1. Other sources claim he was stoned to death.
2. Evidently the disguise was intended to protect Polydamas in case any of Philotas' or Parmenio's supporters had gotten wind of the assassination order and were seeking to intercept him. Guards had also been posted around the camp by Alexander from the moment of Philotas' arrest to ensure that no one could leave to inform Parmenio.
3. Again the point seems to be Alexander's efforts to preserve the secrecy of the mission.

before his arrival was announced he changed back into Macedonian clothing and went to the tent of Cleander, one of the royal generals, around the fourth watch. After giving him Alexander's letter, the two men decided to go together to visit Parmenio at first light. . . .

Parmenio was walking in a wooded grove, on either side of him the officers who were now under orders, by royal writ, to kill him. They had decided to do the deed at the moment when Parmenio was reading the letters given to him by Polydamas. Polydamas now approached, and Parmenio saw him; his face displayed his joy, and he ran to embrace the visitor. After they had greeted one another, Polydamas handed over the letter written by the king. Parmenio asked, as he unsealed the letter, what the king happened to be doing, and Polydamas said that he would learn this from the letter. When he had read it Parmenio said, "The king is making ready a campaign against the Arachosians! The man never stops. But he should take time out for the sake of his health, now that so much glory has been won." Then he started reading a second letter, happy, as was clear from his expression, because it was inscribed with Philotas' name.[4] At that moment Cleander opened him up with a sword thrust to his side, then struck him a second blow in the throat. The others ran him through when he was already dead.

b. The capture of Bessus

Philotas and Parmenio had thus been eliminated, and Alexander's officers in Media had passed the first major test he had imposed on them, an order to assassinate a revered senior commander. Some five years later they, too, were executed, on Alexander's orders—a bitter reward for their loyalty.

The pursuit of Bessus now resumed, leading the Macedonians into the outermost reaches of the Persian realm, Bactria and Sogdiana (parts of present-day Afghanistan, Uzbekistan, and Tajikistan). To reach his quarry from an unexpected quarter, Alexander brought his army across the Hindu Kush mountain range in the spring of 329, exposing them to ills formerly unknown to inhabitants of the Aegean: frostbite, altitude sickness, and the rigors of a rocky landscape that provided food for neither men nor horses. Even the most rugged Macedonian highlander who had grown up amid the ridges of the Balkans must have felt a long way from home by this time.

4. According to Curtius, Alexander had falsified the letter using the seal-ring of the dead Philotas, in the belief that Parmenio would feel more at ease and would let his guard down if he thought Polydamas carried word from his son.

Bessus retreated from his native Bactria to the neighboring province of Sogdiana, where he expected to find an ally in that region's satrap, Spitamenes. But learning of the speed and determination of Alexander's advance, Spitamenes chose to avoid a showdown with Alexander and had Bessus put under arrest. A message was sent to Alexander telling him where the captive could be found, and the Macedonians took custody of Bessus, the last man alive who could dispute Alexander's claim to the Persian throne. Bessus was sent for trial to Zariaspa (also called Bactra), the capital city of Bactria, which now also became the regional headquarters of the Macedonian army. Though Alexander had triumphed over his principal foe, he had not nearly overcome all local resistance; nor had he heard the last of Spitamenes, who would turn against Alexander and lead a long and effective guerrilla insurgency against the Macedonians.

The account of the punishment of Bessus (below) leads Arrian into a famous series of meditations on the changes now taking place in Alexander's character and behavior. His basic theme in this portion of his narrative is the time-honored question, what does it profit a man to gain the whole world but lose his immortal soul? Arrian's interest in this theme leads him to group together a series of episodes that in his view revealed the corrosive effect of power on Alexander's nature, even though these episodes were not contiguous in time. The excerpts below thus follow Arrian's thematic arrangement even when this violates chronology (as explained in more detail in the footnotes).

[Arrian IV.7] Alexander now reached Zariaspa, where he remained until the worst of winter[5] had passed. Phrataphernes, the satrap of Parthyaea, now came to him with Stasanor, who had been sent to Areia to arrest Arsaces. They were escorting the latter, bound in chains, along with Brazanes, whom Bessus had appointed as satrap of Parthyaea, and some others who had revolted with Bessus. At the same time, Epocillus, Melamnidas, and Ptolemy, the commander of the Thracians, had arrived, having escorted the allies to the coast along with the treasure sent with Menes. Asander also arrived at that time, as did Nearchus, leading an army of Greek mercenaries.[6]

---

5. The winter of 329–328 B.C.E.
6. Nearchus, a boyhood friend of Alexander, would go on to play a leading role in his Indian campaign, including that of admiral of the Indian Ocean fleet. His log of the fleet's voyage served as the basis of another of Arrian's writings, the *Indica*.

Calling an assembly of those who were present, Alexander had Bessus brought before them. After accusing him of having betrayed Darius, he commanded that Bessus' nose and the tips of his ears be cut off and that he be taken to Ecbatana to be put to death in the assembly of the Medes and Persians. For my part, I do not approve of that excessive punishment. I consider the mutilation of the extremities to be barbaric, and I admit that Alexander was led on gradually to emulate the luxuriousness of the Medes and Persians and the barbarian kings' disinclination to associate with their subjects on an equal footing.[7] I by no means commend the fact that Alexander, though a descendant of Heracles, substituted the apparel of the Medes for traditional Macedonian dress,[8] or that he was not ashamed to substitute the tiara of the conquered Persians for the headgear that he, their conqueror, had long worn. I can commend none of this, but I surmise that one need look no further than Alexander's great successes for convincing proof that neither strength, nor illustrious birth, nor uninterrupted success in war even greater than Alexander's—even if a man should circumnavigate Libya and Asia and conquer them (as Alexander meant to do), or add Europe, as the third part of his empire, to Asia and Libya—none of these things, I surmise, can foster a man's happiness unless that man, whose achievements are seemingly so great, should at the same time possess the power to govern his passions.

c. The war with Spitamenes

All during the year 328 and part of 327, Alexander's forces in Bactria and Sogdiana were harassed by tribal guerrillas under the command of Spitamenes, the former satrap of Sogdiana, now turned rebel chieftain. Using

---

7. Arrian moves rapidly from a condemnation of mutilation of prisoners to a larger consideration of other "barbarian" practices Alexander began to use during his sojourn in Asia.

8. Alexander began wearing certain items from the Persian royal garb before the time of Bessus' mutilation, in the autumn of 330, combining these with his own traditional Macedonian dress. Various assessments have been made of his motives, but Arrian is surely correct when he says later (see page 172 below) that his new composite style of dress was designed to demonstrate authority over both western and eastern sections of his empire. In the present

hit-and-run tactics and hiding between attacks, the guerrillas inflicted some
of the worst losses the Macedonians had yet experienced, including the
slaughter of an entire garrison force perhaps several thousand strong.
Alexander spent the better part of two years scouring the region in an effort
to eliminate opposition and founding "cities," most of which were little more
than forts, to establish a permanent Greco-Macedonian presence. Greek-
named towns now sprang up in places no Greek had ever before visited;
the present-day Afghan city of Kandahar, for instance, still preserves in tangled form its original name, Alexandria. A scattering of European soldiers
and settlers were left behind in each to oversee the outposts of the new
empire; many of these tried to flee at the first opportunity. Some, however,
stayed in sufficient numbers to establish thriving communities, such as at
the large and prosperous Greek city discovered recently at the site called
Ai-Khanoum.

The war against Spitamenes forced Alexander to develop new tactics and
strategies unlike those he had used before on traditional battlefields. In the
end, though, his greatest asset, as always, was his unstoppable determination and drive. Late in 328 he threatened to carry the war into territory inhabited by the nomadic Massagetae, among whom Spitamenes had taken
refuge. Convinced that nothing else would keep Alexander out of their territory, the Massagetae killed Spitamenes and had his head delivered to the
Macedonian camp.

Amid these perils and losses, as well as the harshness of the climatic extremes in Central Asia, the mood of the army grew increasingly tense. At the
end of 328 and the beginning of 327, the drinking parties that formed the
mainstay of social activity among the Companions became strained and
edgy, to judge by two incidents that broke out during them, as related by Arrian below.

d. The death of Cleitus

[IV.8] Here it will not be out of place for me to relate the tragedy of
Cleitus, son of Dropides, and the dismay it caused Alexander. . . .
Among the Macedonians there was a day held sacred to Dionysus, and
on that day, every year, Alexander performed a sacrifice in the god's
honor. But that year, they say, Alexander neglected Dionysus, it having for some reason occurred to him to sacrifice to the Dioscuri. The
carousal went on far into the night (for by now Alexander's carousals

---

passage, however, he focuses on the moral failing involved in taking on the
luxurious raiment of an Asian monarch.

had become more barbarian in character),[9] and on that occasion there was some talk about the Dioscuri and how their paternity, stolen from Tyndareus, had been traced to Zeus. And some of the company, the sort of men who are forever corrupting and undermining the affairs of kings, sought to flatter Alexander and maintained that Castor and Pollux did not deserve to be compared with Alexander and his exploits. Even Heracles was not left out of the discussion, for they said that jealousy proved an obstacle for living men and prevented their being properly honored by their friends.

It had long been clear that Cleitus was oppressed by Alexander's adoption of a more barbarian way of life and by his flatterers' remarks. On this occasion (as he, too, was affected by the wine), he would not allow them to show disrespect for religion or seek to bestow a graceless grace on Alexander by depreciating the past exploits of heroes. Accordingly, he remarked that the present company were exaggerating the importance and wonderfulness of Alexander's exploits, and that in any case Alexander had not achieved his conquests all by himself: they were in large part the work of the Macedonians. Alexander was vexed at Cleitus' words. Nor do I commend what he said, for I think it sufficient, when such drinking is under way, for a man to keep his views to himself without stooping, as others do, to flattery. But when some of the company also touched on Philip's career, asserting unjustly that he had not accomplished anything great or marvelous, hoping thereby to curry favor with Alexander, Cleitus could no longer contain himself. Claiming that Philip's deeds ranked highest, he belittled those of Alexander—Cleitus was by now quite drunk—and said a great deal more, casting in Alexander's teeth that *he* had saved his life during the cavalry action against the Persians at the Granicus.[10]

9. Another critique of Alexander's character based on "lifestyle" issues, similar to the remarks on clothing above. Barbarians were known in the Hellenic world for drinking immoderately and in particular for downing wine unmixed with water (a drink capable of causing madness, according to some Greeks). According to Arrian, Alexander had begun to abandon the restrained, genteel habits of the Greek symposium in favor of wild, drunken debauches. The charge of drunkenness was in antiquity and remains today one of the principal attacks made on Alexander by his detractors, though, as in all such characterological matters, there is room for argument about the severity of his alcoholism.

10. See page 40 above.

And finally, extending his right hand haughtily, he said, "This was the hand, Alexander, that saved you then."

Alexander reportedly could no longer bear Cleitus' drunken insolence. He leaped up in a fury and was restrained by his fellow drinkers. But Cleitus would not stop baiting Alexander. Alexander shouted for his shield-bearers.[11] When no one obeyed, he said that this was exactly what had happened to Darius when he was arrested by Bessus and his followers and led away, a king in name only. Alexander's Companions were no longer able to restrain him. Some say that on leaping up he snatched a spear from one of his bodyguards and struck Cleitus with it, killing him; others say he used a pike snatched from one of the guards. Aristobulus does not say how the drinking bout got started but maintains that Cleitus had only himself to blame. For when Alexander, infuriated, leaped up as though he would destroy him, Cleitus was spirited away through the door and over the wall and ditch of the citadel where this was happening by Ptolemy, Alexander's bodyguard. But in his obstinacy Cleitus came back and fell in with Alexander, who was calling out Cleitus' name, and said, "Here is Cleitus, Alexander!" And at that moment, struck by the pike, Cleitus died.

[IV.9] For my part, I utterly deplore the insolence Cleitus showed his king, and I pity Alexander that he showed himself mastered on that occasion by two vices, namely anger and drunkenness, neither of which should get the better of a sensible man. But I commend Alexander's conduct in the aftermath, for he recognized immediately that he had committed a savage act. There are some who report that he leaned the pike against the wall, intending to fall on it, as now that he had killed his friend while drunk it was dishonorable for him to live. But most writers offer a different account and say that Alexander took to his bed and lay there moaning and calling out Cleitus' name and that of Cleitus' sister Lanice, who had nursed him, saying that he had after all made her a fine return for her nursing when he became a man. For she had seen two of her own sons die fighting for him, and he had himself killed her brother with his own hand. Again and again he called himself his friend's murderer and went without food and drink for three days and completely neglected his person.

11. The shield-bearers acted as a royal bodyguard; by summoning them Alexander revealed that he suspected a plot on his life.

In light of these events some of the prophets sang in Homeric fashion of the wrath of Dionysus, because Alexander had neglected the god's honors. Persuaded with some difficulty by his Companions, Alexander took food and gave some slight attention to his person. He also made an offering to Dionysus, as he was not unwilling to have the calamity attributed to a god's wrath rather than his own vice. I commend Alexander highly for neither brazening out an iniquitous act nor proving baser still by becoming a defender or advocate of his offensive conduct. Instead, he conceded that, being human after all, he had stumbled.

There are some who say that Anaxarchus the sophist was summoned to console Alexander. Finding the king moaning on his bed, Anaxarchus laughed and said that Alexander had not appreciated that this was why the ancient sages made Justice sit beside Zeus, namely, to show that anything done by Zeus was done with justice. It therefore followed that the acts of a great king should be considered just, first by the king himself and then by the rest of humankind. Anaxarchus' words gave Alexander comfort on that occasion, though in my view he did Alexander an injury greater than the misfortune then afflicting him if he held *that* to be the view of a wise man, that the king's duty is not, after all, to act justly after diligent reflection, but that *anything* done by a king, and in whatever manner, is to be considered just.

e. The *proskynesis* crisis

Arrian continues his serial discussion of Alexander's moral transgression by leaping ahead in time to the next relevant episode, the crisis over the king's attempt to introduce a ritual called proskynesis, *here translated "obeisance," into his court.*

Proskynesis *was a Persian display of respect, performed by bowing low before a person of high rank or, in some cases, prostrating oneself on the ground. At the Achaemenid court it was required of all who approached the person of the Great King. The Greeks, however, had always felt repelled by the idea of giving to a man the honors normally due to the gods, and some had refused to perform the ritual even on pain of death. Alexander's attempt to impose* proskynesis *at his court thus created a cultural rift among his inner circle: the high-ranking Persians who had joined his train considered it normal and natural, and those Macedonians who agreed with his policy of Persification were willing to accept it, but others who had already been disturbed by Alexander's adoption of Persian royal dress saw this as a further extension of a worrisome change in the king's personality. To what degree such a change was occurring is a matter of considerable debate; as in the case of the wardrobe, it is possible that Alexander sought to impose symbols of authority that his new Persian subjects would recognize and accept, without himself craving the superhuman stature they conferred. Arrian, however, clearly took a more serious view of the matter, as seen in his presentation of the episode below.*

It is reported that Alexander wanted his subjects to make obeisance to him (the underlying idea being that Ammon, and not Philip, was his father) and was now showing his admiration for Persian and Median ways by changing his apparel and adopting new arrangements with regard to all other aspects of his attendance. And as his suite included many flatterers, notably the sophist Anaxarchus and Agis of Argos, an epic poet, there was no lack of men willing to grant him that token of submission.

[IV.10] It is said that Callisthenes of Olynthus,[12] who had attended Aristotle's lectures and affected a rather clownish manner, disapproved of this. Here I agree with Callisthenes, though I find his other views unreasonable if what has been written is true and he actually declared that Alexander and his exploits depended on him and his history; and that he had appeared on the scene not to acquire renown from Alexander, but to convey the latter's renown to humankind; and, accordingly, that Alexander's association with divinity depended not on Olympias' tales about his birth but on what he, Callisthenes, would write and publish about him. . . .

With regard to Callisthenes' opposition to Alexander on the question of obeisance, the following story is prevalent. It had been agreed between Alexander and the sophists and the most illustrious Persians and Medes in his suite to introduce the topic at a drinking party. Anaxarchus[13] opened the discussion by saying that Alexander would more justly be considered a god than Dionysus or Heracles,[14]

---

12. See Glossary for more on Callisthenes, the Greek intellectual appointed by Alexander as his official historian.
13. Another court philosopher, like Callisthenes, but more inclined to flatter Alexander, as in his servile response to the killing of Cleitus (see page 103 above).
14. Heracles and Dionysus are the two figures in Greek mythology who had become gods though only half-immortal by birth. Alexander's campaign came increasingly to be seen as a rivalry with these two divinities as he moved

not only in view of his many extraordinary exploits, but also because Dionysus was a Theban (and therefore unrelated to the Macedonians), while Heracles was an Argive and had no ties to Macedonia except his kinship with Alexander, who was his descendant; it would be more just for the Macedonians to pay divine honors to a king who was one of their own. And, in any case, there could be no doubt that once he had departed the human sphere they would honor Alexander as a god. Would it not be more just to honor him while he lived than after his death, when the honor would be of no benefit to him?

[IV.11] When these and similar remarks were made by Anaxarchus, all who shared his opinion applauded his speech and were indeed ready to begin making obeisance. But the Macedonians, who were for the most part vexed at his speech, kept silent. Callisthenes now interrupted and said, "Anaxarchus, I declare that Alexander is unworthy of none of the honors that are due a human being. But the honors accorded to men have been distinguished from those accorded to the gods in a great many ways: the building of temples and the setting up of statues and precincts have been given to the gods, and hymns are composed in their honor, whereas eulogies are composed for human beings. But nowhere is the distinction more plainly marked than in the custom of obeisance. For human beings greet one another with a kiss, but divinity, I suppose because it is seated on high and must not be touched, is honored with obeisance, and choruses are established for the gods, and paeans are sung to them. And this is not at all surprising, since even the gods themselves receive a variety of different honors; and, in fact, other honors, distinct from those paid to the gods, are paid to heroes. It would therefore be unreasonable to confound all these things and cast human beings in an arrogant light by offering them excessive honors, or to degrade the gods unduly (if that is conceivable) by according them the honors paid to human beings. For Alexander would surely not tolerate it if some private citizen thrust himself into royal honors by means of an unjust election or vote. By the same token, the gods would have even more right to be vexed with human beings who thrust themselves into divine honors or tolerate being thrust into them by others.

---

eastward, into territories that only they were thought to have conquered previously. Heracles also was considered to be an ancestor of Alexander through his father's line.

"By any standard, Alexander both is and is thought to be the bravest of brave men, the most kingly of kings, the commander most worthy to command. And you, of all people, Anaxarchus, should become a proponent of these arguments and an opponent of their opposites, since you associate with Alexander in order to instruct and educate him. Accordingly, it was wrong of you to take the lead in this discussion. Instead you ought to recall that you are not associating with or advising Cambyses, or even Xerxes,[15] but a son of Philip, a member of the house of Heracles and Aeacus, whose ancestors came to Macedonia from Argos and have continued to rule the Macedonians not by force but by law. Now Heracles himself did not receive divine honors from the Greeks during his lifetime, nor did he receive them after his death until permission was given by the god at Delphi to honor him as a god. If, however, because our discussion takes place in a barbarian country, one must think barbarian thoughts, I think fit to remind you, Alexander, of the purpose of this entire expedition, namely, to annex Asia to Greece. Only reflect! Will you, on your return there, also compel the Greeks, the freest of men, to make obeisance, or will you leave the Greeks alone but impose that dishonor on the Macedonians? Or will you make some ultimate distinction when it comes to honors and be honored by the Greeks and Macedonians with human honors in the Greek manner, while receiving barbarian honors only from the barbarians?

"But if it is said about Cyrus, son of Cambyses, that he was the first man to have obeisance made him, and that after him that indignity became an institution among the Persians and Medes, one should bear in mind that the Scythians, men who were poor but independent, taught that very Cyrus a lesson[16]—a lesson other Scythians later taught Darius, and the Athenians and Spartans taught Xerxes, and Clearchus and Xenophon and their Ten Thousand taught Artaxerxes, and Alexander taught *this* Darius, without having his people prostrating themselves before him."

15. Former Persian kings.
16. A branch of the Scythian race, the Massagetae, had defeated and killed Cyrus the Great some two centuries before this, at least according to Herodotus. The object lesson drawn by Callisthenes from this and the subsequent examples was that European peoples, though poorer, less numerous, and less hierarchically organized than the Persians, had always been able to prevail when the two cultures met on the battlefield.

[IV.12] In making these and similar remarks Callisthenes greatly irritated Alexander, though what he said pleased the Macedonians. Realizing this, Alexander sent word to the Macedonians telling them to think no more of obeisance.[17] But in the silence that followed these words, the most distinguished Persians stood up and made obeisance in order. When Leonnatus, one of the Companions, judged that one of the Persians had made obeisance in a clumsy manner, he mocked the man for his poor form. Alexander lost his temper with Leonnatus on that occasion, though they were later reconciled. The following story has also been recorded. Alexander was passing around a golden drinking cup, first to those with whom he had come to an agreement about obeisance. The first man to drain the cup stood up, made obeisance, and was kissed by Alexander. Each man did the same as the cup came around to him. When the cup came to Callisthenes, he drained it and approached Alexander to kiss him, though he had not made obeisance. As Alexander happened to be talking to Hephaestion at the time, he did not notice whether Callisthenes had performed his obeisance. But when Callisthenes approached to kiss Alexander, Demetrius, son of Pythonax, one of the Companions, mentioned that Callisthenes was approaching without having made obeisance. And Alexander did not allow Callisthenes to kiss him, whereupon the latter said, "I'll go away a kiss the poorer."

For my part, I commend none of these manifestations of Alexander's arrogance at the time or Callisthenes' tactlessness. I consider it sufficient, however, for a man to conduct himself with discretion and to exalt his king's affairs as far as lies in his power, once he has seen fit to attend him. Accordingly, I find it understandable that Alexander conceived an aversion for Callisthenes, given the latter's ill-timed outspokenness and high-handed fatuity. I imagine that this was why those who accused Callisthenes were readily believed—both those who claimed he had taken part in the pages' conspiracy and those who maintained that he had stirred them up to plot against Alexander. The plot came about in the following way.[18]

17. From this sentence it appears that Alexander was not actually present at the foregoing debate but closeted in a separate room.
18. The account of the pages' conspiracy that follows has been moved by Arrian from its correct chronological position in order to juxtapose it with the obeisance debate, since Callisthenes figures prominently in both episodes. In fact, the events related below occurred in the spring of 327 B.C.E., just before

f. The conspiracy of the pages

[IV.13] Since Philip's day it had been the custom for all the sons of Macedonian officers, when they reached adolescence, to be enrolled in the king's service. In addition to administering to his personal needs, the pages were entrusted with the task of watching over him when he slept. Whenever he went riding, they would receive the horses from the grooms, lead them up and help the king mount in the Persian manner, and accompany him in the rivalry of the hunt. One of their number was Hermolaus, son of Sopolis, who was thought to have an interest in philosophy and for that reason was a disciple of Callisthenes. There is a story about Hermolaus to the effect that in the course of a hunt, when a wild boar was attacking Alexander, Hermolaus struck the boar first. The wounded beast fell, and Alexander, having missed his opportunity, lost his temper with Hermolaus and in his anger ordered that he be whipped in the presence of the other pages; he also took away Hermolaus' horse.

Grieved at the insult, Hermolaus told Sostratus, son of Amyntas, his comrade and lover, that his life would not be worth living unless he took vengeance on Alexander for the insult. Sostratus, as he was Hermolaus' lover, did not hesitate to join him. These two succeeded in enlisting the participation of Antipater,[19] son of Asclepiodorus (who had been the satrap of Syria); Epimenes, son of Arsaeus; Anticles, son of Theocritus; and Philotas, son of Carsis the Thracian. When the night watch came around to Antipater, the conspirators agreed to kill Alexander that night. They planned to attack him while he slept.

But it turned out, according to some writers, that without any prompting Alexander continued to drink until it was day, though Aristobulus tells the following story.[20] A Syrian woman, possessed by the gods, used to follow Alexander about. At first she elicited nothing but

---

the invasion of India. Thus the sequence covered by Arrian in IV.8–14, from the death of Cleitus to the conspiracy of the pages, spans more than a year of historical time.

19. A different Antipater than the regent to whom Alexander had entrusted government of Macedonia and Greece.

20. The dispute between the sources probably has much to do with the unwillingness of some writers, including Aristobulus, to portray Alexander as having a drinking problem.

ridicule from Alexander and the members of his suite. But when everything she said in her inspired state turned out to be true, she was no longer ignored by Alexander but was allowed access to him night and day, and often sat nearby while he slept. On the present occasion, when Alexander left the carousal, the woman, who was in an inspired state, met him and begged him to return and drink the night away. And as Alexander regarded this as an omen, he returned and drank, and thus the pages' conspiracy failed.

The next day, Epimenes, son of Arsaeus, one of the conspirators, spoke of the affair to his lover, Charicles, son of Menander. Charicles then spoke of it to Eurylochus, Epimenes' brother, whereupon Eurylochus went to Alexander's tent and communicated the entire affair to his bodyguard, Ptolemy, son of Lagus. Ptolemy informed Alexander, who ordered the arrest of those named by Eurylochus. Under torture the pages confessed their plot and named some others as fellow conspirators.

[IV.14] According to Aristobulus, the pages claimed that Callisthenes had induced them to make the attempt, and Ptolemy concurs.[21] Most writers, however, view the matter differently and say that because Callisthenes had already incurred Alexander's hatred, and because Hermolaus was especially friendly to Callisthenes, Alexander had no difficulty believing the worst about Callisthenes. A number of writers have also recorded that when Hermolaus was summoned before the Macedonians he admitted that he had conspired, and he asserted that it was no longer possible for a free man to bear Alexander's insolence, of which he recounted all the instances: Philotas' wrongful end and the still more unlawful end of Parmenio and the others who were put to death at the time, the drunken slaying of Cleitus, the Median apparel, the plan (not yet discarded) to require his subjects to make obeisance to him, and his drinking and sleeping habits.[22] Unable to bear these things any longer, he had wanted to free himself and the other Macedonians. Hermolaus and his fellow prisoners were stoned to death by those present at the hearing. Aristobulus says that Callisthenes, bound in shackles, was carried about in the army's train

21. Further evidence that Arrian's two main sources were eager to exonerate Alexander and protect his reputation.
22. An interesting piece of evidence pertaining to the alcoholism question. According to some sources, Alexander's late-night drinking parties were often followed by all-day sleeps.

and subsequently died of disease.[23] Ptolemy, on the other hand, relates that he was tortured and hung. Thus, even the accounts of wholly trustworthy narrators, men who kept company with Alexander at the time, do not agree with regard to public events of which these men had personal knowledge. Though many different versions of these events have been reported, let what I have set down suffice. Though these incidents occurred a little later, I have set them down alongside the story of Alexander and Cleitus in the belief that, for the purposes of my narrative, it is more appropriate to include them here.

g. The Sogdian and Chorienian rocks

The territories of Bactria and Sogdiana had been pacified and reorganized on Greco-Macedonian lines by the spring of 327, with the exception of two fortresslike settlements atop nearly inaccessible rock plateaus. The leaders of these two settlements had been adherents of Bessus and were determined not to submit to his captor; both had laid in enough supplies to withstand years of siege warfare. Alexander tackled the first of these two rocks, the so-called Sogdian Rock ruled by Oxyartes, as described below.

[IV.18] In spring Alexander advanced to the rock in Sogdiana, as he had been informed that many of the Sogdianians had fled there for refuge. The wife and daughters of Oxyartes the Bactrian were said to have fled to the rock as well, Oxyartes having conveyed them there for safekeeping on the assumption that the place was impregnable. For Oxyartes had also revolted from Alexander.

Alexander supposed that once the rock had been taken, the Sogdianians who were ready to revolt would have nowhere else to turn. But when he had marched to the rock, he found that the approach was steep on all sides and that the barbarians had gathered in the provisions necessary for a long siege. A heavy snow, which made the ascent more difficult for the Macedonians, had at the same time brought the

---

23. The sources presenting this version of the story claim that Alexander was planning to have Callisthenes put on trial back in Greece when circumstances permitted. If true, this suggests that Alexander felt that Callisthenes, a philosopher and a nephew of Aristotle whose fate would be closely watched in the Greek world, had to be accorded more civil rights than Philotas and other perceived enemies. But most historians believe he was summarily executed on the spot.

barbarians an abundant supply of water. But even so, Alexander decided to attack the place. For an arrogant remark made by the barbarians had fired his ambition. When they had been summoned to discuss terms, and he had offered them the opportunity to withdraw in safety to their homes if they surrendered the place to him, they had laughed and in their native language urged any of Alexander's soldiers who would capture the place to seek wings, since no other men were of concern to them. Thereupon Alexander announced a reward of twelve talents for the first man to scale the mountain. The rewards for the second and third men were announced in turn, and finally a reward of three hundred darics was promised to the last man to reach the top. The Macedonians, who were already exceptionally eager, were spurred on still more by the proclamation.

[IV.19] When everyone who had acquired rock-climbing expertise in Alexander's sieges had assembled—they numbered nearly three hundred—and had prepared small iron pegs (the ones used to secure their tents) to be fixed in the snow wherever it looked compact and where any bare ground showed through, and had bound the pegs to strong linen cords, they went out at night to the sheerest face of the rock, where the fewest guards had been posted. When they had fixed some of the pegs in the ground where it was visible, others in the snow where it was least likely to break up, they pulled themselves up at various parts of the rock. Some thirty men perished in the ascent, and their bodies were not recovered for burial, as they had fallen here and there in the snow. The rest, having ascended near dawn and reached the mountain's peak, waved scraps of muslin toward the Macedonians' camp as Alexander had instructed them to do. Alexander sent a herald and ordered him to shout to the barbarians' advance guard to delay no longer, but to give themselves up, as Alexander had indeed found the men with wings, and the heights of the mountain were in their hands. And as he spoke, the herald pointed to the soldiers atop the crest.

The barbarians were astounded by the unexpectedness of the sight. Suspecting that even more of Alexander's men, armed to the teeth, were in possession of the heights, they gave themselves up, so terrified were they at the sight of those few Macedonians. Thereupon, many of the barbarians' wives and children were captured, including Oxyartes' wife and children.

Oxyartes had a virgin daughter of marriageable age. Her name was Roxane, and the men who served with Alexander said she was the most beautiful woman they had seen in Asia after Darius' wife. It is said that when Alexander saw her he fell in love with her. But though he had fallen in love, he was reluctant to rape her like a captive; nor did he consider it beneath his dignity to marry her. And I find more to commend than blame in this action of Alexander. Somehow in the case of Darius' wife, who was said to be the most beautiful woman in Asia, either Alexander did not find himself attracted to her or he restrained himself, though he was a young man at the very peak of his success, when men are apt to run wild. But Alexander respected and spared her, showing great self-control and a perfectly understandable desire to be well thought of.

[IV.20] There is also a story that shortly after the battle of Issus the eunuch who had watched over Darius' wife eluded his captors and went to Darius. When Darius saw him, he asked first whether his daughters, wife, and mother were alive. When he heard that they were and that his wife and mother were addressed as queens and were waited on as deferentially as at Darius' court, Darius asked whether his wife had remained faithful to him. On learning that she had, he asked whether Alexander ever forced himself on her, whereupon the eunuch, swearing an oath, said, "Sir, your wife is just as you left her, and Alexander is the best and most temperate of men." On hearing this, Darius raised his hands to the sky and uttered this prayer: "Zeus the King, to whom it has been entrusted to manage the affairs of kings among men, I earnestly entreat you to preserve my sovereignty over the Persians and Medes, as you granted it to me. But if in your sight I am no longer king of Asia, give my power to no one but Alexander." Thus temperate actions are not overlooked even by one's enemies.

When Oxyartes learned that his daughters were captured and that Alexander was taking an interest in his daughter Roxane, he took courage and came to Alexander, who treated him honorably, as was reasonable in such happy circumstances.

Having concluded an alliance by marriage with Oxyartes—a more cogent explanation for Alexander's wooing of Roxane than the grand passion described by Arrian and all other ancient accounts—Alexander turned his attention to the second of the two Sogdian fortresses, known as the Rock of Chorienes after the name of its ruler. Here the army's engineers faced a task almost as formidable as at the island city of Tyre: a plateau ringed by sheer cliffs many hundred feet high, with a ravine at the base that needed to be filled in before a mound could be raised atop it. "Nevertheless," says Arrian,

"Alexander took on the job, having gotten so far along in daring and success that he thought every place had to be open to scaling and capture by him." Inexorably, with antlike determination, the soldiers began filling in the ravine, all the while using screens to protect themselves from the missiles hurled from above. When they had raised a mound high enough to bring the citadel within catapult range, a distressed Chorienes asked that his neighbor Oxyartes, who had recently been in similar straits, be allowed to ascend the rock for a parley. Oxyartes, now Alexander's father-in-law, gave Chorienes stern advice, saying that he could not escape Alexander's onslaught, whereas he would certainly meet with generous and humane treatment if he surrendered. Chorienes accordingly submitted to Alexander and concluded a friendship pact whereby he was allowed to retain his position of power on the rock.

VII

The Invasion of India

(Spring 327–Summer 325 B.C.E.)

a. The capture of Aornos Rock

With Sogdiana now totally under control of pro-Macedonian leaders, Alexander embarked on a further leg of his journey of conquest, an invasion of the lands the Greek world called India.

The region east of the Hindu Kush had been known to the Greeks for centuries, but only in a vague and distorted way that minimized its size and extent while wildly exaggerating its wealth and exoticism. Why Alexander was determined to go there is unclear. Arrian says typically that "a longing seized him" to explore these virtually unknown lands, and this explanation probably comes nearest the truth. There was also the lure of opportunity: an Indian ruler whom the Greeks dubbed Taxiles, after his capital city Taxila, sent an offer of alliance and provision to Alexander in Sogdiana, in the hopes of enlisting the new regional superpower to help him fight his neighbors. Finally, Alexander might have explained his strategy as a reconquest of all Persian lands, since parts of western India had at one time been a loosely connected province of the Achaemenid empire. Whatever the exact mixture of motives, Alexander for a second time hauled his army—perhaps over one hundred thousand now, including all the camp followers who had joined in its train—across the Hindu Kush in the spring of 327, headed for a place few of his men ever expected, or now desired, to see.

Once across the mountains, Alexander faced yet another "impregnable" fortress to test his determination and his engineering skill.

[Arrian IV.28] When the inhabitants of Bazira learned [of Alexander's capture of a neighboring town], they felt their predicament was hopeless. They left the city near midnight and fled to the rock. The other barbarians did the same: leaving their cities, they all fled to the so-called Aornos Rock. This rock is an enormous landmark in the region. According to legend, not even Heracles, son of Zeus, had been able to capture it. I cannot say positively whether the Theban, Tyrian, or

Egyptian Heracles actually reached India; I rather think he did not, but when people want to exaggerate their difficulties, they say that not even Heracles could have overcome them. Accordingly, I am of the opinion that Heracles' name became associated with the rock as a boast.

They say that the rock's circumference measures nearly twenty-five miles and that its height at its lowest measures a mile and a quarter. There is but one way up, and it is handmade and rugged. At the peak there is a plentiful, spring-fed supply of pure water, a wood, and enough fertile soil for a thousand men to cultivate.

When Alexander heard the place described, a longing seized him to capture this mountain too, not least on account of the Heracles legend. . . . After reaching Embolima, a city near Aornos Rock, he left Craterus there with a division of the army, having ordered him to supply the place with as much food as possible and everything else needed for a long stay so that the Macedonians, making the city their base of operations, might wear out the rock's occupiers with a long siege if they could not capture them in the initial assault. Taking the archers, the Agrianians, Coenus' battalion (having selected from the other phalanx the nimblest and best-armed men), some two hundred of the Companion Cavalry, and nearly a hundred mounted bowmen, Alexander led them toward the rock. On that day he encamped at a site he considered suitable; the next day, advancing a little farther toward the rock, he again encamped.

[IV.29] At that point some of the neighboring tribesmen came to him, surrendered themselves, and promised to guide him to the most vulnerable part of the rock, where he could easily capture the place. Using these men as guides, Alexander sent his bodyguard, Ptolemy, son of Lagus,[1] in command of the Agrianians and the light-armed troops (including some chosen shield-bearers), having instructed him, when he had captured the place, to secure possession with a strong guard and to send a signal that it was in his hands. Taking a rugged and barely passable road, Ptolemy gained possession of the place without attracting the barbarians' notice. When he had fortified it all around with a palisade and a ditch, he held up a torch from a spot where it was likely to be seen by Alexander. The flame was seen at once, and on the following day Alexander led the army forward. But

---

1. The same Ptolemy whose account of the Alexander story was adopted by Arrian as one of two principal sources of information.

because the barbarians were mounting a defense, and the terrain was rough, he was unable to make headway. When the barbarians learned that Alexander was in difficulty, they turned and attacked Ptolemy and his men. A fierce battle was fought between the barbarians and Macedonians, the Indians striving to tear down the palisade, Ptolemy to protect his position. The barbarians, getting the worst of it in an exchange of spears and arrows, withdrew at nightfall.

Selecting one of the Indian deserters who was especially trustworthy and knowledgeable about the region, Alexander sent him with a letter to Ptolemy, instructing him to attack the barbarians from the heights when Alexander attacked the rock, and not to be content merely to hold the place under guard. Assailed from both sides, the Indians would then be caught between two fires. Alexander himself, starting from the camp as soon as it was day, led the army along the route by which Ptolemy had ascended unseen, having calculated that if, after forcing his way, he joined up with Ptolemy and his detachment, his task would pose no further difficulty. And so it turned out. Until midday the battle was fierce, the Macedonians forcing their way up the ascent, the barbarians assailing them as they advanced. But when the Macedonians did not give way, and one company came up after another, fresh troops relieving the men who had fought earlier, they managed to get the ascent under their control near evening and joined up with Ptolemy's detachment. Thereafter, the entire army, reunited, advanced against the rock itself. But as it was still impossible for them to attack, they suspended their efforts for that day.

At dawn Alexander ordered each soldier to cut a hundred stakes. When these had been cut, he himself began heaping up a large mound, starting from the crest of the hill where they were encamped and extending to the rock. For it seemed to him that from the mound their arrows could reach the rock's defenders, as could the missiles discharged from engines. Every man took part in the work of raising the mound, and Alexander himself stood by as a supervisor—commending the work where it was being performed with zeal, chastising whenever it failed to progress swiftly.

[IV.30] On the first day, the army raised the mound about two hundred yards. The next day the slingers, hurling stones at the Indians from the rising mound and discharging missiles from the engines, repulsed the Indian skirmishers who sallied out against the Macedonians at work on the mound. The work went on without interruption for three days. On the fourth, a few of the Macedonians, forcing their way, gained possession of a small hill on the same level as the rock. Losing no time, Alexander extended the mound, as he wished to join it to the hill that the few Macedonians were now holding for him.

The Indians were astounded at the indescribable daring of the Macedonians who had forced their way to the hill. Observing that the mound was now attached to it, they abstained from further resistance. Sending their heralds to Alexander, they affirmed their willingness to give up the rock if he would make peace with them. They were actually planning to spend the day prolonging the negotiations and to disperse that night, each tribe to its own settlement. When Alexander got wind of this, he gave the barbarians time for their retreat and the removal of the guard that surrounded the place on all sides. He himself waited until they had started their withdrawal, whereupon he took some seven hundred of the bodyguards and shield-bearers to the abandoned part of the rock. He himself scaled it first, and the Macedonians, drawing one another up at various points, came up after him. At a signal they turned on the retreating barbarians, killing many of them in the flight. The rest, withdrawing in terror along the cliffs, hurled themselves over the edge and perished.

The rock Heracles had failed to capture was in Alexander's hands, and he sacrificed on it and established a garrison there, placing Sisicottus in charge. (Sisicottus had long ago deserted from the Indians to Bessus in Bactra, and when Alexander had taken possession of Bactria, Sisicottus had joined forces with him and shown himself especially trustworthy.)

b. The Nysa revels

[V.1] In the country Alexander invaded between the Cophen and Indus rivers, a city known as Nysa was said to have been settled. The city was said to be a creation of Dionysus, who founded it after he had subdued the Indians[2]—whoever that Dionysus may have been, and whenever and from wherever he made war on the Indians. For I am unable to determine whether or not the Theban Dionysus, starting

---

2. Late Greek legends, most of them probably derived from the model established by Alexander, held that Dionysus had led a campaign of conquest through India and other eastern lands in mythic times. The opening lines of Euripides' *Bacchae* trace Dionysus' journeys as far east as Bactria, though not to India.

from Thebes or the Lydian Tmolus, led an army against the Indians, attacked so many warlike tribes unknown to the Greeks of that period, but subdued none of them by force except the Indians. Of course, one must not examine ancient tales about the divine too minutely. For stories likely to strike their hearers as incredible do not seem wholly implausible when a divine element is added.

When Alexander attacked Nysa, the Nysaeans sent him their best and wisest citizen, a man named Acuphis, and with him thirty envoys of the highest renown, to entreat Alexander to leave the city in the god's keeping. When the envoys entered Alexander's tent, they found him seated, covered with dust from the road, wearing his armor and helmet and holding his spear. Astonished at the sight, they fell to the ground and kept silent for a long time. When Alexander raised them up and urged them to take courage, Acuphis began and spoke as follows:

"Sire, the Nysaeans entreat you, out of respect for Dionysus, to leave them free and independent. For when Dionysus had subdued the Indians and was returning to the Greek sea, he founded this city (peopling it with soldiers past fighting, who were also his revelers) as a memorial of his wandering and ascendancy, just as *you* founded an Alexandria near the Caucasus and another in Egypt. By now you have founded many more, and will found others in course of time, as your exploits outnumber those of our founder.

"Dionysus named the city after Nysa, his nurse, and named the country Nysaea. And the mountain that lies near the city he named Merus, as legend has it that Dionysus grew in Zeus' thigh.[3] Since then we have inhabited Nysa as a free city and have governed ourselves in an independent and orderly manner. Let this be your proof that Dionysus founded Nysa: ivy, which grows nowhere else in India, grows in our country."

[V.2] It gratified Alexander to hear all these details, and he was ready to believe the stories told about the wandering of Dionysus. He also wanted Nysa to be a creation of Dionysus, since he had himself now reached the point Dionysus had reached and would go even farther. He also thought that the Macedonians, faced with the prospect of rivaling Dionysus' exploits, would not decline to join him in further toils.[4] He granted the inhabitants of Nysa their freedom and

---

3. The Greek word for "thigh" is *meros*.
4. An unusual case in which Arrian presents Alexander's unspoken thoughts.

independence. When he inquired about their laws and learned that they were governed by an aristocracy, he expressed his approval and required them to send him some three hundred of their horsemen. As for the men who led their government (who numbered three hundred), he ordered a hundred to be selected and sent to him. Acuphis, whom Alexander appointed as governor of Nysaea, was to select them. On hearing this, Acuphis is said to have smiled. When Alexander asked him why he laughed, Acuphis replied, "How, sire, should a single city, deprived of a hundred good men, still be governed well? If you care for the Nysaeans, take the three hundred horsemen—take more, if you wish—but in place of the hundred you ordered to be chosen from the best men, take twice the number of inferior men, so that when you return you may find the city in the same good order." As what he said seemed reasonable, Acuphis persuaded Alexander, who ordered him to send the horsemen, but no longer to ask for the hundred chosen men, nor even to request others in their stead. But Acuphis was obliged to send him his son and his daughter's son.

A sudden desire seized Alexander to visit the place where certain memorials of Dionysus, as the Nysaeans boasted, were to be seen. He went to Mount Merus with the Companion Cavalry and the infantry *agema* and saw that the thickly shaded mountain abounded in ivy and laurel and had groves of all kinds and all manner of wild beasts. The Macedonians, glad to see the ivy (which they had not seen for a long time, as there was none elsewhere in India, not even where there were vines), eagerly fashioned wreaths from it, donned them at once, and sang Dionysus' praises, calling out the god's various names.[5] Alexander sacrificed there to Dionysus and feasted with his Companions. Some have also reported (if anyone can find this credible) that many of the prominent Macedonians in Alexander's suite, having crowned

---

The mythic rivals with whom Alexander had striven up to this point were Heracles, Perseus, and Achilles; in India, Dionysus joined their retinue.

5. The ivy plant was thought to grow only in European lands, and so the Macedonians, finding it here in India, were powerfully struck by its associations with their homeland. Consider how a native New Englander might feel if, after years of wandering among palm groves, he or she suddenly came upon a stand of maple trees. The fact that the ivy plant was sacred to Dionysus, the presiding deity of the drinking parties that stood at the center of Greco-Macedonian social life, also helps explain the army's emotional response to its appearance here.

themselves with ivy and invoked the god, were possessed by Dionysus, honored the god with cries of "Evoi!" and flew into a Bacchic
frenzy.

[V.3] One is free to believe or disbelieve those tales, however one
wishes to take them. For my part, I do not wholly agree with Eratosthenes of Cyrene, who says that everything the Macedonians attributed to the gods was exaggerated to please Alexander. For example,
he says that when the Macedonians saw a cave in the land of the Parapamisadae[6] and heard some local legend or invented one themselves,
they spread a report that this was in fact the cave in which Prometheus
had been imprisoned, and that the eagle had visited it to feast on his
entrails,[7] and that Heracles, on his arrival, had killed the eagle and
freed Prometheus from his bonds. In their telling, the Macedonians
transferred the Caucasus range from the Black Sea to the eastern re-
gions of the earth, and the land of the Parapamisadae to India, calling
Mount Parapamisus the Caucasus for the sake of Alexander's reputation, so that he would actually have crossed the Caucasus. And in India, when they saw oxen branded with a club, they conjectured that
Heracles had reached India.[8] Eratosthenes is equally skeptical about
the wandering of Dionysus. In my own view, the authenticity of these
stories should remain in question.

When Alexander arrived at the Indus, he found the bridge Hephaestion had built for him,[9] several small vessels, and two thirty-oared
ships.

c. The war with Porus

*Upon entering the region known today as the Punjab, defined by the five
rivers flowing together to form the Indus, Alexander followed through on his
bargain with the local ruler Taxiles: a secure base of operations in Taxila,
plus provisions for the army, in exchange for assistance in overcoming Porus,*

6. The Parapamisadae are, roughly, the mountains of the Hindu Kush. See
the map on pages xxviii–xxix.
7. The reference is to the myth of Prometheus' punishment for the theft of
fire. Aeschylus and other early Greek writers located the site of Prometheus'
imprisonment in the Caucasus range, a region that to them signified the edge
of the world.
8. The club was the weapon associated with Heracles.
9. A large detachment under Hephaestion had been sent ahead some time
earlier, before the siege of Aornos, to secure passage across the Indus.

*Taxiles' powerful enemy to the east. Alexander's war with Porus was to cul-
minate in his last and perhaps greatest battle, known to history as the battle
of the Hydaspes. It is commemorated on a famous medallion issued by
Alexander showing a Macedonian soldier brandishing his spear at a retreating elephant.*

*Before describing that battle and the elaborate shell game that preceded
it, however, Arrian pauses to note some of the discoveries made in India by
Alexander's army. This far-eastern land had been known to the Greeks only
through fables and bizarre legends, so the first arrival there of a European
military expedition had great scientific significance.*

[V.4] Let me record the following undisputed facts about the Indus:
it is the largest river in Asia and Europe except the Ganges, another
Indian river. The Indus' springs are on this side of Mount Parapamisus (or Caucasus), and the river empties into the great sea south
of India. The Indus is double-mouthed, and both its outlets are covered with shoal water, as are the five outlets of the Danube. It forms
a delta similar to the delta in Egypt. . . .

At dawn Alexander and his army crossed the Indus into India. I
have not, in this history, recorded the Indians' customs, nor whether
the country produces any extraordinary animals, nor the quantity or
kind of fish or sea monsters to be found in the Indus, Hydaspes,
Ganges, or other Indian rivers; nor have I mentioned the ants that
mine their gold, nor the guardian dragons, nor all the other tales that
have been written (more for pleasure than for describing what actually exists),[10] as I presume that all the bizarre tales invented about the
Indians will not be verified or refuted by anyone. But Alexander and
those who shared his campaigns tested most of them—as many, at any
rate, as they did not themselves invent. They proved that none of the
Indians had gold[11] (none of the tribes, at any rate, that Alexander
reached with his army, and he reached a great many); that they had
no taste for luxurious living; that they were physically tall, in fact the

10. Exotic tales of "Indian wonders" had been popular among the Greeks
ever since they first became aware of India in the sixth century B.C.E. The
story of "the ants that mine their gold" can be found in Herodotus' account
of India, III.102.
11. The idea that India was rich in gold had been widely accepted by the classical Greek world. Herodotus claimed that the Indians paid tribute to the Persian king in gold dust.

tallest men in Asia, most of them eight feet tall or nearly so; that they were blacker than all the other races except the Ethiopians; and that they were by far the noblest warriors among the inhabitants of Asia at that time.

[V.8] When he had crossed the Indus, Alexander sacrificed according to custom. Setting out from the river, he reached Taxila, a large and prosperous city, the largest between the Indus and the Hydaspes. The local Indians and Taxiles, the city's governor, received him in a friendly manner, and Alexander added to their domain as much of the neighboring territory as they requested. He then advanced toward the river Hydaspes.

For he had received word that Porus,[12] who was now at the far bank of the Hydaspes with his entire army, was determined either to prevent Alexander from crossing or to attack him if he tried to cross. When Alexander learned this, he sent Coenus, son of Polemocrates, back to the Indus with orders to dismantle all the vessels at the crossing there and to convey them to the Hydaspes.[13] The vessels were dismantled and brought to him—the shorter vessels were cut in two, the thirty-oared vessels in three—and the sections were conveyed on carts as far as the bank of the Hydaspes. There the vessels were rebuilt, and the assembled fleet was seen again at the Hydaspes. Taking the force with which he had reached Taxila, and five thousand of the Indians Taxiles and the local governors had brought him, Alexander advanced to the Hydaspes.

[V.9] Alexander encamped at the bank of the Hydaspes, and Porus was observed on the opposite bank with his entire army and his troop of elephants. Remaining in position where he saw that Alexander had encamped, Porus guarded the crossing himself and posted guards at all the other points where the river was easier to ford, appointing commanders for each, as he intended to prevent the Macedonians from crossing. When Alexander observed this, he decided to move the army frequently, in order to keep Porus in doubt. He

---

12. Porus, or Paurava in his own language, was to be the last great opponent Alexander faced. He ruled a large kingdom east of the Hydaspes, though Bosworth maintains that his military strength has been greatly exaggerated by the ancient sources so as to magnify Alexander's achievement in defeating him (*Commentary* II.263).

13. By Alexander's order, the ships built to protect the Indus crossing were constructed in sections that could be disassembled for portage over land.

divided the army into many parts, some of which he himself led up and down the countryside, plundering enemy territory or looking for points where the river appeared more fordable. Having appointed various commanders to the other divisions, he frequently sent them off in different directions.

As grain was being conveyed to Alexander's camp from all quarters on his side of the Hydaspes, it was clear to Porus that Alexander meant to remain at the bank until winter, when the water level would drop and he could cross at many points. Meanwhile, Alexander's vessels, sailing up and down the river, and the hides filled with hay, and the bank teeming here with cavalry, there with infantry, allowed Porus no rest, nor could he even select a single position suitable for a guard and concentrate his forces there. For the time being, all the Indian rivers were swollen and turbid, and their currents were swift, as it was the season of the year, after the summer solstice,[14] when it rains constantly in India, and the snows of the Caucasus, where the springs of most of the rivers lie, melt and greatly increase their volumes. But in winter, when they are straitened, the rivers become small and clear, and except for the Indus, the Ganges, and perhaps some others, it is possible to ford them at various points. The Hydaspes, at any rate, becomes fordable.

[V.10] Accordingly, Alexander declared openly that he would await that season if he were prevented from crossing immediately. But he lay in wait nonetheless, in the hope that he might somehow steal across swiftly without being detected. He realized that he would be unable to cross where Porus himself had encamped by the bank of the Hydaspes. For in addition to Porus' large number of elephants, a vast army, drawn up and armed to the teeth, would attack his men as they emerged from the river. And he imagined that his horses would refuse to step on the opposite bank, as the elephants would immediately charge, and the sight and sound of the beasts would terrify them. And even prior to this, his horses would not remain on the hide floats ferrying them across, but would panic and leap into the water when they caught sight of the elephants on the other side. Accordingly, Alexander planned to steal across in the following manner. He made a nightly practice of leading a large body of cavalrymen here and there along the bank and of having the men raise a shout and a war cry and

14. An error in chronology; Arrian later states (V.19, page 132), correctly, that the battle of the Hydaspes took place in May.

create an uproar of the kind associated with a body of troops ready to make a crossing. Porus, on the other side, would then march with his elephants to the point opposite the hubbub. Thus Alexander got Porus into the habit of making flank marches. But when this had been going on for a long time, and nothing occurred beyond the shouting and the war cry, Porus gave up responding to the sallies of Alexander's cavalrymen. Judging that there was no cause for alarm, he remained in camp, though he saw to it that scouts were posted everywhere along the bank. And once Alexander had allayed Porus' fear of the nightly ventures, he contrived as follows.

[V.11] A promontory jutted out from the bank of the Hydaspes where the river bent at a marked angle. The promontory itself was thick with copse wood of all kinds, and across from it, in the river, lay a deserted island, wooded and untrodden. After inspecting the island opposite the promontory, Alexander decided that as both places were wooded and suitable for concealing the attempt, he would try to transport the army across at that point. The promontory and the island were both nearly twenty miles from the great camp. Alexander had stationed guards all along the bank at intervals that made it possible for them to see one another and to hear orders easily, no matter where they were issued. For many nights, shouting was heard on all sides and fires were burning.

When Alexander had decided to attempt the passage, preparations for crossing went forward openly throughout the camp. Craterus was left behind in camp with his own hipparchy, the Arachosian cavalry and horsemen from the Parapamisadae, the battalions of Alcetus and Polyperchon (from the Macedonian phalanx), the governors of the local Indian tribes, and their five thousand men. He had been ordered not to cross the stream until Porus had left camp to attack them or until he learned that Porus had fled and Alexander's men had won a victory. "If Porus takes part of his army to attack me, and the rest of his men are left in camp with the elephants, stay where you are. If, on the other hand, Porus leads all his elephants against me and leaves part of his army in camp, make haste to cross. For only the elephants make it impracticable to disembark the horses; there will be no trouble facing the rest of Porus' force."

[V.12] Such were Craterus' instructions. Between the island and the great camp where he had been left behind, Meleager, Attalus, and Gorgias had been posted with the mercenary horsemen and foot soldiers. These men were also instructed to cross in sections, after dividing the army, once they saw the Indians engaged in battle.

Having selected the *agema* of the Companions, the hipparchies of Hephaestion, Perdiccas, and Demetrius, the cavalry of the Bactrians and Sogdianians and the Scythian horsemen, the mounted bowmen of the Dahae, and from the phalanx the shield-bearers, the battalions of Cleitus and Coenus, the archers, and the Agrianians, Alexander led his men forward without attracting attention, keeping a good distance from the bank lest he be seen taking them to the island and the promontory where he had decided to attempt a crossing. And there, during the night, the hide floats that had been brought to the place much earlier were filled with hay and carefully stitched together.[15]

A heavy rain fell that night and helped to conceal Alexander's preparations and his attempt to cross, as the thunder and rain drowned out the clash of arms and the noise occasioned by the shouting of instructions. Most of the vessels, which had been cut in pieces, had been conveyed to that spot, reassembled in secret, and concealed in the woods, including the thirty-oared ships. Near dawn, the wind and the rain subsided, and when his cavalry had embarked on the hide floats, and all the foot soldiers the vessels could accommodate had boarded, they crossed by way of the island, lest they be observed by Porus' spies before they had sailed past the island and were a short distance from the bank.

[V.13] Embarking on a thirty-oared ship, Alexander crossed the stream with Ptolemy, the bodyguards Perdiccas and Lysimachus, Seleucus (a Companion who later became king),[16] and half the shield-bearers. Other thirty-oared ships carried the rest of the shield-bearers. When they sailed by the island, they openly attacked the bank, and the Indian scouts, observing their onslaught, rode to Porus as fast as their horses could carry them. Having disembarked first and

---

15. The use of stuffed hides as floats to permit river crossings was by now one of Alexander's oldest ruses; he had used it in his very first campaign, to cross the Danube (see above, page 22). The rafts constructed on this occasion had to be more substantial than those used at the Danube, in order to carry the horses across.

16. Seleucus, one of the so-called Successors who divided up Alexander's kingdom, mastered much of Asia and had himself crowned king in 305 B.C.E.

taken with him the troops from the other thirty-oared ships, Alexander marshaled the horsemen as they disembarked (they had been ordered to disembark first) and led them forward in battle order. But in his ignorance of the area, he had unknowingly disembarked not onto firm ground but onto an island; it, too, was large, which was chiefly why he had not realized it was an island. A narrow channel of the river separated the island from the other bank. Meanwhile, the pouring rain, which continued through much of the night, swelled the stream, with the result that Alexander's cavalry at first did not find a ford, and there was some concern that in order to cross, another effort, equal to their first, would be required. But when a ford was discovered, he led his men across it, though with difficulty: for where the water was deepest it was over the chests of the foot soldiers, while the horses barely kept their heads above water.[17] When he had also crossed that expanse of water, he led the cavalry *agema* and the strongest men selected from the other hipparchies to the right wing. He posted the mounted bowmen in front of the entire cavalry. As for the infantry, he posted the royal shield-bearers, under Seleucus' command, next to the cavalry. Beside the shield-bearers he posted the royal *agema*, and beside the *agema* the rest of the shield-bearers in an order corresponding to the rotation of commands for that day. At both ends of the phalanx he posted the archers, the Agrianians, and the javelin men.

[V.14] Having thus arrayed his army, he commanded the infantry (a force numbering almost six thousand) to follow in good order at a marching pace. As he felt himself superior in cavalry, he took only the horsemen (who numbered nearly five thousand) and led them forward at a brisk pace. He ordered Tauron, the archers' commander, to bring his men up with the cavalry and to deploy them rapidly as well. He had decided that if Porus' men attacked him with their full strength, he would either overcome them easily, attacking with his cavalry, or fight them off until the infantry joined the action. But

17. If things went as Arrian here records, it took exceptional determination on Alexander's part to go forward with this second crossing; most commanders would have abandoned the whole operation after discovering the topographical error that had placed the army on an island instead of on the opposite bank, after the element of surprise had already been lost. But what Arrian fails to note is that the imminent arrival of Abisares, one of Porus' allies, made the timing of Alexander's attack urgent.

if, in their astonishment at the extraordinary daring of the crossing, the Indians should flee, he would follow closely on their heels; for the greater the slaughter in the retreat, the easier his task in the aftermath. Aristobulus says that Porus' son arrived with nearly sixty chariots before Alexander made his last crossing from the small island, and that he would have been able to prevent Alexander's crossing (which was difficult even with no one preventing it) if the Indians had leaped down from their chariots and attacked Alexander's men as they landed. Instead, Porus' son drove by with his chariots and thereby enabled Alexander to cross in safety. Alexander sent the mounted bowmen out against Porus' men, who were routed easily after sustaining casualties. Others say that a battle also took place at the landing site between the Indians who had arrived with Porus' son and Alexander and his cavalry.

[V.15] The Indians fled when they caught sight of Alexander himself and his mass of horsemen, who were attacking not in line but squadron by squadron. Up to four hundred Indian horsemen fell, as did Porus' son. The chariots were captured with their horses; they had proved heavy in the retreat and were of no use in the action itself on account of the mud.

When he was told how many horsemen had arrived in safety after the flight, and was informed that Alexander, with great drive, had led his army across the river, and that his son had died in the battle, Porus was still in doubt, since the men who had been left behind with Craterus in the great camp opposite were clearly attempting to cross the river. Accordingly, Porus chose to advance against Alexander himself and to contend, with his entire army, against the most powerful body of Macedonians and the king himself, though he left a few of the elephants with a modest force at the camp to scare Craterus' cavalry away from the bank. Taking his entire cavalry (up to four thousand horsemen), all his chariots (three hundred), two hundred elephants, and the serviceable portion of his infantry (nearly thirty thousand men),[18] Porus advanced against Alexander. When he lighted upon an

18. The size of Porus' forces is very much in dispute among historians. It seems clear that Arrian has exaggerated the number of elephants available to Porus, if not the other units. Bosworth believes that numerical superiority in this battle, unlike in previous ones, was on Alexander's side, at least in the crucial cavalry contingents (*Commentary* II.292).

area where no mud was visible—a sandy level plain, with firm footing for the charges and wheelings about of his cavalry—he arrayed his forces. First he drew the elephants out in a line, each animal placed less than a hundred feet from the next, so that the line of elephants, drawn out to a width equal to that of the enemy's infantry phalanx, might terrify Alexander's horsemen on all sides. In any event, Porus did not expect that any of the enemy would dare to thrust themselves into the spaces between the elephants—not their cavalry (given the horses' fear), still less the foot soldiers; for they would be barred head on by the onslaught of heavily armed Indians and would be trampled underfoot when the elephants wheeled on them. Next, Porus posted the foot soldiers, not on the same line as the elephants, but in a second line behind them, the companies posted in the intervals between the beasts. He had also stationed foot soldiers at the wings even beyond the elephants. Past the foot soldiers at each wing he posted the cavalry, and in front of the cavalry, likewise at each wing, the chariots.

[V.16] Such was Porus' battle array. As soon as Alexander saw the Indians drawn up in order, he halted his own cavalry in order to await the infantry who were still approaching. But when the phalanx, marching on the double, had joined him, he did not immediately marshal the troops and lead them forward, lest he deliver up exhausted and panting men to the unwearied barbarians. Instead, he circled the infantrymen with his cavalry, giving the former an interval in which to catch their breath. Yet when he saw the Indians' battle order, he decided not to lead his men opposite their center, where the elephants had been thrown forward and the phalanx had been drawn up in close formation in the intervals between the beasts; for he shrank from the combination of forces that Porus, who had calculated carefully, had posted there. Instead, as his cavalry was superior to that of Porus, he took most of it and rode past the enemy's left wing, intending to launch his attack there. He sent Coenus to the right[19] with his own and Demetrius' hipparchy, having ordered him to keep close behind the barbarians once the latter caught sight of the column of cavalry opposite them and sought to bring their own cavalry against them. He

---

19. Arrian's failure to specify whether he means "Alexander's right" or "the Indian right" has caused considerable confusion about the subsequent course of the battle; indeed, P. A. Brunt regards the resulting sequence of events as "hopelessly obscure" due to this ambiguity (note to Loeb edition of Arrian, 2.49).

assigned the command of the infantry phalanx to Seleucus, Antigenes, and Tauron and ordered them not to join the action until they saw that the enemy's infantry phalanx and horsemen were thrown into disorder by his cavalry.

When he was within range of the enemy's missiles, he sent the mounted bowmen, who numbered nearly a thousand, against the Indians' left wing, so as to confuse the Indians stationed there with the rain of arrows and the cavalry charge. Alexander swiftly overtook the barbarians' left with the Companion Cavalry, making haste to attack them in flank while they were still in disarray and before their cavalry was drawn up in line.

[V.17] Meanwhile, the Indians had brought their horsemen together from all sides and were riding parallel to Alexander and drawing out their line to match his progress. Coenus and his men, following Alexander's instructions, appeared behind them. Once the Indians saw this, they were forced to deploy their cavalry in two directions, one part (the largest and strongest) turning toward Alexander, the other toward Coenus and his men. This tactic upset the Indians' lines and their presence of mind. Alexander, having seen his opportunity in the very wheeling about of their cavalry, attacked the men opposite him, and as a result the Indians did not even await the attack of his horsemen, but were driven back to their elephants as to a friendly wall. At that point, the commanders of the elephants led the beasts against the cavalry, and the Macedonian phalanx itself met the advancing elephants, hurled their javelins at the men mounted upon them, and shot at the beasts themselves, standing around them on all sides. The action was like none of their previous battles; for the beasts sallied out against the battalions of foot soldiers and ravaged them wherever they turned (though the Macedonian phalanx was in close formation), while the Indian horsemen, seeing the battle joined with their infantry, turned back and charged the cavalry. But when Alexander's men regained the upper hand (for they far surpassed the Indians in strength and experience), the Indians were again forced back to the elephants.

At that point, Alexander's entire cavalry united in one troop, not in response to an order, but in consequence of the engagement itself; and wherever it assaulted the Indian ranks, they suffered heavy casualties. As the elephants were now confined in a narrow space, their friends were injured by them no less than the enemy—trampled underfoot when the beasts wheeled and shoved. As the Indian horsemen were also confined in a narrow space near the elephants, they suffered a heavy slaughter. Meanwhile, most of the elephants' commanders had been struck down by javelins, and the elephants themselves, some of them wounded, others overcome by their toils and bereft of commanders, no longer remained in formation. Driven senseless by their misery, they attacked friends and foes alike and thrust themselves in all directions, trampling and killing. As the Macedonians were attacking the beasts in an open field and at their own discretion, they gave ground when charged; but when the beasts turned away, the men kept close to them and hurled their javelins, whereas the Indians who wheeled about near the elephants were now incurring more harm from them than were the Macedonians.

When the beasts were worn out and their charges were no longer vigorous—when they merely trumpeted and retired, like ships backing water—Alexander completely surrounded their entire unit with his cavalry and gave the signal for the foot soldiers to lock their shields, draw themselves into the tightest possible formation, and advance the phalanx. And thus all but a few of the Indian horsemen were cut to pieces in the action. Their foot soldiers were already being cut down, as the Macedonians were attacking them from every side. At that point, where a gap appeared in Alexander's cavalry, all the Indians turned and fled.

[V.18] At the same time, Craterus and all the other officers of Alexander's army who had been left behind at the bank crossed the stream when they saw Alexander prevailing decisively. These men achieved no less of a slaughter in the Indians' retreat, having arrived fresh for the pursuit as replacements for Alexander's exhausted men.

Almost twenty thousand Indian foot soldiers and some three thousand horsemen were killed. All their chariots were cut to pieces. Two of Porus' sons died, as did Spitaces, the nomarch of the local Indians, the officers in charge of the elephants and chariots, and all the cavalry commanders and generals of Porus' army . . . and all the elephants that did not perish there were captured. On Alexander's side, about eighty of the eight thousand foot soldiers who had taken part in the initial assault were killed. As for the cavalry, ten of the mounted bowmen (who were the first to engage in the action), about twenty Companions, and some two hundred other horsemen perished.

Porus had performed great exploits in the battle, not only as a general but as a noble soldier. And when he saw the slaughter of his horsemen, some of his elephants fallen there, and others, bereft of their commanders, wandering pitiably, and learned that most of his infantry had perished, he did not emulate Darius the great king, who retreated, the first of his men to flee. Instead, Porus stood his ground as long as any portion of the Indian force remained in the field, and he contended until, wounded at the right shoulder, the only part of him that was exposed as he ranged over the battlefield (for his breastplate, which was remarkable for its strength and joint work—as those who saw it later on were able to learn—protected the rest of his body from missiles), he withdrew, having turned his elephant about. Catching sight of Porus—a great man who had acquitted himself nobly in the battle—Alexander was eager to save him. First he sent Taxiles the Indian to him, and Taxiles, having ridden up to what seemed to him a safe distance from Porus' elephant, demanded that he halt the beast (since escape was now out of the question) and listen to Alexander's proposals. When Porus caught sight of Taxiles, his old enemy, he wheeled about and made ready to hurl his javelin at him; and Porus might have killed Taxiles if the latter had not anticipated him and ridden off to a distance. But even then Alexander did not grow angry with Porus, but sent others to him in turn, and in particular Meroes, an Indian, because he learned that the man was an old friend. When Porus had heard Meroes out, he was overcome by thirst. He halted his elephant and dismounted, and when he had quenched his thirst and recovered himself he urged Meroes to conduct him to Alexander at once.

[V.19] Meroes complied. When Alexander learned that Porus was approaching, he met him in front of the line with a few of the Companions. Halting his horse, he marveled at Porus' height (which appeared to exceed eight feet), his beauty, and the fact that his spirit was plainly unbowed: he approached Alexander as one brave man would approach another, having contended honorably against another king on behalf of his kingdom. Alexander spoke first and urged Porus to say what he hoped would befall him. Porus is said to have replied, "Treat me like a king, Alexander." Pleased with the response, Alexander said, "That will be done, Porus, on my own account. But on *your* account, say what would be to your liking." Porus replied that everything was contained in that wish. And Alexander, even more pleased with this response, granted Porus sovereignty over the very Indians he had been ruling and added another country more extensive than Porus' former domain. Thus he had treated a brave man like a king, and thereafter enjoyed the man's unswerving loyalty. So ended the battle against Porus and the Indians beyond the Hydaspes, which took place in the month of Munychion during Hegemon's archonship at Athens.

At the battlefield and at a site from which he set out to cross the Hydaspes, Alexander founded two cities. He named one of them Nicaea, in honor of his victory over the Indians, the other Bucephala, in memory of his horse Bucephalas, who died there. The horse had not been wounded but had succumbed to the heat and old age (he was about thirty years old) after years of sharing Alexander's toils and dangers. Enormous in stature and noble in spirit, Bucephalas had been mounted only by Alexander; the horse had declined to carry all other riders. He had been branded with a sign: an ox-head, which some say was the source of his name. Others say that though the rest of his body was black, his head was marked with a white shape that resembled an ox-head. Bucephalas went missing once in the Uxians' country, whereupon Alexander issued a general proclamation stating that he would kill each and every Uxian unless they brought back his horse. The horse was brought back as soon as the proclamation was issued, so great was Alexander's regard for Bucephalas, and so great the barbarians' fear of Alexander. May this serve as my brief tribute to Bucephalas for Alexander's sake.

d. The Hyphasis mutiny

With Porus thus defeated, his would-be ally against Alexander, Abisares, soon surrendered, and most other leaders and cities beyond the Hydaspes also came over to Alexander's side. At Sangala, however, where resisters had gathered, Alexander mounted a siege that had unusually bloody consequences: according to Arrian, some seventeen thousand Indians perished in the course of the fight, including those who tried to escape but were too old or sick to get to safety. Even if the numbers are, inevitably, exaggerated, Alexander's operations in India were becoming increasingly harsh, in proportion to his army's increasing isolation and distance from home. Here in India, amid unfamiliar political alliances, linked to his homeland by a long and tenuous route, Alexander seems to have decided to use tactics that would terrorize potential enemies into submission. Perhaps he was also looking ahead to the difficulties of holding and governing such distant territories once he had led the army back toward the west.

But when would he lead them westward? This question, burning in the minds of his troops for a long time already, blazed out into the open on the west bank of the river Hyphasis, when it became clear that Alexander intended to cross. As Arrian reports, Alexander was determined not to end his campaign until all enemies had been eliminated; but his army did not share this ambition. Many soldiers had served under Alexander for ten years of nearly continuous fighting, and few had wanted to go any farther than the boundaries of the Persian empire, as they had done by crossing the Hindu Kush. Now they were headed into territory controlled by a powerful king who owned many elephants, the one weapon of war they had learned to dread. Adding further to their discontent (a factor mentioned by Diodorus but not by Arrian) were the monsoon rains, a phenomenon unknown to Europeans, which had drenched them day after day since before the battle with Porus. At the Hyphasis their discontent took the form of open mutiny.

The speeches Arrian assigns to Alexander and the spokesman for the mutineers, Coenus, give fascinating insight into the mindset of both the king and his followers as they stood at the easternmost point yet reached by inhabitants of Europe. Unfortunately, no one knows for certain what materials (if any) Arrian drew on when he composed these speeches and therefore what authenticity their sentiments have. One recent authority, P. A. Brunt, believes that the speeches in Arrian are ultimately based on the report of Aristobulus, who heard them himself and preserved some of their original content. Bosworth, however, argues in his discussion of these speeches in Commentary, *volume 2, that they form a rhetorical exercise devised by Arrian to explore the problem of the limits of empire. Perhaps the speeches below should be regarded, like those found in Thucydides'* History, *as reconstructions of what the parties involved* should *have said, given their outlooks on the circumstances that faced them—except that Arrian lacks Thucydides' depth of insight into foreign policy problems.*

[V.25] The country beyond the Hyphasis River was said to be prosperous and its inhabitants able farmers and brave fighters whose domestic affairs were conducted in an orderly manner; the people were ruled by their best men, who governed equitably.[20] These Indians also had many more elephants than any of their countrymen—elephants of surpassing size and courage. These reports stirred Alexander's desire to advance. But the Macedonians had by now grown quite weary of their king's plans, seeing him charging from labor to labor, danger to danger. Various meetings were held in the camp; in some (the meetings of the most moderate), the men merely lamented their lot;

20. The native guides accompanying Alexander seem to have informed him about the prosperous Nanda kingdom located in the Ganges River valley, a larger and more powerful state than those he had encountered thus far along the Indus and its tributaries.

in others, they positively refused to follow Alexander any farther. When Alexander learned of this, he summoned his battalion officers before the soldiers' agitation and faintheartedness could increase, and spoke as follows:

"I have noticed, Macedonians and allies, that you no longer follow me into dangers with the same zeal. I have called you together so that I may either persuade you to follow me onward or be persuaded by you to turn back. If you find fault with any of your previous exertions or with me as your leader, there is no point in my saying anything more. But if, through those exertions, we now control Ionia, the Hellespont, both Phrygias, the Cappadocians, Paphlagonia, Lydia, Caria, Lycia, Pamphylia, Phoenicia, Egypt, the Greek region of Libya, part of Arabia, Syria (including both Hollow Syria and Mesopotamia), and Babylon; the Susians, Persians, and Medes and their subject nations, as well as the nations they did *not* rule, namely those beyond the Caspian Gates, beyond the Caucasus, beyond the Tanais, the Bactrians, the Hyrcanians, and the Hyrcanian Sea; if we drove the Scythians all the way to the desert; and if, in addition, the river Indus flows through our realm, as well as the Hydaspes, Acesines, and Hydraotes, why do you shrink from adding the Hyphasis and the tribes beyond it to our Macedonian empire? Are you afraid that other barbarians may withstand your attack? Some of them, after all, come over willingly, while others, attempting to flee, are captured; and those who flee hand over their country abandoned, whereupon *we* hand it over to our allies and those who have joined us of their own accord.

[V.26] "As for a limit to one's labors, I, for one, do not recognize any for a high-minded man, except that the labors themselves should lead to noble accomplishments. If anyone longs to hear when our fighting will come to an end, let him know that we are not far from the Ganges and the eastern sea,[21] with which, I promise you, the Hyrcanian Sea will turn out to be joined. For the great sea girdles the entire earth.[22] I will show the Macedonians and their allies that the

21. The "eastern sea" Alexander here imagines to be a short march away would turn out to be the Pacific Ocean, still thousands of miles distant. Greek geographical doctrine of Alexander's day vastly underestimated the extent of Asia; Aristotle believed that the eastern edge of the continent was visible from atop the Hindu Kush (*Meteorologica* I.350a22–3).
22. More Greek geographical doctrine, the circumambient nature of the

waters of the Indian and Persian gulfs flow together as do the waters of the Hyrcanian and Indian seas. From the Persian Gulf our fleet will sail around to Africa as far as the Pillars of Heracles.[23] And from the Pillars all of Libya becomes ours, and all of Asia, and our empire's boundaries become those that god has set for the earth.

"But if we turn back now, many warlike races will be left unconquered between the Hyphasis and the eastern sea, and many others northward to the Hyrcanian Sea, and the Scythian tribes not far beyond them.[24] Accordingly, it is to be feared that if we turn back, the tribes we do not now hold securely may be stirred to rebel, on our departure, by those not yet under our control.[25] And then many of our toils *will* be profitless, or there will be a need for new toils and dangers. Only stand fast, Macedonians and allies! For I assure you that those who labor and face dangers achieve noble deeds, and it is sweet to live bravely and die leaving behind an immortal fame. Or are you unaware that our ancestor,[26] not content to remain in Tiryns or Argos, or even in the Peloponnese or Thebes, attained such renown that from a man he became, or was thought to become, a god? Even the labors of Dionysus, a more delicate god than Heracles, were not few in number. But *we* have passed even beyond Nysa. And Aornos Rock, which Heracles did not succeed in capturing, belongs to us. Add what still remains of Asia—relatively little—to the many territories you have already acquired. After all, what great or noble thing would we ourselves have accomplished had we sat in Macedonia and thought it

---

"river" known in ancient times as Ocean. Alexander's point here, and in the sentence following, is that the Macedonians can easily secure the remainder of Asia and attain a natural, easily defensible eastern boundary to their empire.
23. The Pillars of Heracles are the straits of Gibraltar. Alexander describes an empire delimited by oceans in both the far east and the far west.
24. The Scythians, some of whom had aided Spitamenes in his guerrilla war against Alexander, had been left unconquered when Alexander departed Sogdiana (see page 100 above). A line of forts had been established along the Tanais River to keep the Scythians from molesting the northern reaches of the new empire.
25. An interesting doctrine that does in fact correspond to the way Alexander conducted his campaign and the plans he was making for future expansion at his death. Opposition from outside the empire was deemed responsible for internal sedition and was therefore made a higher priority.
26. Heracles, from whom Alexander was supposedly descended.

sufficient only to maintain our own country without toil and repulse our Thracian neighbors or the Illyrians or Triballians or any of the Greeks who were not friendly to us?

"Certainly, if while you were toiling and running risks I had been issuing orders as your leader but holding aloof from toil and danger myself, it would not be unreasonable for your spirits to flag first—if you had borne the toils alone and reaped their rewards for others. But as it is, we have *shared* the toils, have shared *equally* in the dangers, and the prizes are set up for us all. The country is yours, and you govern it as satraps.[27] As for treasure, the larger share is coming to you now, and when we have traversed Asia—then, by Zeus, when I have not merely fulfilled but exceeded your hopes of wealth, I will send home those who wish to return to their own country or will lead them back myself, and make those who remain here the envy of those who depart."

[V.27] When Alexander had made these and similar points, there was a prolonged silence. The officers did not dare to contradict the king openly, but were unwilling to agree with him. Meanwhile, Alexander repeatedly urged anyone to speak who wished to—if anyone actually held an opposing view. But even so, the silence persisted. Then, after a long time, Coenus, son of Polemocrates,[28] took courage and spoke thus:

"Since you yourself, sire, do not wish to lead the Macedonians by decree, but declare that on persuading them you will lead them onward, or on being persuaded you will not resort to force, I will speak not on behalf of those of us here who have been honored above the rest, and who have for the most part already received the rewards of our labors and in light of our preeminence are eager to satisfy you in everything, but on behalf of the majority of the army.[29] But even while

27. Several Macedonians had indeed received appointment as satraps, though in many cases those offices went to local leaders or to members of the Persian ruling class.

28. Coenus is described later by Arrian (VI.2, not in this volume) as "one of the most loyal and trusted of the Companions." He died in India, apparently of disease, not long after the above speech was delivered, a circumstance that has led a few scholars to wonder whether Alexander had him killed for sedition. But no ancient sources entertain any suspicion of this.

29. Coenus here acknowledges the class tensions between the officers, like himself, who mostly fought as cavalry and received an outsized share of the spoils of war, and the rank-and-file soldiers of the infantry phalanx, who did

speaking on their behalf I will speak not to please them, but to say what I consider to be expedient for you under the present circumstances and especially conducive to your safety in the future. My age gives me the right not to conceal what I consider to be the best course, as does the rank to which you have raised me and the unhesitating boldness I have shown in the toils and dangers we have encountered thus far.

"To the very degree that the successes achieved by you, as our leader, and by those who set out with you from home have been numerous and great, I consider it expedient to set some limit to our toils and dangers. For you surely see how many of the Macedonians and Greeks set out with you and how many of us are left. You sent the Thessalians home from Bactria, perceiving that they were no longer eager for our toils,[30] and you were right to do so. Of the other Greeks, those who inhabit the cities you founded do not remain where they are entirely of their own will. As for those who have continued to share our toils and dangers, both they and the Macedonian forces have lost some of their comrades in battle, while others, who from wounds are past fighting, have been left behind in various places in Asia. But most have died of disease, and the few who are left are not as vigorous physically as they were, and have grown even wearier in spirit. Among them all there is a longing for parents (among those, at any rate, whose parents are still living), a longing for wives and children, and a longing for their homeland, which they may be pardoned for longing to see, since thanks to the honor you have afforded them they will return important instead of lowly, wealthy instead of poor.

"Do not lead them onward now against their will. For you may find that unwilling combatants will not prove equally formidable in the field. But return, if you wish, to your own country, and when you have seen your mother and settled the Greeks' affairs and brought these many great victories to your father's house, make a fresh start— launch a new expedition, if you like, against those same Indian races who dwell in the east, or to the Black Sea, or, if you prefer, against Carthage and the Libyan tribes who dwell beyond the Carthaginians. These things are for you, as our commander, to decide. Other Macedonians and other Greeks will follow you—young men instead of old,

---

not gain the same benefits. Later, after Alexander's death, these tensions became aggravated enough to create a virtual state of civil war within the army.
30. See page 89 above.

unwearied instead of exhausted, who from inexperience will have no immediate fear of war and will harbor eager hopes for the future. And they will likely be even more eager to follow you when they see that your former comrades-in-arms have returned to their settlements, wealthy now instead of poor, famous now instead of obscure. If anything is to be accounted noble, sire, it is to exercise self-control in prosperity. For while *you* are in command of such an army we have nothing to fear from our enemies, but it is not in men's power to anticipate and thereby guard against what comes from god."

[V.28] By the time Coenus had finished speaking, his hearers were in an uproar. Many even shed tears, making it plainer still that they had no heart for further dangers and would be glad to turn back. Vexed at Coenus' frankness and at the timidity of his other officers, Alexander broke up the assembly. The next day, he called the same men together and angrily declared that he himself would go on, but would force no Macedonian to accompany him, as he would have men who would follow their king voluntarily. Those who wished to return home were free to depart and to tell their families that they had come back after deserting their king among his enemies. So saying, he returned to his tent and admitted none of the Companions, either on that day or for the next two days, as he was waiting to see whether some change of heart of the kind that often occurs in a mass of soldiers would move the Macedonians and allies and make them readier to obey. A great silence now fell on the camp.[31] Yet the men, though clearly grieved by Alexander's anger, were not swayed by it. According to Ptolemy, Alexander continued to perform sacrifices for the crossing, but the omens were not favorable. Then, as everything seemed to favor retreat, he assembled his senior Companions and those who were especially close to him and announced to the army that he had decided to turn back.

[V.29] The soldiery sent up a shout of the kind a motley crowd *would* send up in its joy, and most of the men shed tears. Some even approached the royal tent and called down many blessings on Alexander because he had allowed himself to be conquered only by themselves. Thereupon, Alexander divided the army into units and ordered the men to build twelve altars, equal in height to the largest movable

31. Arrian has created some confusion in the chronology by mentioning the three days of Alexander's self-seclusion. He here returns us to the scene of the assembly, moments after the end of Coenus' speech.

towers but somewhat wider, as thank offerings to the gods who had brought him so far as a conqueror, and as memorials of his labors. When the altars had been built, he performed sacrifices on them in the customary manner and held a competition in athletics and horsemanship. He gave the territory as far as the Hyphasis to Porus to govern, and he himself turned back toward the Hydraotes. After crossing that river, he proceeded back to the Acesines. There he found that the city he had ordered Hephaestion to fortify was completely built. Peopling it with all the neighboring tribesmen who volunteered to settle there and the mercenaries who were past fighting, he made ready for his voyage to the great sea.[32]

e. The Indus voyage and the attack on the Malli

Alexander had lost the test of wills on the Hyphasis and reluctantly put an eastern terminus to his campaign of conquest. The army was put to work building twelve massive altars to the Olympian gods—still undiscovered to this day—and, according to some sources at least, a set of supersized camp beds and horse stalls, designed to frighten external enemies into imagining a race of Macedonian giants. Sacrifices were offered and games and feasts were held, and then, to the delight of the army, the journey homeward began.

But Alexander did not intend to simply retrace his steps. Ever eager for further conquest, exploration, and development, he planned a route that would take him down the Indus River to the sea and assembled a great fleet of perhaps more than a thousand ships to carry a portion of the army down the river while the rest marched alongside. Not coincidentally, this route took him into territory controlled by the most entrenched, virulent anti-Macedonian opposition ever encountered in India, the religiously inspired warriors of the Malli and Oxydracae. The Macedonians who cheered their commander's decision to turn back from the Hyphasis were soon to find that some of the harshest fighting they had ever experienced still lay ahead of them.

Indeed, there are signs in the ancient reports of this campaign that the soldiery had grown unwilling to face great risks in new confrontations. When Alexander ordered them to scale the mud-brick walls of the resisting Malli towns, they held back; dismayed, he resorted to shaming them by rushing up onto the walls himself, even if that meant exposing himself to the arrows and spears of those within. This perilous dynamic culminated in the incident related below.

32. The Indian Ocean (see below).

[VI.8] Alexander marched to the Malli's largest city, as he had learned that many Malli from other cities had sought refuge there. But even that city had been abandoned by the Indians when they learned that Alexander was approaching. Having crossed the Hydraotes and stationed themselves along its banks (as these were high), they were waiting to bar Alexander's way. Informed of this, Alexander took the entire cavalry with him and proceeded to the place where the Malli had reportedly taken up a position. When he reached the river and saw the enemy troops drawn up on the opposite side, he immediately advanced into the water, accompanied only by the cavalry. When the Indians saw Alexander in the middle of the river, they retreated rapidly from the bank (though they maintained their formation), and Alexander pursued them with only his cavalry. But once the Indians, who numbered roughly fifty thousand, noticed that only horsemen were pursuing them, they wheeled about and fought fiercely. Alexander noted their phalanx drawn up in close formation, and as his own infantry had not yet arrived, he encircled and charged the Indians but avoided coming to close quarters with them. Just then the Agrianians joined him with the chosen units of light-armed troops under his own command and the archers. The infantry phalanx was also seen approaching at no great distance. When all these formidable units were pressing close, the Indians turned and fled headlong to the strongest city in the region, and Alexander, in close pursuit, killed many.

The fugitives were confined in the city, and as soon as Alexander reached it he surrounded it with horsemen. When his infantry joined him, he encamped that day around the wall, since only a few hours of daylight remained and his army was exhausted, the foot soldiers by their long march and the uninterrupted pursuit, the horsemen mainly by the fording of the river.

[VI.9] The next day, after dividing the army in two, Alexander led one division up to assault the wall; Perdiccas brought up the other. At that point the Indians did not await the Macedonians' onslaught, but left the city walls and fled together to the citadel.

Alexander and his men, having broken apart a gate, entered the city far in advance of the others. Perdiccas' division came later and scaled the walls with difficulty. Only a few of his men carried ladders, for when they saw the walls deserted by the defenders, they imagined that the city had been taken. But when the citadel was seen to be in their enemies' hands, and many had been stationed before it to fight them off, some of the Macedonians set about undermining the wall, while others, placing ladders wherever it was practicable, made an attempt on the citadel. When Alexander suspected that the Macedonians bringing the ladders were shirking, he snatched a ladder from one of them, placed it against the wall, and ascended, huddled under his shield. Peucestas climbed up after him, carrying the sacred shield, which Alexander had taken from the temple of Athena in Troy and kept with him, and which was carried before him in battle. After Peucestas, Leonnatus, the bodyguard, ascended by the same ladder. Abreas, one of the men who received double pay, ascended by another.

The king was now near the wall's rampart. Propping his shield on it, he thrust some of the Indians back into the city; on slaying others with his sword, he had cleared that part of the wall. The shield-bearers, grown fearful on the king's behalf, hastily forced their way up the same ladder and broke it, and consequently the men who were on their way up fell down and made it impossible for the others to climb up.

Standing on the wall, Alexander was being assailed all around from the nearby towers (since none of the Indians dared to come near him) and also by the men in the citadel, who were hurling their javelins from a fairly short distance, as there happened to be a mound near the wall at that point.

Conspicuous as Alexander was by the brightness of his arms and by his extraordinary daring, he decided that if he remained where he was he would be running a risk, though not performing any noteworthy exploit, whereas if he leaped down inside the wall he might strike fear into the Indians; and even if this tactic failed, since he had to risk his life in any case, he would die nobly, having performed exploits that would command the admiration of future generations. With this in mind, he leaped down from the wall into the citadel. Thereupon, planting himself firmly against the wall, he killed a number of men who engaged him at close quarters, including the Indians' leader, who attacked him boldly and whom he struck with his sword. Throwing stones, he held off one man after another, and anyone who came close he dispatched with his sword. The barbarians were no longer willing to come near him, but surrounding him on all sides assailed him with any missile they happened to have or had taken up at the moment.

[VI.10] At that point Peucestas and Abreas, the man who received double pay, and after them Leonnatus, the only men who

reached the top of the wall before the ladders broke, also leaped down
to defend the king. Abreas now fell, struck in the face by an arrow, and
Alexander himself was also struck, the arrow piercing his breastplate
and entering his chest above the breast. According to Ptolemy,
Alexander's breath and blood spouted together from the wound. As
long as his blood was still warm, Alexander defended himself, though
he was in a bad way. But when a sudden hemorrhage accompanied an
exhalation, he was overcome with vertigo and faintness, and collapsed, slumping over his shield. Peucestas, who bestrode him when
he fell and protected him with the sacred shield from Troy, and Leonnatus, on the other side, were both hit as well, and Alexander was near
death from loss of blood. For at that point the Macedonians' assault
was faltering. Those who saw Alexander assailed on the wall and leaping into the citadel were roused by devotion and fear lest the king suffer harm taking senseless risks. As their ladders were broken, they
devised various means of scaling the wall: some of them, fixing pegs
in it, as it was earthen, and hanging on by these, crept up with difficulty; the others climbed up over them. The first man to scale the wall
threw himself down into the city, where he saw the king lying, and
everyone raised a wail and a war cry. A desperate battle was already
being fought around Alexander, his men taking turns protecting him
with a shield, when some of the Macedonians, having broken the bar
with which the gate in the curtain wall was secured, entered the city
a few at a time. The rest, leaning their shoulders against the gate
where it was ajar and thrusting it inward, threw open the citadel.

[VI.11] At that point, while some were dispatching the Indians
(all of whom were killed, including women and children), others
carried the king away on his shield. He was in a bad way, and it was
not yet known if he could live. Some have written that Critodemus, a
doctor from Cos, of the family of the Asclepiads, made an incision and
drew the arrow from the wound. Others have written that as no doctor was present in the emergency, Perdiccas, the bodyguard, made an
incision with his sword at Alexander's urging and extracted the arrow.
The extraction was accompanied by a heavy loss of blood, whereupon
Alexander fainted again, which retarded further blood loss. A great
many other versions of this episode have been recorded, and tradition, having taken up the story and passed it on, preserves even to our
day the same elements that were reported falsely from the start. Nor
will it cease passing these falsehoods on to others unless it is deterred
by this history.

[VI.12] While Alexander remained there to be treated for his wound, the first report to reach the camp from which he had set out against the Malli was that he had died of it. At first, as the news passed from one to another, the entire army raised a wail. When the wailing ceased, the troops grew discouraged and were at a loss to know who would command the army (as a great many officers were held in equal esteem both by Alexander himself and the Macedonians), and how they would get home safely, surrounded as they were by so many war-like tribes, some of whom had not yet come over to them and whom they guessed would fight stoutly to obtain their freedom, while others would revolt once their fear of Alexander had been dispelled. As for the rivers the Macedonians would encounter on their homeward journey, the troops imagined they would be unfordable. Everything seemed to them impracticable and impossible if they had lost Alexander. When word came that Alexander was alive, they scarcely credited it, as they doubted he was likely to live. And when a letter arrived from him saying he would soon come down to the camp, most of them in their terror did not think it genuine, but guessed that it had been forged by his bodyguards and commanders.

[VI.13] With this in mind, and with an eye to preventing unrest in the army, Alexander had himself conveyed to the banks of the river Hydraotes as soon as his condition permitted. He sailed down the river, and when the ship carrying the king drew near the camp, Alexander gave orders for his tent to be removed from the stern so that he might be clearly seen by one and all. The men were still in doubt, thinking it was really Alexander's corpse being conveyed, until the ship touched at the bank and Alexander held up his hand to the multitude. The soldiers sent up a shout, some of them lifting their hands to the sky, others toward Alexander himself. Many even wept spontaneously at the unhoped-for sight of him. Some of his shield-bearers brought out a litter, as he was to be carried from the ship, but he ordered them to bring him his horse. When on mounting he was seen again, the entire army burst into applause, and the banks and all the nearby glens reechoed with the sound. Nearing his tent he dismounted, so as to be seen walking as well. The soldiers approached him from all sides, some touching his hands, others his knees, still others his clothes, some also merely to set eyes on him from close at hand, speak a kind word, and depart. Some were flinging garlands, others all kinds of flowers, as many as the land of India brought forth at that season.

Nearchus[33] relates that some of Alexander's friends were severe with him, reproaching him because he ran risks out in front of the army, behavior they considered more appropriate to a soldier than a general. I have the impression that Alexander was annoyed by their remarks because he recognized that they were true and that he had deserved his friends' criticism. But Alexander was mastered by battle rage and the love of glory, as others are mastered by some other pleasure, and lacked the strength to keep clear of danger. Nearchus relates that a certain elderly Boeotian (he does not mention the man's name) learned that Alexander was vexed by his friends' reproaches and stern looks. The man approached him and, speaking in the Boeotian dialect, said, "Alexander, deeds are the work of men." He also added a line of iambic verse, something to the effect that to act is to suffer. The man found immediate favor with Alexander and thereafter became his close friend.

Invalided by his wound, Alexander was placed on a cot on the deck of his ship, where the troops could still see him as the expedition made its way south. Five months' travel took them to the head of the Indus delta; during the journey, further unrest and rebellion in the surrounding region had to be dealt with, often by means of harsh measures such as mass slaughter and public executions. Indeed, this stage of the campaign saw some of the worst atrocities ever committed by the Macedonians, if Bosworth's highly critical account (Alexander and the East) *is to be believed. Other perils beset the fleet from an unexpected quarter: the strong tides of the Indus delta, a phenomenon unknown to those hailing from the near-tideless Mediterranean, damaged some of the ships and thoroughly bewildered those aboard them.*

f. The Gedrosia march

As the expedition neared the mouth of the Indus, Alexander, now recovering his strength, sailed out in a single vessel onto the "great sea," a body of water he thought contiguous with the great Ocean stretching around the east of Asia toward the Caspian. (Another, even more misguided geographic notion had already been abandoned by this point: Alexander's idea that the Indus and Nile were part of the same river system.) From the ship he made sacrifice to Poseidon, asking for a favorable voyage for his Indian Ocean

---

33. Arrian here cites a different source from his two principal ones. Nearchus of Crete was a boyhood friend of Alexander who joined the expedition in India and went on to write an account of his experiences there.

fleet, about to depart on a journey of exploration along the near-desert coast of Gedrosia. Nearchus, a Cretan who had been a boyhood friend of Alexander, was appointed admiral of the fleet; his log later served as the basis of Arrian's Indica, *another major source of information about Alexander's Asian campaigns.*

Alexander planned to march through Gedrosia with a large portion of his army, keeping in contact with the fleet at prearranged stations so as to supply it with fresh water, while the fleet in turn supplied the army with food. He knew that the landscape through which he would travel was largely uninhabited. Only with support from the land could Nearchus safely complete his task—to establish a vital sea link between the central and eastern portions of his empire and open a trade route that would avoid the towering Hindu Kush. Alexander might easily have delegated the well-digging mission to a subordinate. But the Gedrosian desert (modern-day Makran, overlapping Pakistan and Iran) was said to have defeated all previous conquerors, including Queen Semiramis of the Assyrians, and so Alexander's tireless "yearning"(which some would characterize as megalomania) once again drove him to compete against his greatest predecessors. He personally took command of the Gedrosian march, detailing Craterus to bring his heavy equipment, companies of decommissioned veterans, and various other contingents along a more hospitable route, through Areia and Drangiana.

Things went awry from the beginning. Nearchus' fleet was detained at the Indus for nearly a month by contrary winds, forcing it to miss the schedule of rendezvous with Alexander and the army. Alexander, too, was unable to keep to his plan, being forced by the rugged landscape to turn inland and to lose sight of the coast. Neither the fleet nor the army were adequately provisioned to make the journey out of contact with the other; both had thoroughly miserable passages. That of Alexander is recounted below.

[VI.24] Alexander proceeded to Gedrosia and reached its capital, Pura, a full sixty days after starting from Ora. Most of the chroniclers of Alexander's career say that all the hardships his troops suffered in Asia, even taken together, do not deserve to be compared with the hardships of that march. They say that Alexander had not been ignorant of the journey's difficulty (only Nearchus maintains otherwise); on the contrary, he had heard that no previous army had ever gotten safely across that region except for Semiramis, when she fled from the Indians. The local people say that she escaped with only twenty of her soldiers, and that Cyrus, son of Cambyses, escaped with only seven. For Cyrus, too, was said to have arrived there with the intention of invading India, though before he could do so he lost most of his army through the desolation and difficulty of that route. When these incidents were reported to Alexander, he was roused to rival Cyrus and Semiramis. It was for this reason and also to be able to provision the fleet from near at hand that Alexander chose that route, according to Nearchus.

The burning heat and the lack of water destroyed a great part of the army and particularly the pack animals. The deep and scorching sand killed off the beasts, and many succumbed to thirst. For they encountered lofty hills of deep, loosely compacted sand, which did not support their weight but engulfed them as if they were stepping in mud, or rather, in untrodden snow. Moreover, in the climbs and descents, the horses and mules were even more afflicted by the unevenness of their path and its instability. The army was particularly oppressed by the long marches, as scarcity of water (which was not to be found at regular intervals) dictated the lengths of the marches. Whenever they could cover the necessary distance at night and reached water in the morning, their hardship was not utterly unrelieved; but when their journey was prolonged, and they were caught marching by day, they languished in the heat and were afflicted with a never-ending thirst.

[VI.25] The destruction of the pack animals was widespread and was the deliberate work of the army. Banding together whenever their provisions ran out, the men would slaughter most of their horses and mules, consume their flesh, and say that the animals had died of thirst or exhaustion. And there was no one to establish the truth of what had occurred, both because of the labor involved and the fact that everyone was transgressing in the same way. Alexander was not unaware of what was happening but found it preferable, under the circumstances, to feign ignorance rather than knowingly condone what the men were doing.

It was no longer easy to transport the troops who were weakened by disease or who were left behind from exhaustion on their marches, as not only had pack animals become scarce, but the men had themselves cut the wagons to pieces, both because these could not be dragged due to the depth of the sand and because in their first marches they had for that reason been compelled not to take the shortest routes but those easiest for the pack animals. So some of the men were left behind on account of disease, others on account of exhaustion or heat or an inability to tolerate thirst. And there were none to transport them or to remain and take care of them, as the march was conducted in great haste, and in the concern for the army as a whole, the needs of individuals were necessarily neglected. Some were also overcome by sleep on the marches, since the men generally marched at night. Later, when they arose to depart, those who were still able to do so followed in the army's tracks, and those few were saved, but most perished in the sand like men who fall overboard at sea.

The army met with another misfortune that especially affected the men, the horses, and the pack animals. Rain is brought to Gedrosia, as to India, by the monsoons, and it falls not on the Gedrosians' plains but in their mountains, where clouds are borne by the wind and pour forth rain without passing over the mountains' crests. The army had encamped near a stream bed that contained a scanty supply of water (it was on account of the water that the site had been chosen). Near the second watch of the night, the stream filled up with rains unseen by the army. It overflowed with such force that it drowned most of the women and children accompanying the army and destroyed all the royal furniture and all the pack animals that were still alive. The men themselves barely got away safely with their weapons, and not even with all of them.

Many even died from drinking too much water, when in their exhaustion and thirst they came upon a plentiful supply. For this reason Alexander did not generally encamp the army near water sources but at a distance of roughly twelve miles or so, so that the men and animals might not perish, falling in throngs on the water; he was also concerned to prevent the men who drank excessively from treading in the springs or the streams and ruining the water for the rest of the army.

[VI.26] At this point a noble deed of Alexander's, perhaps his noblest, should not, it seems to me, be lost sight of, whether it was performed in that region or even earlier among the Parapamisadae, as some have reported. The army was marching across the sands in the already scorching heat, as it had to cover the distance to a source of water that lay ahead. Alexander himself, though badly afflicted with thirst, was nevertheless leading the way on foot, so that the other soldiers might bear their toils more lightly, as they generally do when hardship is shared equally. At that point, some of the light-armed troops who had turned away from the army in search of water found a shallow gully in which a little had pooled: a small, scanty spring. Collecting the water easily, they went in haste to Alexander, as though bearing some great treasure. As they drew near him, they poured the water into a helmet and brought it to the king. Alexander received it and commended the men who had brought it, but took it and poured it out in the sight of all. And the entire army was so encouraged by this gesture that one would have guessed that everyone had drunk the water that Alexander had poured out. For this deed—a testament to his endurance and generalship—I especially commend Alexander.

The following incident befell the army in that region. The guides of the march at last declared that they no longer recalled the route, its signs having been blown away by the wind. For there was nothing, in the masses of sand heaped up equally on all sides, by which to discern the route—no ordinary trees or any solid hill. For they had not made a practice of relying on the stars at night or the sun by day to guide their journey, the way the Phoenician sailors navigate by the Little Bear, the rest of humankind by the Great Bear. At that point, as Alexander realized he should lead the army to the left, he took some horsemen with him and went on ahead. When these men's horses were exhausted by the heat, he left most of them behind, rode away with five, and found the sea. When he had had the gravel scraped away on the beach, he found sweet, clear water, whereupon the entire army joined him. For seven days they marched beside the sea, fetching water from the shore. Then, as the guides now recognized the route, he led the army into the interior.

VIII

The Final Phase

(Autumn 325–Spring 323 B.C.E.)

Alexander reached Carmania, where plentiful supplies could again be obtained, with only a portion of the army he had led into the desert. How great the losses were is a matter of dispute. Some ancient sources reckoned that three out of four soldiers perished in Gedrosia, but this is surely an exaggeration. By any reckoning, the whole episode was a disaster, by far Alexander's worst error in judgment. One saving grace, however, was that Nearchus had brought the fleet through intact, as Alexander discovered in Carmania, when members of his corps who were out foraging bumped into his childhood friend, now barely recognizable in his ragged, exhausted condition.

Alexander vented his wrath over the Gedrosia disaster by conducting a purge of his satrapal appointees (as described below, page 154), several of whom he suspected of having held back requested provisions in hopes of starving his army to death (others had proved rebellious or merely incompetent). All the deposed officials were executed, one of them supposedly by Alexander's own hand. There were to be few peaceful retirements or honorable discharges from this imperial administration; rather, like a Mafia capo, Alexander made examples out of the underlings who displeased him so as to frighten others into upright behavior.

One wayward administrator who had incurred Alexander's displeasure managed to get away safely to Greece, and his departure could have had serious consequences. Harpalus, a Macedonian noble and one of Alexander's oldest friends, had already deserted once before but was taken back into full confidence by Alexander in 331 B.C.E. In his post as royal treasurer, stationed in Babylon, he had led a notorious high life subsidized by embezzled funds, including expensive Greek courtesans and imported delicacies. Now, in 324, he grabbed several thousand talents out of the treasury, hired a band of mercenaries, and made for Athens, hoping to stir up an anti-Macedonian revolution right in Alexander's backyard. But the Athenians once again chose not to risk an open break with Alexander, the same choice they had made during the Theban revolt in 335 and the revolt of King Agis in 331.

They seized Harpalus' money and refused to grant the man refuge from the Macedonians hotly seeking his head. Harpalus fled to Crete, where he was murdered by a friend. Thus ended the life of the only known defector from within Alexander's circle of trusted friends.

The satrapal purge and the defection of Harpalus highlighted the problems Alexander faced in his effort to stabilize the empire internally, now that most external opposition had been neutralized. One threat to stability was the ready availability of mercenary soldiers, such as those hired by Harpalus, who knew no loyalty to Macedonia or any other state and who would lend their polished fighting skills to anyone with money to pay them. Many such soldiers of fortune had become stateless by supporting the losing faction in one of the endless political rivalries afflicting fourth-century Greece. So Alexander resolved at about this time (early 324) to repatriate these wandering mercenaries to their home cities, in the hopes they would become settled and take their place in a peaceful, prosperous Macedonian order. His "Exiles' Decree" was announced to the collective Greek states at the Olympic festival of 324 and was greeted by some with dismay, in large part because it violated the principle of Greek political autonomy agreed to in the settlement made after the battle of Chaeronea. (Some scholars believe that the Exiles' Decree was accompanied by a second proclamation in which Alexander demanded to be worshiped as a god, but the evidence for this is not conclusive.) Discontent with this decree, especially strong at Athens—which stood to lose an important colony thereby—helped fuel the last Greek rebellion against Macedonian rule, the so-called Lamian War of 323–322. But these events take us well past the point we have reached in Arrian's narrative.

With the arrival of the army back in the heartland of the Persian empire, and with all external opposition in Asia defeated, Alexander's life story entered what was to be its final phase. Arrian pauses at the beginning of this phase to contemplate the king's remarkable nature, which he regarded as akin to that of the tragic heroes of Greek drama: innately noble and admirable but marred by flaws that grew in their dimensions as his power increased. In a kind of philosophic digression Arrian highlights Alexander's weaknesses by contrasting him with figures of immense moral strength, the Brahmans or Indian sages Alexander had met in Taxila, and in particular Calanus, a Brahman who had joined the Macedonian train. The encounter with these religious mystics had made a deep impression on Alexander, to judge by all our surviving sources (though the more fanciful ones went overboard by giving Alexander a desire to convert to their monastic way of life). In the following section, Arrian—himself a military commander who had studied with an ascetic sage, Epictetus—explores the dichotomy between the code of heroic action exemplified by Alexander and the Zen-like "way of peace" represented by the Brahmans.

a. The death of Calanus

[Arrian VII.1] When Alexander reached Pasargadae and Persepolis, a sudden longing seized him to sail down the Euphrates and Tigris to the Persian Sea and to see the rivers' outlets and the sea into which they emptied, as he had done at the Indus. Some say that Alexander was planning to circumnavigate most of Arabia, Ethiopia, and Libya, sail past the nomads beyond Mount Atlas to Gadeira, and proceed into the Mediterranean. After subjugating Libya and Carthage, he would indeed have earned the right to call himself king of all of Asia. (As the kings of the Persians and Medes had ruled not even the smallest fraction of Asia,[1] they had not been justified in calling themselves Great Kings.) Thereafter, according to some sources, he planned to sail into the Black Sea to Scythia and Lake Maeotis; others say he meant to sail to Sicily and the headland of Iapygia, as he was already unsettled by the Romans' growing renown.[2]

For my part, I cannot ascertain with any accuracy what plans Alexander was revolving, nor is it my concern to guess, though I can confidently assert that he would have planned nothing trivial or insignificant, nor would he have kept still no matter what he had already acquired, even if he had added Europe to Asia or the British Isles to Europe. Instead, he would have sought beyond them for something unknown, vying with himself in the absence of any other rival.

It is with this in mind that I commend the Indian sages, some of whom Alexander reportedly encountered in the open air in the meadow where they were accustomed to pass their time discussing philosophy. It is said that at the sight of Alexander and his army they merely stomped on the ground with their feet. When Alexander inquired, through interpreters, what the gesture meant, they replied, "King Alexander, each man can have only so much land as this on

1. This statement and the one preceding it rely on the standard Greek use of the term "Asia" to include Africa, as well.
2. There has been much debate about the authenticity of the "last plans" attributed to Alexander, both here and in Diodorus. At the time of his death Alexander was preparing a naval expedition against the Arabians, and quite possibly he also contemplated a naval war with Carthage somewhere down the road (see page 137 above). The idea of an attack on the nascent power of Rome is more fanciful, however, and probably sprang from the desire of the Romans for their nation to have some part, however peripheral, in the Alexander story.

which we are standing. Like the rest of us, you are only human, except that in your restlessness and arrogance you travel so far from home, making trouble for yourself and others. Well, you will soon be dead and will have as much land as will suffice to bury your corpse."

[VII.2] At the time, Alexander commended the speakers and their remarks, though he acted otherwise and in a manner contrary to what he commended. He is also said to have admired Diogenes of Sinope.[3] Coming upon Diogenes lying in the sun at the Isthmus, Alexander halted with his shield-bearers and infantry companions and asked the man if he needed anything. Diogenes replied that he needed nothing, other than for Alexander and his men to step aside, as they were blocking the sun.

Thus we can see that Alexander was not wholly removed from a better way of thinking, but he was, to a great degree, overpowered by ambition. When he arrived in Taxila and saw the Indian sages who go naked,[4] he was seized by a desire to have one of them join his suite, as he admired their endurance.[5] The oldest sage, whose name was Dandamis (the others were his disciples), said that he would neither join Alexander himself nor would he allow the others to do so. He is reported to have replied that if Alexander was really a son of Zeus, then so was *he*. He said he needed nothing from Alexander, as he was content with his lot; and from what he could see, Alexander's men were wandering at length over land and sea for no good reason, nor was there any limit to their many wanderings. In any event, he desired nothing Alexander had the power to bestow, nor was he afraid to be deprived of anything under Alexander's control. While he lived, the land of India, bearing its fruit in season, was all he needed, and when

3. Diogenes of Sinope was one of the early leaders of the Cynic school of philosophy, which held that all social customs were artificial and advocated an ascetic lifestyle unbound by civilized conventions. Diogenes famously lived in a large ceramic jar outside Corinth and mocked the values of those around him. The legend of his encounter with Alexander is almost certainly fictitious.

4. "Gymnosophists" or "Naked Sages" became a standard Greek and Roman term denoting various sects of ascetic Indian devotees, including Hindu, Jain, and later Buddhist orders. No one has been able to identify what sect Alexander and his men encountered in Taxila; a number of religious schools were centered there.

5. The yogic rituals of these ascetics included standing on one leg for hours at a time or exposing oneself naked to the elements (see Strabo XV.1.63–5).

he died he would depart his body, an unseemly companion. The result was that Alexander did not, after all, try to coerce him, recognizing that the man was free.

But Calanus, one of the local sages, was persuaded to join Alexander's suite. According to Megasthenes' account,[6] the sages themselves said that Calanus was notably lacking in self-control. They reproached him because he abandoned the happiness to be gained with them and served a master other than god.

[VII.3] I have mentioned these incidents because in any history of Alexander it is essential to speak of Calanus. It is said that Calanus' health deteriorated in Persia, though he had never been ill previously. But he refused to live the life of an invalid and told Alexander that he was content to die as he was, before experiencing any suffering that would force him to change his way of life. For a long time Alexander tried to argue with him, but when he saw that Calanus would not yield, and would die in some other way if he were not humored, he ordered a pyre to be built according to Calanus' instructions and ordered Ptolemy, his bodyguard, to take charge of it. Some say that Calanus was preceded by an escort of horses and men, some wearing armor, others carrying all manner of incense for the pyre. Others say that the men carried gold and silver cups and royal robes. A horse was prepared for Calanus himself, as his illness made it impossible for him to walk. But as he could not even ride, he was conveyed on a litter, crowned with garlands in the Indian fashion and chanting Indian songs, which his countrymen say were hymns in praise of their gods. It is said that the horse that had been provided for his use was of the royal Nesaean breed, and that before he mounted the pyre he presented it to Lysimachus, one of his disciples. As for the cups and rugs Alexander had ordered to be thrown on the pyre in his honor, Calanus distributed them among his followers.[7]

6. Megasthenes went to India two decades after Alexander's death as the ambassador of Seleucus Nicator, the Companion who had gone on to seize sovereignty over Asia after Alexander's death. He wrote an account of his observations of Indian life and government.

7. The idea that an Indian ascetic would have had "disciples" and "followers" among Alexander's army is intriguing. Some scholars have suggested that developments in Greek philosophy at about this time, such as the evolution of the Cynic and Skeptic movements, were influenced by the Greco-Macedonian encounter with Indian religion.

Then, on mounting the pyre he lay down in a decorous manner in sight of the entire army. Alexander did not think it decent to witness such a spectacle (the man having been his friend), but the rest were amazed to see that Calanus remained motionless in the fire. When the fire was kindled by those to whom the duty had been given, Nearchus says that trumpets blared, by Alexander's order, and the troops shouted "Alalai!" as they used to do when marching into battle, and the elephants chimed in with their high-pitched war cry in honor of Calanus.

Competent writers have recorded these details about Calanus the Indian, which are not utterly without value for humankind, or at least for anyone who cares to comprehend how powerful and unconquerable is the human will to accomplish whatever it desires.

b. The Susa weddings

With the surviving remnants of the army he had brought through Gedrosia, rejoined now by the divisions who had marched a safer route under Craterus, Alexander made his way back through the Persian capital cities he had plundered after the battle of Gaugamela, almost seven years earlier. In Pasargadae he was distressed to find the tomb of Cyrus the Great, the founder of the Persian empire, lying in ruins, and ordered Aristobulus, who later wrote one of the two memoirs on which Arrian relied, to restore it. Symbolically he may have seen this project as a way of identifying himself with Cyrus or of promising the future restoration of the empire's greatness. He also revisited the charred shell of the palace of Persepolis, the building that had burnt down under his occupation (see pages 87–8 above), where he reportedly expressed regret at the destruction he had caused.

In the spring of 324 Alexander arrived at Susa, the third and greatest of the Persian imperial capitals, and undertook one of his most enigmatic projects.

[VII.4] On reaching Susa, Alexander arrested Abulites and his son Oxathres and had them put to death for abusing their power.[8] Many offenses had indeed been committed by those in control of the territories conquered by Alexander—offenses against temples, tombs, and

---

8. These were Persians whom Alexander had appointed as satraps of two eastern provinces. According to Plutarch's *Life of Alexander* (chapter 68), the king himself executed Oxathres by running him through with a lance.

the inhabitants themselves. For the king's expedition to India had been prolonged, and people doubted he would return home safe from all those tribes and elephants. They imagined he would perish beyond the Indus, Hydaspes, Acesines, and Hyphasis. The disasters that befell him in Gedrosia further encouraged the satraps in Persia to reject the idea of his return. And it cannot be denied that at that period Alexander is said to have become quicker to accept accusations as wholly trustworthy and to impose severe punishments on those who were convicted even of minor offenses, on the assumption that in the same state of mind they might commit serious ones.[9]

He also held weddings at Susa for himself and his Companions.[10] He himself married Darius' eldest daughter, Barsine, and, according to Aristobulus, another wife as well—Parysatis, the youngest of Ochus' daughters.[11] He was already married to Roxane, the daughter of Oxyartes the Bactrian. To Hephaestion he gave another daughter of Darius—Drypetis, his own wife's sister, as he wanted Hephaestion's children and his own to be cousins. To Craterus he gave Amastrine, the daughter of Oxyartes, Darius' brother. To Perdiccas he gave the daughter of Atropates, the Median satrap. To Ptolemy his bodyguard and to Eumenes his royal secretary he gave the daughters of Artabazus—Artacama and Artonis. To Nearchus he gave the daughter of Barsine and Mentor, to Seleucus the daughter of Spitamenes the Bactrian.[12] In like manner he gave the other Companions the

9. An interesting insight into Alexander's psychological state at the end of his life. Some historians have concluded from statements such as this that Alexander was in fact developing severe paranoia, aggravated by late-stage alcoholism, at this point.

10. These Susa weddings form a further stage in the highly controversial Persification policy Alexander had been pursuing since 330. Having already blended Europeans and Persians in his imperial administration and in his armed forces, Alexander now sought to force intermarriage between the leadership of the two peoples, uniting their interests more closely than ever and (hopefully) producing a new generation of mixed-race children. In practice, nearly all the Companions renounced their Persian wives after Alexander's death.

11. Ochus is another name for Artaxerxes III, the Persian king from 358 to 338. By marrying daughters from two different royal lines of the Persians, Alexander sought to guarantee that his hoped-for offspring would have unquestioned legitimacy.

12. This unlikely union, between a Macedonian general and the daughter of

Persians' and Medes' most distinguished daughters—about eighty in number.

The weddings were held in the Persian manner. Chairs were placed in order for the bridegrooms, and after the toasts were drunk, the brides arrived and each sat down beside her bridegroom. The grooms took their brides by the hand and kissed them. The king was the first to do so (as all the weddings took place at the same time). Alexander's conduct on that occasion was felt to be particularly generous and amiable. On receiving their wives, each man led his own away. All the brides received dowries from Alexander, and he commanded all other Macedonians who had married Asian wives to have their names registered. There turned out to be more than ten thousand, and these men, too, received wedding gifts from Alexander.

[VII.5] He also thought it an opportune moment to pay off all his soldiers' debts. Accordingly, he ordered his clerks to record how much each man owed, with the idea that they would receive the money. At first only a few registered their names, as the soldiers feared that this was a test—a way for Alexander to discover which of his men were not getting by on their pay and which were living extravagantly. When it was reported that few of the men were registering and that those who held promissory notes were hoping to conceal the fact, Alexander reproached the men for their distrust. He declared that the king should speak nothing but the truth to his subjects, and that none of them should ever imagine he would do otherwise. He had tables set up in the camp with money on them and instructed his clerks to pay the debt of any man who presented a promissory note but not to take down his name. The soldiers now believed that Alexander was speaking the truth, and were more thankful that their names had not been made known than that their debts had been cleared. This gift to the army is said to have amounted to twenty thousand talents.

Alexander also bestowed a number of other gifts in recognition either of rank or of conspicuous courage in the field. He awarded golden crowns to those who had distinguished themselves for valor, presenting the first to Peucestas for having covered him with a shield, the next to Leonnatus for having done the same and in recognition of

---

the rebel chief who had harassed Alexander's army for nearly two years, is the one Susa marriage known to have endured and produced children, the future rulers of the Seleucid kingdom in Asia.

the risks he had run in India and the victory won in Ora. (With the force that had been left with him, Leonnatus had taken a stand against the Oritan rebels and their neighbors and overpowered them in battle. He was also thought to have put Ora's affairs in good order.) Alexander also crowned Nearchus, who had now arrived at Susa, for his voyage from India through the great sea. Onesicritus, the pilot of the royal ship, was also crowned, as were Hephaestion and all the other bodyguards.

c. The mutiny at Opis

[VII.6] Alexander also received visits from the satraps of his newly founded cities and the other territory taken in war. They brought with them about thirty thousand adolescent boys, all the same age, whom Alexander called his Epigoni.[13] They had been issued Macedonian arms and were trained for war in the Macedonian manner. Their arrival is said to have vexed the Macedonians, who felt that Alexander was doing his utmost to lessen his future dependence on his countrymen.

Indeed, the Macedonians were highly distressed at the sight of Alexander's Median apparel, and the fact that the weddings had been performed in the Persian manner offended most of them, even those who had themselves taken part as bridegrooms, notwithstanding that they had been greatly honored that the king had treated them as equals. They were also vexed at Peucestas, the satrap of the Persians, who had taken to wearing Persian apparel and speaking Persian to please Alexander. It also grieved them that Bactrian, Sogdianian, Arachosian, Zangarian, Areian, and Parthyaean cavalrymen (and Persian cavalrymen, the so-called Euacae) were distributed into the Companion Cavalry if they were plainly preeminent in rank, appearance, or some other quality. Furthermore, a fifth cavalry regiment had been created. It was not entirely barbarian, but when the whole cavalry was

13. The word "Epigoni" loosely translates as "successors" or "trainees." These Persian youth formed the first corps of foreign troops who were trained to occupy the central positions in the battle line, which had always, up until now, belonged to Macedonians. Alexander had come to realize that his country's small population could not forever fill the ranks of the new imperial army, and perhaps he also foresaw that a mixed armed force would be more successful than an all-European one in pacifying Asian provinces.

increased in size, barbarians were enrolled in it, and the *agema* now included Cophen, the son of Artabazus; Hydarnes and Artiboles, the sons of Mazaeus; Sisines and Phradasmenes, the sons of Phrataphernes, the satrap of Parthyaea and Hyrcania; Itanes, the son of Oxyartes and brother of Roxane, Alexander's wife; and the brothers Aegobares and Mithrobaeus. Hystaspes the Bactrian had been appointed as their commander, and they had been issued Macedonian spears instead of barbarian javelins.

All these developments troubled the Macedonians, who felt that Alexander was becoming utterly barbarian in spirit and regarded Macedonian customs and the Macedonians themselves with disrespect.

After making a naval excursion down the Euphrates River and into the Persian Gulf, Alexander brought his army to Opis on the banks of the Tigris. There, the resentment his native Macedonians had long felt over his plan to "Persify" his forces finally broke out into the open.

[VII.8] On reaching Opis, Alexander assembled the Macedonians and announced that he was discharging from the army all who, through age or disability, were unfit to serve. He was sending them home, and as they departed he would give them enough to arouse the envy of the Macedonians at home and excite their desire to share the same dangers and toils.

Alexander undoubtedly assumed his words would please the Macedonians. But as they felt they had already been slighted by Alexander and were considered useless in war, they were vexed yet again, and not unreasonably, by his words. Throughout the whole army the men had been exasperated on many other occasions. By now they had often been pained by Alexander's Persian apparel, as it conveyed the same message, and by his supplying the Epigoni with Macedonian equipment and his inclusion of foreign cavalrymen in the ranks of the Companions.[14] Accordingly, they could not bear to sit

14. The integration of elite Persian horsemen into the Companion Cavalry is also referred to in VII.6. Possibly they formed separate units within the larger corps of the Companions, such that in a few cases Macedonian and Persian soldiers were fighting side by side.

silent but charged him to release them all and take his "father" along on his next campaign, referring mockingly to Ammon.

Alexander was quicker to anger at that period,[15] and because the barbarians were now dancing attendance on him, he was no longer as kind to the Macedonians as in the past. As soon as he heard their protests he leaped down from the platform with his officers, ordered them to arrest the principal agitators, and pointed out to the shield-bearers the men they should arrest, thirteen in number. He commanded that they be led away for execution.[16] Thunderstruck, the rest kept silent, whereupon Alexander again mounted the platform and spoke as follows:[17]

[VII.9] "I will speak not to quell your longing for home, Macedonians, for you may go wherever you wish as far as I am concerned, but so you may realize, as you depart, the character of our conduct toward one another.

"I will begin, as is appropriate, with Philip, my father, who took you up when you were helpless wanderers, most of you dressed in hides, pasturing a few flocks in the mountains and in their defense fighting ineptly with your neighbors, the Illyrians, Triballians, and Thracians. He gave you cloaks to wear instead of skins, led you down from the mountains to the plains, and made you a match in battle for your barbarian neighbors, so your safety depended not on your mountain strongholds but on your own courage. He made you city-dwellers,[18] and by means of laws and good customs gave you an orderly way of life. He made you masters of the very barbarians who had

15. A further suggestion, like that in VII.4 (page 155) above, that Alexander's psychological state was deteriorating after the reverses of the preceding year: his failure to convince his men to cross the Hyphasis, his close brush with death in the attack on the Malli, and the Gedrosia disaster.

16. One of the most startling instances of Alexander's arbitrary use of power, not covered up this time by Arrian or his sources.

17. The following speech, like the one Arrian gives to Alexander at the Hyphasis (see pages 134–6 above), has been deemed a complete invention by some historians, containing little if any authentic content. Even as a rhetorical exercise, though, it provides insight into what Arrian believed Alexander *could* have said.

18. The Macedonian capital, Pella, had taken on some of the sophistication of a classical Greek polis during Philip's era.

plundered you earlier of men and property—you who had been their slaves and subjects—and added the greater part of Thrace to Macedonia. Having captured the most advantageous places along the coast, he opened up the country to trade, made it safe for you to work the mines, and made you masters of the Thessalians, who in times past had frightened you half to death. By humbling the Phocians, he made your route into Greece broad and open instead of narrow and difficult.[19] As for the Athenians and Thebans, who were always lying in wait for us, he brought them so low, at a time when I myself was sharing his toils, that instead of our paying tribute to the Athenians and obeying the Thebans, it was *their* turn to look to *us* for their security. On his arrival in the Peloponnese Philip again put state affairs in order. Appointed as leader with absolute power over the rest of Greece for the expedition against Persia, he conferred as much renown on the Macedonian state as on himself.

"Such are the benefits conferred on you by my father. But though substantial when judged by themselves, they appear small when compared with the benefits *I* have conferred. Having inherited from my father a few gold and silver cups, with not even sixty talents in the treasury and with debts incurred by Philip amounting to nearly five hundred talents, I myself borrowed an additional eight hundred and set out from the land from which you were barely able to get a living. Heading straight for the Hellespont, I opened a passage for you, though the Persians then held sway at sea. Overpowering the Persian satraps with my cavalry, I added all of Ionia to your domain and all of Aeolia, both Phrygias and Lydia, and took Miletus by siege. As for all the other countries that came over to me willingly, I seized and gave you them for your own profit. The treasures from Egypt and Cyrene, all of which I acquired without a battle, go to you; Hollow Syria, Palestine, and Mesopotamia are your property; Babylon, Bactra, and Susa are yours; and the wealth of the Lydians, the treasures of the Persians, the riches of India, and the surrounding Ocean are yours. You are satraps, generals, and commanders.

"As for me, what is left to me after these labors except this purple and this diadem?[20] I have acquired nothing in my own name, nor

19. That is, by gaining control over the pass of Thermopylae, a narrow choke point that the Greeks had been easily able to seal off prior to this.
20. The author of the speech apparently forgets that the adoption of royal purple by Alexander was a sore point among his troops.

can anyone point to treasures of my own, but only *your* possessions or all that is guarded on your behalf. For there would be no point in my keeping anything, since I eat the same food as you do and take the same sleep. Though, for that matter, I doubt that my food is as dainty as the fare some of you eat, and I *know* I keep awake and stand watch for you, that you may sleep soundly.[21]

[VII.10] "Now perhaps you feel that it was *you* who were toiling and suffering hardships, while I acquired these treasures as your leader without toil and hardship. But who among you imagines that he has toiled more on my behalf than I have on his? Come on, then— let any of you strip and show his wounds, and I will show mine. For in my own case, there is no part of my body, at least not in front, that has been left unwounded, and there is no weapon, held or hurled, whose marks I do not carry. On the contrary, I have been wounded by the sword when fighting hand to hand, pierced by arrows, struck by missiles from catapults, and hit time and again by rocks and clubs.[22] For *your* sake, for the sake of your renown and your wealth, I lead you, a conquering army, through every land and sea, every river, every mountain, and every plain. I have made the same marriages as you have, and the children of many of you will be related to my own. And if any of you had incurred debts, though you are handsomely paid and have had many opportunities to plunder after a siege, I paid them off without taking the trouble to find out how they were incurred. Most of you have golden crowns—immortal remembrances of your valor and my esteem. And anyone who has died has met with a glorious end and a splendid funeral. Bronze statues of most of your dead comrades stand at home,[23] and their honored parents are exempt from all public duty and tax. For none of you died fleeing the enemy while *I* held command.

"I was now going to send back those of you who are unfit for war, to be envied by those at home. But since you all wish to go, be gone,

---

21. Another point on which the speech's author has not carefully cross-checked his facts; Alexander had long been resented for sleeping late after all-night drinking parties.

22. Plutarch, on two occasions, rather luridly catalogs all the wounds and scars that Alexander's body exhibited; see *Moralia* 327a–b and 341a–c.

23. "Most" is a gross exaggeration here, for it would mean that Macedonia would have been heaped high with bronze statues. Only the soldiers who died at the battle of the Granicus are thought to have been so honored.

all of you, and report, when you get home, that Alexander, your king, who conquered the Persians, Medes, Bactrians, and Sacae, who sub-jugated the Uxians, Arachosians, and Drangians, who acquired the lands of the Parthyaeans, Chorasmians, and Hyrcanians as far as the Caspian Sea, who crossed the Caucasus beyond the Caspian Gates, and the Oxus, the Tanais, and the Indus, too, which none had ever crossed but Dionysus, and the Hydaspes, the Acesines, and the Hydraotes, and who would have crossed the Hyphasis had you not shrunk back, and who burst into the great sea by both outlets of the Indus, and who traversed the Gedrosian desert, which none had crossed with an army, and along the way acquired Carmania and the land of the Oritans, the fleet having already sailed from India to Persia—tell them, why don't you, that when you returned to Susa you abandoned him and departed, turning him over to the protection of the barbarians you had conquered. Such a report may win you renown from men and will doubtless be holy in the sight of god.[24] Away with you!"

[VII.11] So saying, he quickly leaped down from the platform and passed into the palace, where he began to neglect his person and was seen by none of his Companions, not even the next day.[25] On the third day, he called in the foremost Persians and distributed among them the commands of his battalions and directed that only those whom he called his kinsmen were permitted to kiss him.

As for the Macedonians, when Alexander's speech ended[26] they remained in stunned silence near the platform, nor did anyone follow the departing king except the Companions and bodyguards who attended him. Most of them remained where they were; they had no idea what to do or say, but were unwilling to leave. But when they were told about the Persians and Medes, the commands being given

24. The tone here is bitterly sarcastic.

25. This moody withdrawal was a familiar ploy that Alexander had used before—after the killing of Cleitus and amid the Hyphasis mutiny (see pages 102 and 138 above). Alexander may have been consciously emulating his mythic ancestor, Achilles, who withdrew to his tent after being slighted by Agamemnon.

26. Once again, as in his description of events at the Hyphasis (see page 138), Arrian has jumped out of time sequence to show Alexander's long withdrawal into his tent; he then returns to the narrative present with the reaction of the men following the speech.

to the Persians, the barbarian troops being drafted into companies, and the Macedonian names—a Persian *agema*, Persian "infantry companions," other *astheteroi*, a Persian battalion of "silver shields,"[27] and the Companion Cavalry with a new royal *agema*—they could no longer contain themselves but ran together to the palace, flung their weapons before the door (to signal that they were the king's suppliants), and stood before it, shouting and pleading to be admitted. They said they were willing to surrender the men who were responsible for the present disturbance and those who had started the uproar, but they would not depart, day or night, unless Alexander took pity on them.

When this had been reported to Alexander, he hurried out. Seeing them so downcast and hearing most of them wailing piteously, he, too, shed tears. He stepped forward as if to speak, while they remained in the posture of suppliants. One of them, a man named Callines, who was distinguished by age and rank (he was a commander of the Companion Cavalry), said, "Sire, what grieves the Macedonians is that you have now made some of the Persians your kinsmen, and that Persians are called 'kinsmen of Alexander' and may kiss you, but none of the Macedonians has yet enjoyed that honor."

Breaking in, Alexander said, "But I consider all of you my kinsmen and from now on I will call you so." At these words Callines approached and kissed Alexander, and anyone else who wished to do so kissed him as well. They then retrieved their weapons and returned to camp, shouting and chanting their song of triumph.

Alexander now performed a sacrifice to the gods to whom he customarily sacrificed, and held a public banquet. He seated all the Macedonians around him, and next to them the Persians, and next to *them* the other foreigners notable for rank or some other merit. Drawing wine from the same bowl, Alexander and those around him poured the same libations, after the Greek seers and the Magi had led the way. Along with other requests, Alexander prayed that the Macedonians and Persians of his empire might enjoy concord and fellowship. It is said that nine thousand men attended the banquet and that all of them poured the same libation and joined in a song of victory.[28]

27. The "silver shields" appear to have been the same company as the shield-bearers, renamed and perhaps reorganized late in Alexander's campaign.
28. This is the famous "loving cup" toast to which Plutarch in antiquity and Sir William Tarn in recent times (*Alexander the Great*) attributed such

Following this tempestuous showdown with his troops and the festive, though doubtless uneasy, reconciliation, Alexander carried through his plan to send thousands of senior Macedonian veterans home and infuse new blood, drawn from the youth of Persia, into his army. Craterus, though ill, was detailed to lead the veterans back to Macedonia and, once there, to assume command of the home front, replacing Antipater, who had loyally kept Macedonia and Greece secure for Alexander for twelve years now. Antipater, in turn, was to gather fresh reinforcements and lead them to Alexander in Babylon. Apparently, Alexander had gotten wind in the letters he received from home of the bad feelings between Antipater and his own mother, Olympias, and sought to get Antipater off the scene before the discord caused serious problems.

From Opis the army moved on to Ecbatana in Syria, where another sharp blow was about to fall on Alexander.

d. The death of Hephaestion

[VII.14] At Ecbatana Alexander performed a sacrifice, as was his custom after successful ventures, and held competitions in athletics and the arts and drinking parties with his Companions. At that point Hephaestion fell ill. It is said that on the seventh day of his illness the stadium was filled with spectators, as it was the day of the boys' athletic competition. When it was reported to Alexander that Hephaestion's condition was grave, he rushed to his friend's side but found him no longer alive.

A variety of accounts have been written about Alexander's grief. All writers agree that it was profound. As for Alexander's conduct on the occasion, reports vary depending on whether the writer was well- or ill-disposed to Hephaestion or to Alexander himself. Among the writers who describe Alexander's unrestrained behavior, some seem to me to think that everything he did or said in his intense grief over his dearest friend was to his credit; others, however, find his conduct shameful—befitting neither a king nor Alexander. Some say that for most of that day, having flung himself onto his friend's body, Alexander moaned and wept and refused to leave until his Companions carried him off by force. Others maintain that he remained on the body

significance. Tarn's notion that the idea of universal brotherhood of all humankind was born at this banquet has largely been rejected by later scholars. Nevertheless, it seems clear that Alexander, acting out of a variety of motivations, was seeking to knit the two ruling peoples of Asia and Europe together.

for the whole day and the whole night. Still others say that he hanged the doctor, Glaucias, because of a drug given by mistake, or because Glaucias, though he had seen Hephaestion drinking heavily, had not intervened. That Alexander cut his hair over the corpse I do not consider improbable given his emulation of Achilles, whom from boyhood he had sought to rival.[29] Some say that Alexander himself drove the chariot on which the body was borne—an implausible report, in my opinion. Others say that Alexander commanded that the temple of Asclepius in Ecbatana be razed—a barbaric act utterly out of character for Alexander, but more in keeping with Xerxes' arrogance toward the gods and the tale about the fetters he lowered into the Hellespont with the actual intention of punishing it.[30]

Another story, one that strikes me as not completely implausible, has it that when Alexander marched to Babylon, many ambassadors from Greece met him on the way, including a deputation from Epidaurus. When these men had obtained what they requested from Alexander, he gave them an offering to convey to Asclepius,[31] adding, "though Asclepius has not treated me fairly, as he failed to save my companion, whom I valued as I do my own life."

Most writers have reported that Alexander gave orders that a hero's rites were always to be used when sacrificing to Hephaestion.[32] Some say that he also sent envoys to Ammon to ask the god whether it was permissible to sacrifice to Hephaestion as to a god, but the oracle would not allow it.

All the writers agree that for the two days following Hephaestion's death Alexander neither tasted food nor took any care of his

---

29. In Homer's *Iliad* Achilles cuts his hair—a mark of extreme grief—when mourning the death of Patroclus. Alexander and Hephaestion had symbolically assumed the identities of Achilles and Patroclus when passing through Troy at the start of the campaign (see page 35 above).

30. According to Herodotus (*Histories* 7.32ff.), Xerxes, when preparing his invasion of Greece in 480 B.C.E., had thus insulted the Hellespont after a pontoon bridge he was building across it had been destroyed in a storm. Arrian refuses to contemplate the possibility that, having become a new ruler of the Persians, Alexander had become another Xerxes.

31. God of healing and medicine.

32. A "hero" in Greek religious terms is a figure neither entirely divine nor entirely mortal. Heroes such as Achilles, Agamemnon, and Ajax were thought to retain the power to aid the living even after death, and therefore ritual sacrifices were conducted at their tombs.

person, but lay either moaning or in grief-stricken silence. He reportedly ordered a pyre to be made ready for him in Babylon at a cost of ten thousand talents[33] (some say it cost even more) and a period of mourning to be observed throughout the barbarian land. It is said that many of Alexander's Companions dedicated themselves and their weapons to the dead Hephaestion. Eumenes, whose quarrel with Hephaestion we mentioned a little earlier,[34] was the first to come up with this idea, lest he appear to Alexander to be exulting over Hephaestion's death. In order that Hephaestion's name might not be lost to the regiment, Alexander assigned no one else as commander of the Companion Cavalry in Hephaestion's place. The regiment continued to be called Hephaestion's regiment and followed the standard Hephaestion had designed. Alexander planned to hold a competition in athletics and the arts far more distinguished than all previous competitions, both in the number of competitors and the fortune spent on it, as he provided three thousand competitors in all. It was these men, they say, who competed a little later at Alexander's funeral.

e. Alexander's illness and death

Alexander slowly emerged from the paralyzing grief he felt at Hephaestion's death, and his restless energy began to crave new projects. In the winter that ended the year 324 B.C.E., he led a campaign against the Cossaeans, a Mesopotamian hill tribe that had long preyed on travelers and passersby. According to Arrian, neither the harsh weather nor the rough terrain slowed Alexander down, for "nothing in the military sphere was beyond Alexander's powers, once he set out to do it" (VII.15). The Cossaeans were either destroyed or, according to some sources, resettled in cities Alexander had founded.

The king now approached the city of Babylon, which, in all likelihood, he planned to adopt as the capital of his empire; Macedonian Pella was too far to the west and too provincial to serve this purpose. Grand plans were set in motion everywhere for the improvement of the city and for the launching of the next major campaign. Great sums of money were allotted to rebuilding the temple of Bel in the city's center, dredging a vast new harbor, and building and manning a new fleet of warships, a fleet equipped

33. A fantastic sum. The pyre as described by Diodorus (17.115) was seven stories high and bedecked with sculptures at each level. The charred remains of the structure have been uncovered in Babylon's ruins.
34. This was mentioned in a passage not included in this volume.

to sail against Arabia. For Alexander had a new enemy in his sights, the Arabs, allegedly because they, alone among peoples of the known world, had failed to send a delegation to him in Mesopotamia to give tokens of acquiescence.

As Alexander prepared to enter Babylon, he is said to have received various signs and portents warning that disaster awaited him there, especially if he entered the city by its western gate. But the road to the eastern entrance was too muddy and swampy for the army to manage, so Alexander ended up using the western gate anyway. At this point, Arrian writes, his doom was sealed: "A divine force was leading him along the path where, once he passed by, he must die. It was better, perhaps, for him to depart life then, at the height of his fame and most longed for by humankind, before falling victim to the misfortunes that afflict all humanity"(VII.16).

Before Alexander's doom closed in on him, however, he made one more set of arrangements to ensure that Hephaestion received proper honors after death, prompting severe censure from Arrian.

[VII.23] The envoys from Ammon now arrived, whom Alexander had sent to ask how he might appropriately honor Hephaestion. The envoys reported that Ammon had declared it appropriate to sacrifice to him as to a hero. Alexander was pleased with the response, and from then on honored Hephaestion with a hero's rites. He also sent a letter to Cleomenes, a despicable man who had committed many crimes in Egypt. I do not fault the letter for its fond remembrance of the dead Hephaestion, but much of its other content was objectionable. For the letter said that hero's shrines were to be built in Egyptian Alexandria, in the city itself and on the island of Pharos near the lighthouse—shrines that were to be unsurpassed in grandeur and extravagance. Cleomenes was told to see to it that the shrines were named after Hephaestion, and Hephaestion's name was also to be inscribed on all contracts drawn up between merchants. This I cannot fault, except insofar as Alexander was wasting effort on trivial matters. But what follows I utterly deplore. "If I find," ran the letter, "that the temples in Egypt and the shrines of Hephaestion are well-built, I will pardon you for any wrong you have done thus far, and if you misbehave in the future, you will meet with no unpleasantness from me." This message, directed from a great king to a man who held sway over a large and well-populated region, I cannot approve, especially as the man was a villain.

[VII.24] But Alexander's end was near. Aristobulus says that the following incident foreshadowed what was to come. Alexander was

distributing into the Macedonian battalions the troops who had arrived from Persia with Peucestas and from the coast with Philoxenus
and Menander. Feeling thirsty, Alexander departed the council, leaving the royal throne unoccupied. On either side of the throne stood
silver-footed couches on which the Companions who attended him
had been sitting. Now some obscure fellow (some say he was a con-
vict on parole) saw the throne and couches unoccupied and the eunuchs standing near the throne, the Companions having risen with
the king when he went out. Passing through the group of eunuchs,
the man went up and sat on the throne. The eunuchs, in obedience
to some Persian custom, did not remove him but tore their clothes
and beat their chests and faces as at some calamity. When the incident
was reported to Alexander, he gave orders for the culprit to be tortured on the rack, in order to learn whether his action had been part
of a plot. But the man maintained that he had only acted on an impulse. This actually strengthened the seers' impression that disaster
was looming for Alexander.

Not many days later, having made his customary offerings for
good fortune as well as other rites that had been suggested by
prophecy, Alexander feasted with his friends and drank far into the
night. He is also said to have distributed sacrificial victims and wine
throughout the army's regiments and companies of a hundred. Some
have written that when he wanted to leave the drinking bout to go to
bed, he encountered Medius, the most persuasive of the Companions
at the time. Medius asked Alexander to join him in a carousal, as the
party would be a pleasant one.

[VII.25] The royal diaries give the following account. Alexander
drank and caroused with Medius. Then, after rising and bathing, he
slept, dined again with Medius, and again drank far into the night. On
leaving the carousal he bathed. After his bath he took a little food and
slept where he was, as he was already in a fever.[35]

---

35. The cause of Alexander's illness and death has been variously identified as
malaria, scarlet fever, alcoholism aggravated by the lung injury sustained in India (or vice versa), and even syphilis. The theory that he was poisoned by political enemies circulated widely in antiquity, Antipater and his son Cassander
being most often named as the agents (with Aristotle, in some versions, having
prepared the poison, in revenge for the death of Callisthenes). However, Alexander's symptoms, reported in exacting detail below thanks to the record preserved
in the "royal diaries," do not seem to fit the pattern of death by poison.

He was carried out on a couch to make his customary daily offerings; after sacrificing, he lay down in the men's quarters until dark.
At that time he gave his officers instructions about the march and voyage: the infantry were to depart in three days, and those who were accompanying him by sea were to set sail in four. He was then carried
on his couch to the river. He boarded a vessel and sailed across to the
park, where he again bathed and rested. The next day he again bathed
and made his customary offerings. Going to his canopy bed, he lay
down and talked with Medius. He also instructed his officers to meet
him early the next morning. He then took a little food. Carried again
to his canopy bed, he spent the whole night in a fever.

The next day he bathed and sacrificed. He informed Nearchus
and the other officers that the voyage would start in two days' time.
The next day he again bathed and performed the appointed sacrifices;
thereafter his fever never left him. Even so, he called in his officers
and instructed them to prepare for the voyage. He bathed in the
evening, and afterward was already very ill. The next day he was
carried to the building near the bathing pool, where he performed the
appointed sacrifices. Though very ill, he called in his most important
officers and again instructed them about the voyage. The next day he
managed to be carried out to the sacrifices; he made his offerings, and
in spite of his condition continued to instruct his officers about the
voyage. The next day, though ill, he still performed the appointed sacrifices. He instructed the generals to wait in the court, the chiliarchs
and pentacosiarchs outside his door. Now, desperately ill, he was
carried from the park to the palace. When his officers entered, he recognized them but said nothing; his voice was gone. He was gravely ill
with fever that night and day, and his condition remained unchanged
throughout the next night and day.

[VII.26] These events have been recorded in the royal diaries,
where we also read that the soldiers longed to visit him, some in hopes
of seeing him still alive, others because it had been announced that he
was already dead, and I imagine they suspected that his death was being concealed by his bodyguards. But most of his men forced their
way in to see Alexander out of grief and longing for their king. They
say that he had already lost his voice by the time the men moved past
him, but that he greeted each of them, raising his head with difficulty
and making a sign with his eyes. The royal diaries say that Peithon,
Attalus, Demophon, and Peucestas, together with Cleomenes,
Menidas, and Seleucus, passed the night in the temple of Sarapis and

asked the god whether it would be better for Alexander to be brought
to the temple as a suppliant and be cared for by the god. The god's response was that he should not be brought to the temple, as it would
be better for him to remain where he was. His Companions reported
the response, and shortly thereafter Alexander died, as that, after all,
was now "better."

Aristobulus and Ptolemy have nothing more to add. Others have
recorded that when his Companions asked him to whom he was leaving the kingdom, he answered, "To the strongest man."

*Whether or not this last remark is authentic, it is certain that Alexander had
failed to designate or prepare a successor or make any arrangements for a
transfer of executive power. Perhaps he had hoped that Hephaestion would
succeed him and had not made an alternate choice after his friend's sudden
death some months earlier. Or perhaps he believed the legends about his
divine parentage enough to hope that he would never die. Whatever the reason, Alexander's lack of forethought for the future of his empire has been
taken by many historians as unmistakable proof of his megalomania.*

*The king had, however, fathered an heir, though it was not yet known at
the time of his death that Roxane's unborn child was to be a boy. The Companions, desperately seeking some way to preserve a legitimate line of succession, came up with a plan to appoint Perdiccas, one of their number, as
regent until Alexander's child, if male, attained an age at which he could assume the throne. But the rank-and-file troops of the infantry contingents suspected a plot by the nobles to usurp royal power. They backed a member of
the royal family who was already of age, though he was thought to suffer
from mental defects: Arrhidaeus, Alexander's mentally impaired half-
brother, who had accompanied the army all through Asia without playing
any significant part in its campaigns. To avoid the looming rift between army
factions, a compromise was reached by which Arrhidaeus, now known as
Philip III, was made co-regent with Alexander's unborn child, and Perdiccas
became regent for both.*

*This tripartite division of power was little more than a power vacuum,
however, which Alexander's most ambitious generals quickly rushed to fill.
The so-called Successors would go on to battle for supremacy over the next
two decades and more, employing Alexander's highly effective military
strategies and his crack veterans against one another. In the turmoil both
Philip III and Alexander's son by Roxane—officially known as Alexander IV,
though he never spent a day on the throne—were executed, and many of
the other high commanders of the Asian march met violent deaths. When a
stable order finally emerged, the Macedonian empire had been split into*

pieces, never to be reassembled until absorbed by the Romans over the second and first centuries B.C.E.

Indeed, Alexander's empire had existed as a unified whole for only a few months. India had already begun to secede before the Macedonian army had even left its borders, and after 301 it received official independence. Other provinces, including mainland Greece, were plotting or actively undertaking rebellions in the year before Alexander died. The empire's vast territory had been so rapidly aggregated that only a leader of Alexander's stature could have forced it to cohere; and Alexander himself had done too little to bring this cohesion about, preferring new external wars to the more sedate tasks of governance and stabilization. Perhaps the breakup of the empire was therefore inevitable, even if a single legitimate leader had taken over in Alexander's stead.

Ultimately, it was only the force of Alexander's remarkable personality that could hold the tricontinental empire together for even a brief space of time—the personality that ever since has been the focus of so much examination and debate, and about which today's experts still have profound disagreements. Modern readers of Arrian and the other ancient sources on Alexander must form their own opinions. Was this a drunken tyrant with delusions of godhead, wading through blood and slaughter toward his goal of world domination? Or was he a man of superhuman talent and drive who set out to reshape the world after his own ideals, but whose lust for glory undermined his better nature? Modern historians have mostly inclined toward the former view, whereas Arrian preferred the latter. We close this volume with the closing passage of the Anabasis, *in which Arrian formulates his final, glowing assessment of Alexander's nature and achievements.*

[VII.28] Alexander died in the hundred and fourteenth Olympiad, during the archonship of Hegesias at Athens.[36] He lived, according to Aristobulus, for thirty-two years and eight months and reigned for twelve years and those same eight months. He possessed an extraordinary physical beauty and love of toil, proved exceedingly shrewd and courageous, and was unsurpassed in his love of honor, in his zest for danger, and in the strict performance of his religious duties. With regard to bodily pleasures he enjoyed perfect self-control; where pleasures of the mind were concerned, he was insatiable only for praise. He was remarkably clever at seeing at a glance what had to be done when it was not yet obvious, was exceptionally lucky at guessing

36. 323 B.C.E.

what was likely to happen based on the available evidence, and showed outstanding skill at drawing up, arming, and equipping an army. In raising morale—in filling his soldiers with good hopes and dispelling their fear in times of danger by his own fearlessness—he showed himself supremely gifted. All that needed to be done in the open he did with the utmost courage; he also excelled at snatching the advantage from his enemies before they suspected what was coming. He was utterly reliable in honoring promises and agreements, and no one was less likely to be taken in by deceivers. Uncommonly sparing in the use of money for his own pleasures, he spent ungrudgingly for the benefit of others.

[VII.29] If any offense was given by Alexander's sharpness or anger, or if he carried to an extreme his taste for barbarian ways, I do not myself regard it as a serious matter. One might reasonably take into account Alexander's youth, his uninterrupted good fortune, and the fact that those who consort with kings always do and always will exercise a bad influence, given that they are disposed to consider what will please, not what will be for the best. But Alexander is the only ancient king I know of whose nobility moved him to feel remorse for his misdeeds. Most men, if they recognize that they have erred, defend what they have done as if it were perfectly proper. Thinking to conceal their error, they exercise poor judgment. For in my view, the only remedy for a misdeed is for the guilty party to acknowledge his error and show clearly that he repents it. In consequence, those who have suffered obtain some relief from his admission that he acted improperly, while he himself is left with the hope that in the future he will not commit a similar offense if he is manifestly dismayed by his prior offenses.

The fact that Alexander traced his birth to a god does not impress me as a serious fault; it may merely have been a clever means of securing his subjects' respect. He does not seem to me to have been any less illustrious a king than Minos or Aeacus or Rhadamanthys, whose births, traced by the ancients to Zeus, elicited no charge of hubris, or than Theseus, the son of Poseidon, or Ion, the son of Apollo. His Persian apparel strikes me as a tactic adopted with the barbarians in mind, in order that their king might not seem foreign to them in every respect, and with regard to the Macedonians, that he might have some refuge from the native sharpness and arrogance of Macedonia. It seems to me he had the same end in view when he included the Persian "apple-bearers" in the Macedonian squadrons and the Persian nobles in the *agemas*. As for Alexander's carousals, they were prolonged not because he cared for wine—for he did not drink much wine—but out of kindness to his Companions.[37]

[VII.30] Anyone who reproaches Alexander should not simply cite those deeds that deserve to be reproached. Instead, on collecting in one place all that concerns Alexander, let his critic then consider who *he* is and what sort of luck *he* has been favored with that he proposes to reproach Alexander, given who the man became and the enormous success he attained, the undisputed king of both continents whose name reached every land—whereas *he* is a lesser man, toiling at trivial things and not even handling *them* with any ability.

I suppose there was not a race of men nor any city at that time nor any single person whom Alexander's name did not reach. I therefore assume that a man unlike any other in the world would not have been born without the intervention of the gods. Oracles are said to have indicated this at Alexander's death, and various apparitions that were seen and dreams that were dreamed, and the honor in which Alexander has to this day been held by humankind and the memory of him that surpasses the merely human. Even today, after so much time has passed, other oracles in his honor have been proclaimed for the people of Macedonia.

Though I have myself had occasion to find fault in the course of my survey of Alexander's career, I am not ashamed to admire Alexander himself. If I have condemned certain acts of his, I did so out of my regard for truth and also for the benefit of humankind. That, after all, was my purpose in embarking on this history, and I, too, have been favored with help from god.

37. Arrian's forgiving attitude toward the behaviors in the above paragraph stands in sharp contrast to his presentation of them earlier in the text. At IV.7, for example, he explicitly censures the adoption of Persian dress as an arrogant, barbarian affectation (see page 99), without noting the possibility that it was merely a political expedient.

Glossary of Names, Places, Peoples, and Military Terms

All dates are B.C.E. unless otherwise indicated.

Achilles: Mythical hero celebrated in Homer's *Iliad* as the best of the Greek warriors at Troy. Alexander, who thought of himself as a descendant of Achilles on his mother's side, often took this legendary ancestor as his role model.

Aegae: Important Macedonian city (modern-day Vergina), originally the capital of the country, where Philip was assassinated and where members of the royal family were interred. Recent excavations have brought to light a tomb there that may well be Philip's.

agema: The "leading" or advance unit of a military contingent, composed of its most effective troops. Arrian usually uses the term to refer to the elite corps of the Companion Cavalry, those who were at the forefront of the decisive charges in most battles.

Agis III: Spartan king who led a Greek rebellion against Macedonian rule in 331. He was defeated by Antipater's forces and killed in battle.

Alexander of Lyncestis: A potential contender for the Macedonian throne after Philip's death; accused of collaborating with Persia to assassinate Alexander, he was arrested in 333 and executed in 330.

Alexander III, "the Great": Born to Philip and Olympias in 356, he ascended the throne after his father's murder in 336; died in Babylon, probably of disease, in 323. He inherited from his father the most powerful army in the world, along with a plan to use it in an invasion of western Asia. In the period 334–327 Alexander conquered all the territory that had comprised the Persian empire, and then spent two more years marching eastward through India until compelled by his troops to turn homeward. He was thought to have planned further campaigns against Arabia and Carthage, evidently with the goal of subduing the entire known world.

Alexandria: Egyptian city founded by Alexander at the mouth of the Nile in 331; later it became the leading hub of Mediterranean commerce. The same name was also given to numerous other, smaller

174

cities, distinguished as "Alexandria-in-Areia," "Farthest Alexandria," and the like. Alexander's remains were interred here.

Ammon: Egyptian deity generally identified with Zeus. Alexander consulted the oracle of Ammon in Egypt (331) and either believed or claimed that he was descended from the god.

Antipater: Father of Cassander, Alexander's boyhood friend; appointed by Alexander to govern Macedonia's European empire while the Asian campaign was under way.

Aornos: Hilltop settlement in modern-day Pakistan, thought to be impregnable even when assaulted by Heracles due to its natural defenses. Taken by Alexander in 326.

Aristobulus: Minor official serving in the Asian campaign; later the author of a detailed memoir, now lost, on which Arrian relied (along with that of Ptolemy) when composing the *Anabasis.*

Aristotle: Greek philosopher and head of the Peripatetic school; appointed Alexander's tutor for three years starting near the end of 343.

Arrhidaeus: Illegitimate, half-witted son of Philip, half-brother to Alexander; after the death of Alexander ruled briefly as Philip III, under the regency of Perdiccas.

Arrian: A Greek who studied with the Stoic sage Epictetus in his youth, then served Rome as governor of an eastern province and commander of a sizable army. He wrote the *Anabasis of Alexander* sometime in the first half of the second century C.E., along with several other works dealing with both military and spiritual topics.

Arses: Youngest son of Artaxerxes III who came to power briefly after his father's murder. Bagoas, a palace eunuch who poisoned Artaxerxes in 338, also dispatched Arses in 336 (perhaps with the help of Darius III).

Artaxerxes III (Ochus): The last great Persian king, whose long reign (358–338) saw a great consolidation and centralization of imperial power; murdered by the eunuch Bagoas at just the moment when Philip, increasingly his enemy and rival, was preparing to attack.

Athens: Leading naval power in the Aegean and leading supporter of Greek freedom in the face of Philip's hegemony; defeated at the battle of Chaeronea in 338. Torn by foreign policy disputes, Athens stayed out of both the Theban revolt against Macedonia in 335 and the revolt of King Agis in 331; its own rebellion, the so-called Lamian War of 323–322, ended in its final defeat.

Attalus: Son-in-law of Parmenio and uncle of Cleopatra, Philip's fifth wife. Alexander perceived him as an enemy and had him assassinated shortly after coming to power.

Babylon: Mesopotamian city that had become one of the capitals of the Persian empire and was likely to have been Alexander's capital as well. Alexander captured it after his victory at Gaugamela and celebrated the rites of Bel, its chief deity. He returned there in 324 amid warnings that the city would spell doom for him, and he died there in June 323.

Bactria: Northeastern province of the Persian empire comprising what is today northern Afghanistan and southern Uzbekistan and Tajikistan. The final Persian resistance to Alexander's conquest was mounted there, forcing the Macedonians to fight a protracted guerrilla war in 329 and 328. Bactra (sometimes called Zariaspa) was its capital city.

Bessus: Satrap of Bactria and fierce foe of Alexander. He fled Gaugamela with Darius, whom he later deposed in a coup d'état. Hunted by Alexander through Bactria in 329, he was betrayed by his ally Spitamenes and turned over to the Macedonians for execution.

Bucephalas: Prized Thessalian horse named "Ox-head" after a marking or brand on its coat. Tamed by Alexander in 347 and ridden by him throughout his subsequent campaigns, Bucephalas finally died in 326, at the age of thirty, in the battle against Porus.

Calanus: Indian sage encountered by Alexander in the city of Taxila and attracted into the king's retinue. He accompanied Alexander as far as the return to Persia in 324, when he committed a spectacular suicide by burning himself alive in front of the whole army.

Callisthenes: Nephew of Aristotle and court-appointed historian of Alexander's Asian campaign. He composed a now-lost account of events up to 330, in which he seems to have celebrated Alexander as a superhuman figure. In the dissent at court over Alexander's attempt to impose a Persian form of obeisance, Callisthenes became a prominent voice for the opposition. Shortly afterward, he was implicated in the conspiracy of the pages and was probably executed (some sources say he died of disease while awaiting trial).

Cassander: Son of Antipater and boyhood friend of Alexander. He remained in Pella guarding the home front during the Asian campaign, then he joined Alexander in Babylon shortly before the king's death, leading to (probably baseless) rumors that he had collaborated in poisoning him. In the wars of the Successors, Cassander fought to gain control of Macedonia and Greece and succeeded in 316. He ended Alexander's line by executing Olympias, Roxane, and the young Alexander IV.

Chaeronea: The battle that in 338 ended an attempt by Thebes and Athens to prevent Philip from dominating mainland Greece. Alexander led the decisive cavalry charge that smashed the Theban infantry and defeated the Sacred Band.

Cleander: A top Macedonian commander posted to Ecbatana in Media. According to Quintus Curtius, he was recruited by Alexander to help murder Parmenio. Later he was executed on Alexander's orders.

Cleitarchus: Most probably the author of the romanticized, sensationalized history of Alexander's march that was the principal source for the "vulgate" tradition (the works of Diodorus, Quintus Curtius, and Pompeius Trogus). He wrote sometime in the third century B.C.E. but probably did not accompany Alexander in Asia.

Cleitus: A close friend of Alexander and senior officer in the army; saved Alexander's life at the battle of the Granicus by disabling a Persian opponent. In 328 Cleitus pricked Alexander's rage with drunken remarks at a banquet; the king killed him on the spot.

Cleopatra: (1) Fifth wife of Philip and mother of his son Caranus, whom some viewed as a rival to Alexander for the Macedonian throne; killed by Olympias after Philip's death. (2) Daughter of Philip and Olympias, sister of Alexander, whose wedding festivities in 336 were the occasion of her father's murder.

Coenus: High-ranking officer who led a decisive cavalry movement at the battle of the Hydaspes. In the Hyphasis mutiny of 325 he served as spokesman for the troops who did not want to proceed farther eastward. He died of disease shortly thereafter.

Companion Cavalry: The elite corps of horsemen, usually led by Alexander himself, stationed on the right wing of most battle formations and assigned the role of mounting the decisive charges.

Companions: Alexander's trusted inner circle of advisers and friends, consisting of fewer than a hundred Macedonian nobles.

Craterus: A revered officer in Alexander's army who executed many crucial commissions for Alexander, serving virtually as second in command after Parmenio's death. Appointed to lead the veterans homeward from Opis and assume command of the home front from Antipater (323), he played a crucial role in the Lamian War and died in battle in the wars of the Successors.

Cyrus: Founder of the Persian empire in the mid-sixth century. His tomb at Pasargadae was restored by Alexander in 324.

Darius I: King of Persia who ordered the first invasion of Greece in 490.

Darius III: King of Persia starting in 336, the same year Alexander came to the throne; portrayed by Arrian as a coward and a bungler whose flight from battle lost the engagements at Issus and Gaugamela. Assassinated in exile by a group of usurpers led by Bessus, Darius was given burial with full royal honors by Alexander.

Demosthenes: Leading Athenian orator and politician in the third quarter of the fourth century. Spearheaded the opposition, both political and military, to Philip's expansion, and then worked quietly behind the scenes to oppose Alexander. After the defeat of Athens in the Lamian War, he was exiled and hunted as an enemy of Macedonia; he killed himself in 322.

Diodorus Siculus: A Greek writer of the first century C.E., whose *Universal History* contains, in its sixteenth and seventeenth books, an important account of the reigns of Philip and Alexander. His account of the latter figure derives principally from Cleitarchus.

Dionysus: Greek god of wine and drunken revelry, born from the union of Zeus with a mortal, Semele; thought to have "conquered" the far east in mythic times. Taken by Alexander as both a prototype and a rival during the invasion of India.

Gedrosia: Desert region spanning the coast of modern Pakistan and eastern Iran. Alexander marched his army through this land on his return from India in 325; lack of provisions and failure to rendezvous with Nearchus' fleet led to the deaths of many soldiers.

Greek League: Also known as the League of Corinth: a union of mainland Greek states formed in 337 under Philip's leadership. Members were required to abide by decisions passed by the League, to refrain from attacks on other members, and to preserve their own political status quo. Macedonia was not officially a member but was empowered to act as an executive branch, to carry out the League's decisions.

Harpalus: Boyhood friend of Alexander who was appointed to the important post of royal treasurer on the Asian campaign. He defected and fled to Greece in 333, but he was welcomed back by Alexander in 331 and granted amnesty. During the satrapal purge of 324 he again decamped from Babylon, where he had been spending lavishly out of purloined funds, and tried, unsuccessfully, to stir up a revolt against Alexander in Greece. Exiled from Athens, he was murdered by an associate on Crete.

Hellespont: Modern-day strait of Dardanelles and surrounding region; used as a crossing point between Europe and Asia, first by Xerxes marching his armies toward Greece in 480, then by Alexander in 334 leading his forces in the opposite direction.

Hephaestion: Best friend and possibly lover to Alexander during most of the Asian campaign until his death from illness in 324. Mourned extravagantly by Alexander and accorded the rites due to a semidivine being.

Heracles: Son of Zeus by Alcmene, a mortal; by legend, an ancestor of Alexander on his father's side. Alexander deliberately emulated Heracles in many of his exploits and had himself depicted on coins wearing a lion's-skin helmet, Heracles' typical headgear.

Hermolaus: Alleged leader of the pages' conspiracy in 327; executed for his role in the plot. Said to have conceived a hatred for Alexander after receiving an unduly harsh punishment from him, and also to have been inspired with antimonarchic ideas by Callisthenes.

hipparchy: A cavalry contingent comprising about a thousand horsemen.

Illyria: Mountainous region adjacent to Macedonia to the north, approximately comprising present-day Albania. Illyria was long at war with Macedonia until Philip finally subdued it and Alexander confirmed its subjection.

Malli: An Indian people usually identified with the Malavas mentioned in Sanskrit literature. Their fierce resistance to Alexander during his trip down the Indus in 325 resulted in much bloody fighting, including one siege in which Alexander, trapped almost alone within a town's walls, was badly wounded by an arrow in the chest.

Mazaeus: Satrap of Babylon under Darius III, and entrusted by him with important roles in the defense of Mesopotamia and at the battle of Gaugamela. Later reappointed to his old post by Alexander but under Macedonian sovereignty.

Memnon: Greek mercenary general in the employ of Darius III in the opening phase of the Asian campaign. A man of great talent who knew the capability of the Macedonians, Memnon sought to force an early end to the war by stirring up revolt among Alexander's Aegean allies, but he died of illness before this could be accomplished.

Nearchus: A Greek born on Crete who was nonetheless educated alongside Alexander in Macedonia. Summoned to join his old friend in India in 325, Nearchus went on to lead the vast naval expedition along the coast of Gedrosia. A journal of his experiences has been summarized by Arrian in his *Indica*.

Ochus: The preregnal name of Artaxerxes III (see above).

Olympias: Philip's third wife, a princess of the kingdom of Epirus east of Macedonia, and mother of Alexander; said to have been a strong-willed and passionate woman with a taste for bizarre, ecstatic religious rites. She became estranged from Philip by 337, partly due to his affections for Cleopatra (see under Cleopatra). Suspected of having played a part in Philip's assassination.

Parmenio: Senior Macedonian general and right-hand man to both Philip and Alexander until 331 when Alexander posted him to a lesser command in Media; murdered in 330 by Polydamas, Cleander, and others, on Alexander's orders, after his son Philotas had also been executed on conspiracy charges. Portrayed by Arrian as a cautious, circumspect strategist, a foil to Alexander's brash self-confidence.

Pausanias: (1) Lover of Philip, subsequently rejected and made a target of vicious abuse by one of Philip's cronies; assassinated Philip in 336, allegedly to take revenge for both the rejection and the abuse. (2) Another lover of Philip who supplanted Pausanias #1 in his affections.

Pella: Macedonian city established as the national capital under Philip.

Perdiccas: Member of the Companions and trusted friend of Alexander, who held many important commands on the Asian campaign; appointed regent for the two co-monarchs Philip III and Alexander IV, but soon lost power during the wars of the Successors and was killed by his own army.

Persepolis: One of several capital cities of the Persian empire; site of magnificent palaces built under Darius I and Xerxes. The central palace of the complex was destroyed by fire while occupied by Alexander's forces in 331; historians are uncertain whether the fire was deliberately set on Alexander's orders.

Persians: An Iranian people who seized power from their kinsmen, the Medes, in the mid-sixth century. Under the so-called Achaemenid dynasty established by Cyrus, the Persians built an immense empire that by 500 encompassed all of Asia from Turkey to the Indus River, as well as Egypt, North Africa, and parts of eastern Europe. Their attempts to conquer Greece in 490 and 480 were unsuccessful, however. By the fourth century their empire was thought to be in decline, tempting Agesilaus of Sparta to lead a partly successful invasion in 396; later, Alexander succeeded in capturing the entire empire and ending the Achaemenid dynasty.

phalanx: A rank-and-file formation of infantry soldiers designed to present a solid wall of weaponry to an opponent in battle. Devised by the Greeks, perhaps in the ninth century, the phalanx was radically altered in the fourth century, first by Thebes, which experimented with its size and configuration, and then by Macedonia, which armed its soldiers with long *sarissas* and small, shoulder-hung shields.

Philip II: Born in 382, assumed the Macedonian throne in 359, and assassinated by Pausanias in 336. A gifted leader, diplomat, and military strategist, Philip transformed his country from a weak provincial backwater to a superpower in two decades. After winning the battle of Chaeronea, he created the Greek League (or League of Corinth) to unify the Greek cities under his own leadership; he then laid plans for an invasion of Asia to begin in 336. With his third wife, Olympias, he fathered Alexander in 356, and he trained the boy as his successor until mysteriously breaking with him in 338–337. The last of his many marriages, to Cleopatra, raised the possibility that he was seeking a new heir, and it may well have been a factor in his assassination.

Philotas: Son of Parmenio and member of the Companions; accused of conspiracy to murder Alexander in 330 and executed after being forced to confess under torture.

Phoenicians: Seafaring people inhabiting the cities of the Levantine coast (principally Tyre, Sidon, and Gaza) as well as parts of North Africa and the western Mediterranean. Phoenicians served as the principal naval arm of the Persian empire, but they did so without great loyalty to Persia; many deserted to Alexander's side during the early phase of the Asian campaign.

Plutarch: Greek essayist and biographer of the late first–early second centuries C.E., who composed a *Life of Alexander* as one of his many *Parallel Lives.* An enthusiastic partisan of Alexander in his youth, Plutarch took a more mixed view in the *Life,* which is a pastiche of stories drawn from at least half a dozen primary sources.

Polydamas: Low-ranking Macedonian officer chosen by Alexander to carry and execute his order for Parmenio's murder.

Porus: Indian ruler of territories between the Hydaspes and Acesines rivers; Alexander's last great opponent. In 326 Porus brought his large army, which included a hundred or more elephants, into position to block Alexander from crossing the Hydaspes. After weeks of feints and ruses, the Macedonians finally effected a crossing and defeated Porus' forces. After the battle Porus regained his position under Macedonian sovereignty.

Ptolemy, son of Lagus: Boyhood friend of Alexander and member of the Companions who held various minor commands during the Asian campaigns. After Alexander's death he established himself as ruler of Egypt, where he was crowned king in 305 and ruled as Ptolemy I. His dynasty went on to become the longest lived of all the successor kingdoms, finally capitulating to Rome in 31. Sometime in the early third century he composed a history of Alexander's march, which served as one of Arrian's two primary sources.

Quintus Curtius (Rufus): Roman writer of uncertain date, probably the first or early second centuries C.E. His one surviving work, a ten-book history of Alexander (the first two books are lost), belongs to the "vulgate" tradition deriving chiefly from Cleitarchus; it presents Alexander in a sensational and usually negative light.

Roxane: Iranian princess, daughter of Oxyartes (ruler of the Sogdian Rock), married to Alexander in 327; mother of Alexander IV, with whom she was executed by Cassander.

sarissa: The long (perhaps sixteen-foot) lance introduced by Philip as the primary weapon of the Macedonian infantryman. It was held at a point near its butt end and wielded with two hands.

shield-bearers or *hypaspists*: Contingent of the Macedonian infantry used in various special situations: (1) on pursuits, where speed and mobility were paramount, (2) in battle, to fill any possible gaps between the phalanx and the cavalry wings, and (3) as bodyguard of the king in noncombat situations.

Siwah: Oasis in the desert west of Egypt in which an important oracle of Ammon was situated.

Sogdiana: Northeastern province of the Persian empire (overlapping portions of modern-day Uzbekistan and Kirgizia). Theater of Macedonian operations during much of the years 330, 329, and 328.

Sparta: Leading Greek city in the Peloponnese; foe of Macedonia that kept itself aloof from the Greek League and led a failed revolt in 331.

Spitamenes: Satrap of Sogdiana under the Persians who became leader of a guerrilla resistance to the Macedonians in 329–328; finally executed by his allies, the Massagetae, after inflicting much damage on Alexander's forces.

Susa: One of the imperial capitals of Persia; captured, with its vast wealth, by Alexander in 331.

Taxiles: Indian ruler named by the Greeks for his capital city, Taxila (Ambhi or Omphi was his real name); ally and host of Alexander's forces in the Punjab, 327–326.

Thais: Greek courtesan who, according to the "vulgate" accounts, at a drunken banquet gave Alexander the idea for the burning of the Persepolis palace.

Thebes: Infantry superpower of the Greek world in the mid-fourth century, thanks to the military innovations of Epaminondas. Defeated by Philip at the battle of Chaeronea and thereafter secured by a Macedonian garrison. Destroyed by Alexander after a revolt in 335.

Thessalian cavalry: Greek cavalry contingent accompanying Alexander through Asia, approximately equal in size and skill to the Companion Cavalry.

Thrace: Tribal region to the northwest of Macedonia, stretching across the northern Aegean to the Danube. The Thracians were subdued by Philip and contributed a cavalry contingent to the Macedonian army.

Triballians: Warlike Balkan tribe subdued by Philip.

Tyre: Phoenician city commanding the seas off the Levantine coast; thought to be impregnable to all land armies because of its island location until Alexander conquered it in 333.

Xerxes: Persian king who commanded the great land-and-sea invasion of Greece in 480; sacker of Athens.

Bibliographical Note

Those who wish to read further about Alexander have a wealth of recent literature awaiting them. They should be cautioned, however, that the opinions of expert historians remain sharply divided on key questions surrounding Alexander, and every author of a book on the subject makes choices that define his or her perspective. Some writers, for example, believe that Alexander played a key role in the murder of his father, while others reject this possibility. The portrait of a man who became a parricide at age twenty will obviously look very different from that of one who did not.

Among those inclined toward the "dark" portrayal of Alexander are A. B. Bosworth in *Conquest and Empire: The Reign of Alexander the Great* (Cambridge University Press, 1988) and *Alexander and the East: The Tragedy of Triumph* (Oxford University Press, 1996) and, to a lesser extent, Peter Green in *Alexander of Macedon, 356–323 B.C.* (University of California Press, 1991). The more positive sides of Alexander's nature were emphasized by William Tarn in a now largely discredited, but still influential, work, *Alexander the Great* (2 vols., Cambridge University Press, 1948), and, more responsibly, by N. G. L. Hammond in *Alexander the Great: King, Commander and Statesman* (Noyes Press, 1980). Two very recent books that make note of these opposing views without adopting strong positions of their own are *Alexander the Great* by Richard Stoneman (Routledge, 1997) and *Alexander: Destiny and Myth* by Claude Mossé (translated by Janet Lloyd, Johns Hopkins University Press, 2004). Robin Lane Fox takes a mixed view of Alexander in *The Search for Alexander* (Little, Brown, 1980), a book that is also beautifully illustrated. Several further studies were due to appear in the year or two after this volume was completed, as well as two feature-length films.

Several recent scholars have attempted to compile different views of Alexander taken from either ancient or modern sources, or both, to allow readers to make quick comparisons. These include Joseph Roisman, *Alexander the Great: Ancient and Modern Perspectives* (D. C. Heath, 1995); Ian Worthington, *Alexander the Great: A Reader* (Routledge, 2003); and Waldemar Heckel and J. C. Yardley, *Alexander the Great: Historical Sources in Translation* (Blackwell, 2004).

General studies of Macedonia include N. G. L. Hammond's *The Macedonian State: The Origins, Institution and History* (Oxford

University Press, 1989); Eugene Borza's *In the Shadow of Olympus: The Emergence of Macedon* (Princeton University Press, 1992); and James R. Ashley's *The Macedonian Empire* (McFarland, 1998), which focuses in particular on the military side of Philip's and Alexander's reigns.

A complete version of Arrian's *Anabasis* can be found either in the Penguin edition (*The Campaigns of Alexander*, translated by Aubrey de Sélincourt, 1971) or in the dual-language Loeb edition with the translation, notes, and appendices of Philip Brunt: *History of Alexander and Indica* (2 vols., Harvard University Press, 1976). A Landmark edition of the text will soon be available from Pantheon Books.

In addition to all the above sources, I have relied on the following in preparing the notes for this volume: A. B. Bosworth, *A Historical Commentary on Arrian's History of Alexander*, vols. 1–2 (Oxford University Press, 1980 and 1995), cited in the notes as *Commentary;* Francesco Sisti and Andrea Zambrini, *Arriano: Anabasi di Alessandro,* 2 vols. (first vol. by Sisti only; Mondadori, 2001 and 2004); and J. R. Hamilton, *Plutarch, Alexander: A Commentary* (2nd ed., Duckworth, 1999).

Index